Works

THE PRIME MINISTER

THE PRIME MINISTER

BY

ANTHONY TROLLOPE

VOL. II

NEW-YORK
DODD, MEAD & COMPANY
1911

Copyright, 1893,
By Dodd, Mead & Company.

All rights reserved.

CONTENTS.

CHAPTER		PAGE
I.	The Duchess is much Troubled	1
II.	The Two Candidates for Silverbridge	9
III.	"Yes;—a Lie!"	21
IV.	"Yes;—with a Horsewhip in my Hand."	33
V.	"What Business is it of Yours?"	45
VI.	Showing that a Man should not Howl	57
VII.	The Silverbridge Election	65
VIII.	Lopez back in London	85
IX.	The Jolly Blackbird	100
X.	The Horns	109
XI.	Sir Orlando Retires	124
XII.	"Get Round Him."	136
XIII.	"Come and Try It."	146
XIV.	The Value of a Thick Skin	158
XV.	Retribution	166
XVI.	Kauri Gum	187
XVII.	Mr. Wharton intends to make a New Will	198
XVIII.	Mrs. Sexty Parker	209
XIX.	"He wants to get Rich too Quick."	220
XX.	As for Love!	233
XXI.	"Has He Ill-treated You?"	249

CHAPTER		PAGE
XXII.	"Where is Guatemala?"	259
XXIII.	Mr. Slide's Revenge	270
XXIV.	Coddling the Prime Minister	284
XXV.	"I can sleep here to-night, I suppose?"	299
XXVI.	Mr. Hartlepod	312

THE PRIME MINISTER.

CHAPTER I.

THE DUCHESS IS MUCH TROUBLED.

It is hardly possible that one man should turn another out of his house without many people knowing it; and when the one person is a Prime Minister and the other such a major as Major Pountney, the affair is apt to be talked about very widely. The Duke of course never opened his mouth on the subject, except in answer to questions from the Duchess; but all the servants knew it. "Pritchard tells me that you have sent that wretched man out of the house with a flea in his ear," said the Duchess.

"I sent him out of the house, certainly."

"He was hardly worth your anger."

"He is not at all worth my anger;—but I could not sit down to dinner with a man who had insulted me."

"What did he say, Plantagenet? I know it was something about Silverbridge." To this question the Duke gave no answer, but in respect to Silverbridge he was stern as adamant. Two days after the departure of the major it was known to Silverbridge generally that in the event of there being an election the Duke's agent would not as usual suggest a nominee. There was a paragraph on the subject in the county paper, and another in the London Evening Pulpit. The Duke of Omnium,—that he might show his respect to the law, not only as to the letter of the law, but as to the spirit also,—had made it known to his tenantry in and round Silverbridge generally that he would in no way influence their choice of a candidate in the event of an election. But these newspapers did not say a word about Major Pountney.

The clubs of course knew all about it, and no man at any club ever knew more than Captain Gunner. Soon after Christmas he met his friend the major on the steps of the new military club, The Active Service, which was declared by many men in the army to have left all the other military clubs "absolutely nowhere." "Halloa, Punt!" he said, "you seem to have made a mess of it at last down at the Duchess's."

"I wonder what you know about it."

"You had to come away pretty quick, I take it."

"Of course I came away pretty quick." So much as that the major was aware must be known. There were details which he could deny safely, as it would be impossible that they should be supported by evidence, but there were matters which must be admitted. "I'll bet a fiver that beyond that you know nothing about it."

"The Duke ordered you off, I take it."

"After a fashion he did. There are circumstances in which a man cannot help himself." This was diplomatical, because it left the captain to suppose that the Duke was the man who could not help himself.

"Of course I was not there," said Gunner, "and I

can't absolutely know, but I suppose you had been interfering with the Duchess about Silverbridge. Glencora will bear a great deal,—but since she has taken up politics, by George, you had better not touch her there." At last it came to be believed that the major had been turned out by the order of the Duchess, because he had ventured to put himself forward as an opponent to Ferdinand Lopez, and the major felt himself really grateful to his friend the captain for this arrangement of the story. And there came at last to be mixed up with the story some half-understood innuendo that the major's jealousy against Lopez had been of a double nature,—in reference both to the Duchess and the borough,—so that he escaped from much of that disgrace which naturally attaches itself to a man who has been kicked out of another man's house. There was a mystery;—and when there is a mystery a man should never be condemned. Where there is a woman in the case a man cannot be expected to tell the truth. As for calling out or in any way punishing the Prime Minister, that of course was out of the question. And so it went on till at last the major was almost proud of what he had done, and talked about it willingly with mysterious hints, in which practice made him perfect.

But with the Duchess the affair was very serious, so much so that she was driven to call in advice,—not only from her constant friend, Mrs. Finn, but afterwards from Barrington Erle, from Phineas Finn, and lastly even from the Duke of St. Bungay, to whom she was hardly willing to subject herself, the Duke being the special friend of her husband. But the matter became so important to her that she was unable to trifle with it. At Gatherum the expulsion of Major Pountney soon became a forgotten affair. When the Duchess learned the truth she quite approved of the expulsion, only hinting to Barrington Erle that the act of kicking out should have been more absolutely practical. And the loss of Silverbridge, though it hurt her sorely, could be endured. She must write to her friend Ferdinand Lopez, when the time should come, excusing herself as best she might, and must lose the exquisite delight of making a member of Parliament out of her own hand. The newspapers, however, had taken that matter up in the proper spirit, and political capital might to some extent be made of it. The loss of Silverbridge, though it bruised, broke no bones. But the Duke had again expressed himself with unusual sternness respecting her ducal hospitalities, and had reiterated the declaration of his intention to live out the remainder of his period of office in republican simplicity. "We have tried it and it has failed, and let there be an end of it," he said to her. Simple and direct disobedience to such an order was as little in her way as simple or direct obedience. She knew her husband well, and knew how he could be managed and how he could not be managed. When he declared that there should be an "end of it,"—meaning an end of the very system by which she hoped to perpetuate his power, she did not dare to argue with him. And yet he was so wrong! The trial had been no failure. The thing had been done and well done, and had succeeded. Was failure to be presumed because one impertinent puppy had found his way into the house? And then to abandon the system at once, whether it had failed or whether it had succeeded, would be to call the attention of all the world to an acknowledged failure,—to a failure so disreputable that its acknowledgment must lead to the loss of everything! It was known now,—so argued the Duchess to herself,—that she had devoted herself to the work of cementing and consolidating the Coalition by the graceful hospitality which the wealth of herself and her husband enabled her to dispense. She had made herself a Prime Ministress by the manner in which she opened her salons, her banqueting-halls, and her gardens. It had never been done before, and now it had been well done. There had been no failure. And yet everything was to be broken down because his nerves had received a shock!

"Let it die out," Mrs. Finn had said. "The people will come here and will go away, and then, when you are up in London, you will soon fall into your old ways." But this did not suit the new ambition of the Duchess. She had so fed her mind with daring hopes that she could not bear that "it should die out." She had arranged a course of things in her own mind by which she should come to be known as the great Prime Minister's wife; and she had, perhaps unconsciously, applied the epithet more to herself than to her husband. She, too, wished to be written of in memoirs, and to make a niche for herself in history. And now she was told that she was to let it "die out!"

"I suppose he is a little bilious," Barrington Erle had said. "Don't you think he 'll forget all about it when he gets up to London?" The Duchess was sure that her husband would not forget anything. He never did forget anything. "I want him to be told," said the Duchess, "that everybody thinks that he is doing very well. I don't mean about politics exactly, but as to keeping the party together. Don't you think that we have succeeded?" Barrington Erle thought that upon the whole they had succeeded; but suggested at the same time that there were seeds of weakness. "Sir Orlando and Sir Timothy Beeswax are not sound, you know," said Barrington Erle. "He can't make them sounder by shutting himself up like a hermit," said the Duchess. Barrington Erle, who had peculiar privileges of his own, promised that if he could by any means make an occasion, he would let the Duke know that their side of the Coalition was more than contented with the way in which he did his work.

"You don't think we've made a mess of it?" she said to Phineas, asking him a question. "I don't think that the Duke has made a mess of it,—or you," said Phineas, who had come to love the Duchess because his wife loved her. "But it won't go on forever, Duchess." "You know what I 've done," said the Duchess, who took it for granted that Mr. Finn knew all that his wife knew. "Has it answered?" Phineas was silent for a moment. "Of course you will tell me the truth. You won't be so bad as to flatter me now that I am so much in earnest." "I almost think," said Phineas, "that the time has gone by for what one may call drawing-room influences. They used to be very great. Old Lord Brock used them extensively, though by no means as your Grace has done. But the spirit of the world has changed since then." "The spirit of the world never changes," said the Duchess, in her soreness.

But her strongest dependence was on the old Duke. The party at the Castle was almost broken up when she consulted him. She had been so far true to her husband as not to ask another guest to the house since his command;—but they who had been asked before came and went as had been arranged. Then, when the place was nearly empty, and when Locock and Millepois and Pritchard were wondering among themselves at this general collapse, she asked her husband's leave to invite their old friend again for a day or two. "I do so want to see him, and I think he'll come," said the Duchess. The Duke gave his permission with a ready smile,—not because the proposed visitor was his own confidential friend, but because it suited his spirit to grant such a request as to any one after the order that he had given. Had she named Major Pountney, I think he would have smiled and acceded.

The Duke came, and to him she poured out her whole soul. "It has been for him and for his honour that I have done it;—that men and women might know how really gracious he is, and how good. Of course, there has been money spent, but he can afford it without hurting the children. It has been so necessary that with a Coalition people should know each other! There was some little absurd row here. A man who was a mere nobody, one of the travelling butterfly men that fill up spaces and talk to girls, got hold of him and was impertinent. He is so thin-skinned that he could not shake the creature into the dust as you would have done. It annoyed him,—that, and, I think, seeing so many strange faces,—so that he came to me and declared, that as long as he remained in office he would not have another person in the house, either here or in London. He meant it literally, and he meant me to understand it literally. I had to get special leave before I could ask so dear an old friend as your Grace."

"I don't think he would object to me," said the Duke, laughing.

"Of course not. He was only too glad to think you would come. But he took the request as being quite the proper thing. It will kill me if this is to be carried out. After all that I have done, I could show myself nowhere. And it will be so injurious to him! Could not you tell him, Duke? No one else in the world can tell him but you. Nothing unfair has been attempted. No job has been done. I have endeavoured to make his house pleasant to people, in order that they might look upon him with grace and favour. Is that wrong? Is that unbecoming a wife?"

The old Duke patted her on the head as though she were a little girl, and was more comforting to her than her other counsellors. He would say nothing to her husband now;—but they must both be up in London at the meeting of Parliament, and then he would tell his friend that, in his opinion, no sudden change should be made. "This husband of yours is a very peculiar man," he said, smiling. "His honesty is not like the honesty of other men. It is more downright; —more absolutely honest; less capable of bearing even the shadow which the stain from another's dishonesty might throw upon it. Give him credit for all that, and remember that you cannot find everything combined in the same person. He is very practical in some things, but the question is, whether he is not too scrupulous to be practical in all things." At the close of the interview the Duchess kissed him and promised to be guided by him. The occurrences of the last few weeks had softened the Duchess much.

CHAPTER II.

THE TWO CANDIDATES FOR SILVERBRIDGE.

On his arrival in London Ferdinand Lopez found a letter waiting for him from the Duchess. This came into his hand immediately on his reaching the rooms in Belgrave Mansion, and was of course the first object of his care. "That contains my fate," he said to his wife, putting his hand down upon the letter. He had talked to her much of the chance that had come in his way, and had shown himself to be very ambitious of the honour offered to him. She of course had sympathised with him, and was willing to think all good things both of the Duchess and of the Duke, if they would between them put her husband into Parliament. He paused a moment, still holding the letter under his hand. "You would hardly think that I should be such a coward that I don't like to open it," he said.

"You 've got to do it."

"Unless I make you do it for me," he said, holding out the letter to her. "You will have to learn how weak I am. When I am really anxious I become like a child."

"I do not think you are ever weak," she said, caressing him. "If there were a thing to be done you would do it at once. But I 'll open it if you like." Then he tore off the envelope with an air of comic importance and stood for a few minutes while he read it.

"What I first perceive is that there has been a row about it," he said.

"A row about it! What sort of a row?"

"My dear friend the Duchess has not quite hit it off with my less dear friend the Duke."

"She does not say so?"

"Oh dear, no! My friend the Duchess is much too discreet for that;—but I can see that it has been so."

"Are you to be the new member? If that is arranged I don't care a bit about the Duke and Duchess."

"These things do not settle themselves quite so easily as that. I am not to have the seat at any rate without fighting for it. There 's the letter."

The Duchess's letter to her new adherent shall be given, but it must first be understood that many different ideas had passed through the writer's mind between the writing of the letter and the order given by the Prime Minister to his wife concerning the borough. She of course became aware at once that Mr. Lopez must be informed that she could not do for him what she had suggested that she would do. But there was no necessity of writing at the instant. Mr. Grey had not yet vacated the seat, and Mr. Lopez was away on his travels. The month of January was passed in comparative quiet at the Castle, and during that time it became known at Silverbridge that the election would be open. The Duke would not even make a suggestion, and would neither express, nor feel, resentment should a member be returned altogether hostile to his ministry. By degrees the Duchess accustomed herself to this condition of affairs, and as the consternation caused by her husband's very imperious conduct wore off, she began to ask herself whether even yet she need quite give up the game. She could not make a member of Parliament altogether out of her own hand, as she had once fondly hoped she might do; but still she might do something. She would in nothing disobey her husband, but if Mr. Lopez were to stand for Silverbridge, it could not but be known in the borough that Mr. Lopez was her friend. Therefore she wrote the following letter:—

"Gatherum, January, 18—.

"My dear Mr. Lopez,—I remember that you said that you would be home at this time, and therefore I write to you about the borough. Things are changed since you went away, and, I fear, not changed for your advantage.

"We understand that Mr. Grey will apply for the Chiltern Hundreds at the end of March, and that the election will take place in April. No candidate will appear as favoured from hence. We used to run a favourite, and our favourite would sometimes win,—would sometimes even have a walk over; but those good times are gone. All the good times are going, I think. There is no reason that I know why you should not stand as well as any one else. You can be early in the field;—because it is only now known that there will be no Gatherum interest. And I fancy it had already leaked out that you would have been the favourite if there had been a favourite;—which might be beneficial.

"I need hardly say that I do not wish my name to be mentioned in the matter.

"Sincerely yours,
"GLENCORA OMNIUM.

"Sprugeon, the ironmonger, would, I do not doubt, be proud to nominate you."

"I don't understand much about it," said Emily.

"I dare say not. It is not meant that any novice should understand much about it. Of course you will not mention her Grace's letter."

"Certainly not."

"She intends to do the very best she can for me. I have no doubt that some understrapper from the Castle has had some communication with Mr. Sprugeon. The fact is that the Duke won't be seen in it, but that the Duchess does not mean that the borough shall quite slip through their fingers."

"Shall you try it?"

"If I do I must send an agent down to see Mr. Sprugeon on the sly, and the sooner I do so the better. I wonder what your father will say about it?"

"He is an old conservative."

"But would he not like his son-in-law to be in Parliament?"

"I don't know that he would care about it very much. He seems always to laugh at people who want to get into Parliament. But if you have set your heart upon it, Ferdinand——"

"I have not set my heart on spending a great deal of money. When I first thought of Silverbridge the expense would have been almost nothing. It would have been a walk over, as the Duchess calls it. But now there will certainly be a contest."

"Give it up, if you cannot afford it."

"Nothing venture nothing have. You don't think your father would help me in doing it? It would

add almost as much to your position as to mine."
Emily shook her head. She had always heard her
father ridicule the folly of men who spent more than
they could afford in the vanity of writing two letters
after their name, and she now explained that it had
always been so with him. "You would not mind asking him," he said.

"I will ask him if you wish it, certainly." Ever since
their marriage he had been teaching her,—intentionally
teaching her,—that it would be the duty of both of
them to get all they could from her father. She had
learned the lesson, but it had been very distasteful to
her. It had not induced her to think ill of her husband. She was too much engrossed with him, too
much in love with him for that. But she was beginning to feel that the world in general was hard and
greedy and uncomfortable. If it was proper that a
father should give his daughter money when she was
married, why did not her father do so without waiting
to be asked? And yet, if he were unwilling to do so,
would it not be better to leave him to his pleasure in
the matter? But now she began to perceive that her
father was to be regarded as a milch cow, and that
she was to be the dairymaid. Her husband at times
would become terribly anxious on the subject. On
receiving the promise of £3,000 he had been elated,
but since that he had continually talked of what more
her father ought to do for them.

"Perhaps I had better take the bull by the horns,"
he said, "and do it myself. Then I shall find out
whether he really has our interest at heart, or whether
he looks on you as a stranger because you 've gone
away from him."

"I don't think he will look upon me as a stranger."

"We 'll see," said Lopez.

It was not long before he made the experiment. He had called himself a coward as to the opening of the Duchess's letter, but he had in truth always courage for perils of this nature. On the day of their arrival they dined with Mr. Wharton in Manchester Square, and certainly the old man had received his daughter with great delight. He had been courteous also to Lopez, and Emily, amidst the pleasure of his welcome, had forgotten some of her troubles. The three were alone together, and when Emily had asked after her brother, Mr. Wharton had laughed and said that Everett was an ass. "You have not quarrelled with him?" she said. He ridiculed the idea of any quarrel, but again said that Everett was an ass.

After dinner Mr. Wharton and Lopez were left together, as the old man, whether alone or in company, always sat for half an hour sipping port-wine after the manner of his forefathers. Lopez had already determined that he would not let the opportunity escape him, and began his attack at once. "I have been invited, sir," he said with his sweetest smile, "to stand for Silverbridge."

"You too!" said Mr. Wharton. But, though there was a certain amount of satire in the exclamation, it had been good-humoured satire.

"Yes, sir. We all get bit sooner or later, I suppose."

"I never was bit."

"Your sagacity and philosophy have been the wonder of the world, sir. There can be no doubt that in my profession a seat in the House would be of the greatest possible advantage to me. It enables a man to do a great many things which he could not touch without it."

"It may be so. I don't know anything about it."

"And then it is a great honour."

"That depends on how you get it, and how you use it;—very much also on whether you are fit for it."

"I shall get it honestly if I do get it. I hope I may use it well. And as for my fitness, I must leave that to be ascertained when I am there. I am sorry to say there will probably be a contest."

"I suppose so. A seat in Parliament without a contest does not drop into every young man's mouth."

"It very nearly dropped into mine." Then he told his father-in-law almost all the particulars of the offer which had been made him, and of the manner in which the seat was now suggested to him. He somewhat hesitated in the use of the name of the Duchess, leaving an impression on Mr. Wharton that the offer had in truth come from the Duke. "Should there be a contest, would you help me?"

"In what way? I could not canvass at Silverbridge, if you mean that."

"I was not thinking of giving you personal trouble."

"I don't know a soul in the place. I should n't know that there was such a place except that it returns a member of Parliament."

"I meant with money, sir."

"To pay the election bills! No; certainly not. Why should I?"

"For Emily's sake."

"I don't think it would do Emily any good, or you either. It would certainly do me none. It is a kind of luxury that a man should not attempt to enjoy unless he can afford it easily."

"A luxury!"

"Yes, a luxury; just as much as a four-in-hand coach or a yacht. Men go into Parliament because it gives them fashion, position, and power."

"I should go to serve my country."

"Success in your profession I thought you said was your object. Of course you must do as you please. If you ask me for advice, I advise you not to try it. But certainly I will not help you with money. That ass Everett is quarrelling with me at this moment because I won't give him money to go and stand somewhere."

"Not at Silverbridge!"

"I'm sure I can't say. But don't let me do him an injury. To give him his due, he is more reasonable than you, and only wants a promise from me that I will pay electioneering bills for him at the next general election. I have refused him,—though for reasons which I need not mention I think him better fitted for Parliament than you. I must certainly also refuse you. I cannot imagine any circumstances which would induce me to pay a shilling towards getting you into Parliament. If you won't drink any more wine we'll join Emily upstairs."

This had been very plain speaking, and by no means comfortable to Lopez. What of personal discourtesy there had been in the lawyer's words,—and they had not certainly been flattering,—he could throw off from him as meaning nothing. As he could not afford to quarrel with his father-in-law, he thought it probable that he might have to bear a good deal of incivility from the old man. He was quite prepared to bear it as long as he could see a chance of a reward;—though, should there be no such chance he would be ready to avenge it. But there had been a decision in the present refusal which made him quite sure that it would be vain to repeat his request. "I shall find out, sir," he said, "whether it may probably be a costly affair, and if so I shall give it up. You are rather hard upon me as to my motives."

"I only repeated what you told me yourself."

"I am quite sure of my own intentions, and know that I need not be ashamed of them."

"Not if you have plenty of money. It all depends on that. If you have plenty of money, and your fancy goes that way, it is all very well. Come, we'll go upstairs."

The next day he saw Everett Wharton, who welcomed him back with warm affection. "He'll do nothing for me;—nothing at all. I am almost beginning to doubt whether he'll ever speak to me again."

"Nonsense!"

"I tell you everything, you know," said Everett. "In January I lost a little money at whist. They got plunging at the club, and I was in it. I had to tell him, of course. He keeps me so short that I can't stand any blow without going to him like a schoolboy."

"Was it much?"

"No;—to him no more than half-a-crown to you. I had to ask him for a hundred and fifty."

"He refused it!"

"No;—he did n't do that. Had it been ten times as much, if I owed the money, he would pay it. But he blew me up, and talked about gambling,—and—and——"

"I should have taken that as a matter of course."

"But I'm not a gambler. A man now and then may fall into a thing of that kind, and if he's decently well off and don't do it often he can bear it."

"I thought your quarrel had been altogether about Parliament."

"Oh no! He has been always the same about that. He told me that I was going head-foremost to the dogs, and I could n't stand that. I should n't be surprised if he has n't lost more at cards than I have during the last two years." Lopez made an offer to act as go-between, to effect a reconciliation; but Everett declined the offer. "It would be making too much of an absurdity," he said. "When he wants to see me, I suppose he 'll send for me."

Lopez did despatch an agent down to Mr. Sprugeon at Silverbridge, and the agent found that Mr. Sprugeon was a very discreet man. Mr. Sprugeon at first knew little or nothing,—seemed hardly to be aware that there was a member of Parliament for Silverbridge, and declared himself to be indifferent as to the parliamentary character of the borough. But at last he melted a little, and by degrees, over a glass of hot brandy and water with the agent at the Palliser's Arms, confessed to a shade of an opinion that the return of Mr. Lopez for the borough would not be disagreeable to some person or persons who did not live quite a hundred miles away. The instructions given by Lopez to his agent were of the most cautious kind. The agent was merely to feel the ground, make a few inquiries, and do nothing. His client did not intend to stand unless he could see the way to almost certain success with very little outlay. But the agent, perhaps liking the job, did a little outstep his employer's orders. Mr. Sprugeon, when the frost of his first modesty had been thawed, introduced the agent to Mr. Sprout, the maker of cork soles, and Mr. Sprugeon and Mr. Sprout between them had soon decided that Mr. Ferdinand Lopez should be run for the borough as the "Castle" candidate. "The Duke won't interfere," said Sprugeon; "and, of course, the Duke's man of business can't do anything openly;—but the Duke's people will know." Then Mr. Sprout told the agent that there was already another candidate in the field, and in a whisper communicated the gentleman's name. When the agent got back to London, he gave Lopez to understand that he must certainly put himself forward. The borough expected him. Sprugeon and Sprout considered themselves pledged to bring him forward and support him,—on behalf of the Castle. Sprugeon was quite sure that the Castle influence was predominant. The Duke's name had never been mentioned at Silverbridge,—hardly even that of the Duchess. Since the Duke's declaration "The Castle" had taken the part which the old Duke used to play. The agent was quite sure that no one could get in for Silverbridge without having the Castle on his side. No doubt the Duke's declaration had had the ill effect of bringing up a competitor, and thus of causing expense. That could not now be helped. The agent was of opinion that the Duke had had no alternative. The agent hinted that times were changing, and that though dukes were still dukes, and could still exercise ducal influences, they were driven by these changes to act in an altered form. The proclamation had been especially necessary because the Duke was Prime Minister.

The agent did not think that Mr. Lopez should be in the least angry with the Duke. Everything would be done that the Castle could do, and Lopez would be no doubt returned,—though, unfortunately, not without some expense. How much would it cost? Any accurate answer to such a question would be impossible, but probably about £600. It might be £800; —could not possibly be above £1,000. Lopez winced as he heard these sums named, but he did not decline the contest.

Then the name of the opposition candidate was whispered to Lopez. It was Arthur Fletcher! Lopez started, and asked some question as to Mr. Fletcher's interest in the neighbourhood. The Fletchers were connected with the De Courcys, and as soon as the declaration of the Duke had been made known, the De Courcy interest had aroused itself, and had invited that rising young barrister, Arthur Fletcher, to stand for the borough on strictly conservative views. Arthur Fletcher had acceded, and a printed declaration of his purpose and political principles had been just published. "I have beaten him once," said Lopez to himself, "and I think I can beat him again."

CHAPTER III.

"YES;—A LIE!"

"So you went to Happerton after all," said Lopez to his ally, Mr. Sextus Parker. "You could n't believe me when I told you the money was all right! What a cur you are!"

"That 's right;—abuse me."

"Well, it was horrid. Did n't I tell you that it must necessarily injure me with the house? How are two fellows to get on together unless they can put some trust in each other? Even if I did run you into a difficulty, do you really think I 'm ruffian enough to tell you that the money was there if it were untrue?"

Sexty looked like a cur and felt like a cur, as he was being thus abused. He was not angry with his friend for calling him bad names, but only anxious to excuse himself. "I was out of sorts," he said, "and so d——d hippish I did n't know what I was about."

"Brandy and soda!" suggested Lopez.

"Perhaps a little of that;—though, by Jove, it is n't often I do that kind of thing. I don't know a fellow who works harder for his wife and children than I do. But when one sees such things all round one,—a fellow utterly smashed here who had a string of hunters yesterday, and another fellow buying a house in Piccadilly and pulling it down because it is n't big enough, who was contented with a little box at Hornsey last summer, one does n't quite know how to keep one's legs."

"If you want to learn a lesson look at the two men, and see where the difference lies. The one has had some heart about him, and the other has been a coward."

Parker scratched his head, balanced himself on the hind legs of his stool, and tacitly acknowledged the truth of all that his enterprising friend said to him. "Has old Wharton come down well?" at last he asked.

"I have never said a word to old Wharton about money," Lopez replied,—"except as to the cost of this election I was telling you of."

"And he would n't do anything in that?"

"He does n't approve of the thing itself. I don't doubt but that the old gentleman and I shall understand each other before long."

"You 've got the length of his foot."

"But I don't mean to drive him. I can get along without that. He 's an old man, and he can't take his money along with him when he goes the great journey."

"There 's a brother, Lopez,—is n't there?"

"Yes,—there 's a brother; but Wharton has enough for two; and if he were to put either out of his will it would n't be my wife. Old men don't like parting with their money, and he 's like other old men. If it were not so I should n't bother myself coming into the City at all."

"Has he enough for that, Lopez?"

"I suppose he 's worth a quarter of a million."

"By Jove! And where did he get it?"

"Perseverance, sir. Put by a shilling a day, and let

it have its natural increase, and see what it will come to at the end of fifty years. I suppose old Wharton has been putting by two or three thousand out of his professional income, at any rate for the last thirty years, and never for a moment forgetting its natural increase. That's one way to make a fortune."

"It ain't rapid enough for you and me, Lopez."

"No. That was the old-fashioned way, and the most sure. But, as you say, it is not rapid enough; and it robs a man of the power of enjoying his money when he has made it. But it's a very good thing to be closely connected with a man who has already done that kind of thing. There's no doubt about the money when it is there. It does not take to itself wings and fly away."

"But the man who has it sticks to it uncommon hard."

"Of course he does;—but he can't take it away with him."

"He can leave it to hospitals, Lopez. That's the devil!"

"Sexty, my boy, I see you have taken an outlook into human life which does you credit. Yes, he can leave it to hospitals. But why does he leave it to hospitals?"

"Something of being afraid about his soul, I suppose."

"No; I don't believe in that. Such a man as this, who has been hard-fisted all his life, and who has had his eyes thoroughly open, who has made his own money in the sharp intercourse of man to man, and who keeps it to the last gasp,—he does n't believe that he'll do his soul any good by giving it to hospitals when he can't keep it himself any longer. His mind has freed itself from those cobwebs long since. He gives his money to hospitals because the last pleasure of which he is capable is that of spiting his relations. And it is a great pleasure to an old man, when his relations have been disgusted with him for being old and loving his money. I rather think I should do it myself."

"I 'd give myself a chance of going to heaven, I think," said Parker.

"Don't you know that men will rob and cheat on their death-beds, and say their prayers all the time? Old Wharton won't leave his money to hospitals if he 's well handled by those about him."

"And you 'll handle him well;—eh, Lopez?"

"I won't quarrel with him, or tell him that he 's a curmudgeon because he does n't do all that I want him. He 's over seventy, and he can't carry his money with him."

All this left so vivid an impression of the wisdom of his friend on the mind of Sextus Parker, that in spite of the harrowing fears by which he had been tormented on more than one occasion already, he allowed himself to be persuaded into certain fiscal arrangements, by which Lopez would find himself put at ease with reference to money at any rate for the next four months. He had at once told himself that this election would cost him £1,000. When various sums were mentioned in reference to such an affair, safety could alone be found in taking the outside sum;—perhaps might generally be more surely found by adding fifty per cent. to that. He knew that he was wrong about the election, but he assured himself that he had had no alternative. The misfortune had been that the Duke should have made his proclamation about the borough immediately after the offer made by the Duchess. He had been almost forced to send the agent down to inquire;—and the agent, when making his inquiries, had compromised him. He must go on with it now. Perhaps some idea of the pleasantness of increased intimacy with the Duchess of Omnium encouraged him in this way of thinking. The Duchess was up in town in February, and Lopez left a card in Carlton Terrace. On the very next day the card of the Duchess was left for Mr. Lopez at the Belgrave Mansion.

Lopez went into the City every day, leaving home at about eleven o'clock, and not returning much before dinner. The young wife at first found that she hardly knew what to do with her time. Her aunt, Mrs. Roby, was distasteful to her. She had already learned from her husband that he had but little respect for Mrs. Roby. "You remember the sapphire brooch," he had said once. "That was part of the price I had to pay for being allowed to approach you." He was sitting at the time with his arm round her waist, looking out on beautiful scenery and talking of his old difficulties. She could not find it in her heart to be angry with him, but the idea brought to her mind was disagreeable to her. And she was thoroughly angry with Mrs. Roby. Of course in these days Mrs. Roby came to see her, and of course when she was up in Manchester Square, she went to the house round the corner,—but there was no close intimacy between the aunt and the niece. And many of her father's friends, —whom she regarded as the Herefordshire set,—were very cold to her. She had not made herself a glory to Herefordshire, and,—as all these people said,—had broken the heart of the best Herefordshire young man of the day. This made a great falling-off in her acquaintance, which was the more felt as she had never been, as a girl, devoted to a large circle of dearest female friends. She whom she had loved best had been Mary Wharton, and Mary Wharton had refused to be her bridesmaid almost without an expression of regret. She saw her father occasionally. Once he came and dined with them at their rooms, on which occasion Lopez struggled hard to make up a well-sounding party. There were Roby from the Admiralty, and the Happertons, and Sir Timothy Beeswax, with whom Lopez had become acquainted at Gatherum, and old Lord Mongrober. But the barrister, who had dined out a good deal in his time, perceived the effort. Who, that ever with difficulty scraped his dinner guests together, was able afterwards to obliterate the signs of the struggle? It was, however, a first attempt, and Lopez, whose courage was good, thought that he might do better before long. If he could get into the House and make his mark there people then would dine with him fast enough. But while this was going on Emily's life was rather dull. He had provided her with a brougham, and everything around her was even luxurious, but there came upon her gradually a feeling that by her marriage she had divided herself from her own people. She did not for a moment allow this feeling to interfere with her loyalty to him. Had she not known that this division would surely take place? Had she not married him because she loved him better than her own people? So she sat herself down to read Dante,—for they had studied Italian together during their honeymoon, and she had found that he knew the language well. And she was busy with her needle. And she already began to anticipate the happiness which would come to her when a child of his should be lying in her arms.

She was of course much interested about the election. Nothing could as yet be done, because as yet there was no vacancy; but still the subject was discussed daily between them. "Who do you think is going to stand against me?" he said one day with a smile. "A very old friend of yours." She knew at once who the man was, and the blood came to her face. "I think he might as well have left it alone, you know," he said.

"Did he know?" she asked in a whisper.

"Know;—of course he knew. He is doing it on purpose. But I beat him once, old girl, did n't I? And I 'll beat him again." She liked him to call her old girl. She loved the perfect intimacy with which he treated her. But there was something which grated against her feelings in this allusion by him to the other man who had loved her. Of course she had told him the whole story. She had conceived it to be her duty to do so. But then the thing should have been over. It was necessary, perhaps, that he should tell her who was his opponent. It was impossible that she should not know when the fight came. But she did not like to hear him boast that he had beaten Arthur Fletcher once, and that he would beat him again. By doing so he likened the sweet fragrance of her love to the dirty turmoil of an electioneering contest.

He did not understand,—how should he?—that though she had never loved Arthur Fletcher, had never been able to bring herself to love him when all her friends had wished it, her feelings to him were nevertheless those of affectionate friendship;—that she regarded him as being perfect in his way, a thorough gentleman, a man who would not for worlds tell a lie, as most generous among the generous, most noble among the noble. When the other Whartons had thrown her off, he had not been cold to her. That very day, as soon as her husband had left her, she looked again at that little note. "I am as I always have been!" And she remembered that farewell down by the banks of the Wye. "You will always have one,—one besides him,—who will love you best in the world." They were dangerous words for her to remember; but in recalling them to her memory she had often assured herself that they should not be dangerous to her. She was too sure of her own heart to be afraid of danger. She had loved the one man and had not loved the other;—but yet, now, when her husband talked of beating this man again, she could not but remember the words.

She did not think,—or rather had not thought,—that Arthur Fletcher would willingly stand against her husband. It had occurred to her at once that he must first have become a candidate without knowing who would be his opponent. But Ferdinand had assured her as a matter of fact that Fletcher had known all about it. "I suppose in politics men are different," she said to herself. Her husband had evidently supposed that Arthur Fletcher had proposed himself as a candidate for Silverbridge, with the express object of doing an injury to the man who had carried off his love. And she repeated to herself her husband's words, "He is doing it on purpose." She did not like to differ from her husband, but she could hardly bring herself to believe that revenge of this kind should have recommended itself to Arthur Fletcher.

Some little time after this, when she had been settled in London about a month, a letter was brought her, and she at once recognised Arthur Fletcher's writing. She was alone at the time, and it occurred to her at first that perhaps she ought not to open any communication from him without showing it to her husband. But then it seemed that such a hesitation would imply a doubt of the man, and almost a doubt of herself. Why should she fear what any man might write to her? So she opened the letter, and read it,—with infinite pleasure. It was as follows:—

"My dear Mrs. Lopez,—I think it best to make an explanation to you as to a certain coincidence which might possibly be misunderstood unless explained. I find that your husband and I are to be opponents at Silverbridge. I wish to say that I had pledged myself to the borough before I had heard his name as connected with it. I have very old associations with the neighbourhood, and was invited to stand by friends who had known me all my life as soon as it was understood that there would be an open contest. I cannot retire now without breaking faith with my party, nor do I know that there is any reason why I should do so. I should not, however, have come forward had I known that Mr. Lopez was to stand. I think you had better tell him so, and tell him also, with my compliments, that I hope we may fight our political battle with mutual good-fellowship and good-feeling.

"Yours very sincerely,
"Arthur Fletcher."

Emily was very much pleased by this letter, and yet she wept over it. She felt that she understood accurately all the motives that were at work within the man's breast when he was writing it. As to its truth,—of course the letter was gospel to her. Oh,—if the man could become her husband's friend how sweet it would be! Of course she wished, thoroughly wished, that her husband should succeed at Silverbridge. But she could understand that such a contest as this might be carried on without personal animosity. The letter was so like Arthur Fletcher,—so good, so noble, so generous, so true! The moment her husband came in she showed it to him with delight. "I was sure," she said as he was reading the letter, "that he had not known that you were to stand."

"He knew it as well as I did," he replied, and as he spoke there came a dark scowl across his brow. "His writing to you is a piece of infernal impudence."

"Oh, Ferdinand!"

"You don't understand, but I do. He deserves to be horsewhipped for daring to write to you, and if I can come across him he shall have it."

"Oh,—for Heaven's sake!"

"A man who was your rejected lover,—who has been trying to marry you for the last two years, presuming to commence a correspondence with you without your husband's sanction!"

"He meant you to see it. He says I am to tell you."

"Psha! That is simple cowardice. He meant you not to tell me; and then when you had answered him without telling me, he would have had the whip-hand of you."

"Oh, Ferdinand, what evil thoughts you have!"

"You are a child, my dear, and must allow me to dictate to you what you ought to think in such a matter as this. I tell you he knew all about my candidature, and that what he has said here to the contrary is a mere lie;—yes, a lie!" He repeated the word because he saw that she shrank at hearing it; but he did not understand why she shrank,—that the idea of such an accusation against Arthur Fletcher was intolerable to her. "I have never heard of such a thing," he continued. "Do you suppose it is common for men who have been thrown over to write to the ladies who have rejected them immediately after their marriage?"

"Do not the circumstances justify it?"

"No;—they make it infinitely worse. He should have felt himself to be debarred from writing to you, both as being my wife and as being the wife of the man whom he intends to oppose at Silverbridge."

This he said with so much anger that he frightened her. "It is not my fault," she said.

"No; it is not your fault. But you should regard it as a great fault committed by him."

"What am I to do?"

"Give me the letter. You, of course, can do nothing."

"You will not quarrel with him?"

"Certainly I will. I have quarrelled with him already. Do you think I will allow any man to insult my wife without quarrelling with him? What I shall do I cannot yet say, and whatever I may do, you had better not know. I never thought much of these Herefordshire swells who believe themselves to be the very cream of the earth, and now I think less of them than ever."

He was then silent, and slowly she took herself out of the room, and went away to dress. All this was very terrible. He had never been rough to her before, and she could not at all understand why he had been so rough to her now. Surely it was impossible that he should be jealous because her old lover had written to her such a letter as that which she had shown him! And then she was almost stunned by the opinions he had expressed about Fletcher, opinions which she knew,—was sure that she knew,—to be absolutely erroneous. A liar! Oh, heavens! And then the letter itself was so ingenuous and so honest! Anxious as she was to do all that her husband bade her, she could not be guided by him in this matter. And then she remembered his words: "You must allow me to dictate to you what you ought to think." Could it be that marriage meant as much as that,—that a husband was to claim to dictate to his wife what opinions she was to form about this and that person,—about a person she had known so well, whom he had never known? Surely she could only think in accordance with her own experience and her own intelligence! She was certain that Arthur Fletcher was no liar. Not even her own husband could make her think that.

CHAPTER IV.

"YES;—WITH A HORSEWHIP IN MY HAND."

EMILY LOPEZ, when she crept out of her own room and joined her husband just before dinner, was hardly able to speak to him, so thoroughly was she dismayed, and troubled, and horrified, by the manner in which he had taken Arthur Fletcher's letter. While she had been alone she had thought it all over, anxious if possible to bring herself into sympathy with her husband; but the more she thought of it the more evident did it become to her that he was altogether wrong. He was so wrong that it seemed to her that she would be a hypocrite if she pretended to agree with him. There were half-a-dozen accusations conveyed against Mr. Fletcher by her husband's view of the matter. He was a liar, giving a false account of his candidature;—and he was a coward; and an enemy to her, who had laid a plot by which he had hoped to make her act fraudulently towards her own husband, who had endeavoured to creep into a correspondence with her, and so to compromise her! All this, which her husband's mind had so easily conceived, was not only impossible to her, but so horrible that she could not refrain from disgust at her husband's conception. The letter had been left with him, but she remembered every word of it. She was sure that it was an honest letter, meaning no more than had been said,—simply intending to explain to her that he would not willingly have stood in the way of a friend whom he had loved, by interfering with her husband's prospects. And yet she was told that she was to think as her husband bade her think! She could not think so. She could not say that she thought so. If her husband would not credit her judgment, let the matter be referred to her father. Ferdinand would at any rate acknowledge that her father could understand such a matter even if she could not.

During dinner he said nothing on the subject, nor did she. They were attended by a page in buttons whom he had hired to wait upon her, and the meal passed off almost in silence. She looked up at him frequently and saw that his brow was still black. As soon as they were alone she spoke to him, having studied during dinner what words she would first say: "Are you going down to the club to-night?" He had told her that the matter of this election had been taken up at the Progress, and that possibly he might have to meet two or three persons there on this evening. There had been a proposition that the club should bear a part of the expenditure, and he was very solicitous that such an arrangement should be made.

"No," said he, "I shall not go out to-night. I am not sufficiently light-hearted."

"What makes you heavy-hearted, Ferdinand?"

"I should have thought you would have known."

"I suppose I do know,—but I don't know why it should. I don't know why you should be displeased. At any rate, I have done nothing wrong."

"No;—not as to the letter. But it astonishes me that you should be so—so bound to this man that——"

"Bound to him, Ferdinand!"

"No;—you are bound to me. But that you have so much regard for him as not to see that he has grossly insulted you."

"I have a regard for him."

"And you dare to tell me so?"

"Dare! What should I be if I had any feeling which I did not dare to tell you? There is no harm in regarding a man with friendly feelings whom I have now known since I was a child, and whom all my family have loved."

"Your family wanted you to marry him!"

"They did. But I have married you, because I loved you. But I need not think badly of an old friend, because I did not love him. Why should you be angry with him? What can you have to be afraid of?" Then she came and sat on his knee and caressed him.

"It is he that shall be afraid of me," said Lopez. "Let him give the borough up if he means what he says."

"Who could ask him to do that?"

"Not you,—certainly."

"Oh no."

"I can ask him."

"Could you, Ferdinand?"

"Yes;—with a horsewhip in my hand."

"Indeed, indeed you do not know him. Will you do this;—will you tell my father everything, and leave it to him to say whether Mr. Fletcher has behaved badly to you?"

"Certainly not. I will not have any interference from your father between you and me. If I had listened to your father you would not have been here now. Your father is not as yet a friend of mine.

When he comes to know what I can do for myself, and that I can rise higher than these Herefordshire people, then perhaps he may become my friend. But I will consult him in nothing so peculiar to myself as my own wife. And you must understand that in coming to me all obligation from you to him became extinct. Of course he is your father; but in such a matter as this he has no more to say to you than any stranger." After that he hardly spoke to her; but sat for an hour with a book in his hand, and then rose and said that he would go down to the club. "There is so much villainy about," he said, "that a man if he means to do anything must keep himself on the watch."

When she was alone she at once burst into tears; but she soon dried her eyes, and putting down her work, settled herself to think of it all. What did it mean? Why was he thus changed to her? Could it be that he was the same Ferdinand to whom she had given herself, without a doubt as to his personal merit? Every word that he had spoken since she had shown him the letter from Arthur Fletcher had been injurious to her, and offensive. It almost seemed as though he had determined to show himself to be a tyrant to her, and had only put off playing the part till the first convenient opportunity after their honeymoon. But through all this, her ideas were loyal to him. She would obey him in all things where obedience was possible, and would love him better than all the world. Oh yes;—for was he not her husband? Were he to prove himself the worst of men she would still love him. It had been for better or for worse; and as she had repeated the words to herself, she had sworn that if the worst should come, she would still be true.

But she could not bring herself to say that Arthur Fletcher had behaved badly. She could not lie. She knew well that his conduct had been noble and generous. Then unconsciously and involuntarily,—or rather in opposition to her own will and inward efforts,—her mind would draw comparisons between her husband and Arthur Fletcher. There was some peculiar gift, or grace, or acquirement belonging without dispute to the one, and which the other lacked. What was it? She had heard her father say when talking of gentlemen,—of that race of gentlemen with whom it had been his lot to live,—that you could not make a silk purse out of a sow's ear. The use of the proverb had offended her much, for she had known well whom he had then regarded as a silk purse and whom as a sow's ear. But now she perceived that there had been truth in all this, though she was as anxious as ever to think well of her husband, and to endow him with all possible virtues. She had once ventured to form a doctrine for herself, to preach to herself a sermon of her own, and to tell herself that this gift of gentle blood and of gentle nurture, of which her father thought so much, and to which something of divinity was attributed down in Herefordshire, was after all but a weak, spiritless quality. It could exist without intellect, without heart, and with very moderate culture. It was compatible with many littlenesses and with many vices. As for that love of honest, courageous truth which her father was wont to attribute to it, she regarded his theory as based upon legends, as in earlier years was the theory of the courage, and constancy, and loyalty of the knights of those days. The beau ideal of a man which she then pictured to herself was graced, first with intelligence, then with affection, and lastly with ambition. She knew no reason why such a hero as her fancy created should be born of lords and ladies rather than of working mechanics, should be English rather than Spanish or French. The man could not be her hero without education, without attributes to be attained no doubt more easily by the rich than by the poor; but, with that granted, with those attained, she did not see why she, or why the world, should go back beyond the man's own self. Such had been her theories as to men and their attributes, and acting on that, she had given herself and all her happiness into the keeping of Ferdinand Lopez. Now, there was gradually coming upon her a change in her convictions, —a change that was most unwelcome, that she strove to reject,—one which she would not acknowledge that she had adopted even while adopting it. But now,— ay, from the very hour of her marriage,—she had commenced to learn what it was that her father had meant when he spoke of the pleasure of living with gentlemen. Arthur Fletcher certainly was a gentleman. He would not have entertained the suspicion which her husband had expressed. He could not have failed to believe such assertions as had been made. He could never have suggested to his own wife that another man had endeavoured to entrap her into a secret correspondence. She seemed to hear the tones of Arthur Fletcher's voice, as those of her husband still rang in her ear when he bade her remember that she was now removed from her father's control. Every now and then the tears would come to her eyes, and she would sit pondering, listless, and low in heart. Then she would suddenly rouse herself with a shake, and take up her book with a resolve that she would read steadily, would assure herself as she did so that her husband should still be her hero. The intelligence at any rate was there, and, in spite of his roughness, the affection which she craved. And the ambition, too, was there. But, alas, alas! why should such vile suspicions have fouled his mind?

He was late that night, but when he came he kissed her brow as she lay in bed, and she knew that his temper was again smooth. She feigned to be sleepy, though not asleep, as she just put her hand up to his cheek. She did not wish to speak to him again that night, but she was glad to know that in the morning he would smile on her. "Be early at breakfast," he said to her as he left her the next morning, "for I'm going down to Silverbridge to-day."

Then she started up. "To-day!"

"Yes;—by the 11.20. There is plenty of time, only don't be unusually late."

Of course she was something more than usually early, and when she came out she found him reading his paper. "It's all settled now," he said. "Grey has applied for the Hundreds, and Mr. Rattler is to move for the new writ to-morrow. It has come rather sudden at last, as these things always do after long delays. But they say the suddenness is rather in my favour."

"When will the election take place?"

"I suppose in about a fortnight;—perhaps a little longer."

"And must you be at Silverbridge all that time?"

"Oh dear, no. I shall stay there to-night, and perhaps to-morrow night. Of course I shall telegraph to you directly I find how it is to be. I shall see the principal inhabitants, and probably make a speech or two."

"I do so wish I could hear you."

"You'd find it awfully dull work, my girl. And I shall find it awfully dull too. I do not imagine that Mr. Sprugeon and Mr. Sprout will be pleasant companions. Well; I shall stay there a day or two and settle when I am to go down for the absolute canvass. I shall have to go with my hat in my hand to every blessed inhabitant in that dirty little town, and ask them all to be kind enough to drop in a paper for the most humble of their servants, Ferdinand Lopez."

"I suppose all candidates have to do the same."

"Oh yes;—your friend, Master Fletcher, will have to do it." She winced at this. Arthur Fletcher was her friend, but at the present moment he ought not so to have spoken of him. "And from all I hear, he is just the sort of fellow that will like the doing of it. It is odious to me to ask a fellow that I despise for anything."

"Why should you despise them?"

"Low, ignorant, greasy cads, who have no idea of the real meaning of political privileges;—men who would all sell their votes for thirty shillings each, if that game had not been made a little too hot!"

"If they are like that I would not represent them."

"Oh yes, you would;—when you came to understand the world. It's a fine thing to be in Parliament, and that is the way to get in. However, on this visit I shall only see the great men of the town,—the Sprouts and Sprugeons."

"Shall you go to Castle Gatherum?"

"Oh, heavens, no! I may go anywhere now rather than there. The Duke is supposed to be in absolute ignorance of the very names of the candidates, or whether there are candidates. I don't suppose that the word Silverbridge will be even whispered in his ear till the thing is over."

"But you are to get in by his friendship."

"Or by hers;—at least I hope so. I have no doubt that the Sprouts and the Sprugeons have been given to understand by the Lococks and the Pritchards what are the Duchess's wishes, and that it has also been intimated in some subtle way that the Duke is willing to oblige the Duchess. There are ever so many ways, you know, of killing a cat."

"And the expense?" suggested Emily.

"Oh,—ah; the expense. When you come to talk of the expense things are not so pleasant. I never saw such a set of meaningless asses in my life as those men at the club. They talk and talk, but there is not one of them who knows how to do anything. Now at the club over the way they do arrange matters. It's a common cause, and I don't see what right they have to expect that one man should bear all the expense. I've a deuced good mind to leave them in the lurch."

"Don't do it, Ferdinand, if you can't afford it."

"I shall go on with it now. I can't help feeling that I've been a little let in among them. When the Duchess first promised me it was to be a simple walk over. Now that they've got their candidate, they go back from that and open the thing to any comer. I can't tell you what I think of Fletcher for taking advantage of such a chance. And then the political committee at the club coolly say that they've got no money. It isn't honest, you know."

"I don't understand all that," said Emily sadly. Every word that he said about Fletcher cut her to the heart;—not because it grieved her that Fletcher should be abused, but that her husband should condescend to abuse him. She escaped from further conflict at the moment by proclaiming her ignorance of the whole matter; but she knew enough of it to be well aware that Arthur Fletcher had as good a right to stand as her husband, and that her husband lowered himself by personal animosity to the man. Then Lopez took his departure. "Oh, Ferdinand," she said, "I do so hope you may be successful."

"I don't think he can have a chance. From what people say, he must be a fool to try. That is, if the Castle is true to me. I shall know more about it when I come back."

That afternoon she dined with her father, and there met Mrs. Roby. It was of course known that Lopez had gone down to Silverbridge, and Emily learned in Manchester Square that Everett had gone with him. "From all I hear, they 're two fools for their pains," said the lawyer.

"Why, papa?"

"The Duke has given the thing up."

"But still his interest remains."

"No such thing! If there is an honest man in England it is the Duke of Omnium, and when he says a thing he means it. Left to themselves, the people of a little town like Silverbridge are sure to return a conservative. They are half of them small farmers, and of course will go that way if not made to go the other. If the club mean to pay the cost——"

"The club will pay nothing, papa."

"Then I can only hope that Lopez is doing well in his business!" After that nothing further was said about the election, but she perceived that her father was altogether opposed to the idea of her husband being in Parliament, and that his sympathies and even his wishes were on the other side. When Mrs. Roby suggested that it would be a very nice thing for them all to have Ferdinand in Parliament,—she always called him Ferdinand now,—Mr. Wharton railed at her. "Why should it be a nice thing? I wonder whether you have any idea of a meaning in your head when you say that. Do you suppose that a man gets £1,000 a year by going into Parliament?"

"Laws, Mr. Wharton; how uncivil you are! Of course I know that members of Parliament ain't paid."

"Where 's the niceness, then? If a man has his time at his command and has studied the art of legislation it may be nice, because he will be doing his duty;—or if he wants to get into the Government ruck like your brother-in-law, it may be nice;—or if he be an idle man with a large fortune it may be nice to have some place to go to. But why it should be nice for Ferdinand Lopez I cannot understand. Everett has some idea in his head when he talks about Parliament,—though I cannot say that I agree with him." It may easily be understood that after this Emily would say nothing further in Manchester Square as to her husband's prospects at Silverbridge.

Lopez was at Silverbridge for a couple of days, and then returned, as his wife thought, by no means confident of success. He remained in town nearly a week, and during that time he managed to see the Duchess. He had written to her saying that he would do himself the honour of calling on her, and when he came was admitted. But the account he gave to his wife of the visit did not express much satisfaction. It was quite late in the evening before he told her whither he had been. He had intended to keep the matter to himself, and at last spoke of it,—guided by the feeling which induces all men to tell their secrets to their wives,—because it was a comfort to him to talk to some one who would not openly contradict him. "She's a sly creature after all," he said.

"I had always thought that she was too open rather than sly," said his wife.

"People always try to get a character just opposite to what they deserve. When I hear that a man is always to be believed, I know that he is the most dangerous liar going. She hummed and hawed and would not say a word about the borough. She went so far as to tell me that I was n't to say a word about it to her."

"Was n't that best if her husband wished her not to talk of it?"

"It is all humbug and falsehood to the very bottom. She knows that I am spending money about it, and she ought to be on the square with me. She ought to tell me what she can do and what she can't. When I asked her whether Sprugeon might be trusted, she said that she really wished that I would n't say anything more to her about it. I call that dishonest and sly. I should n't at all wonder but that Fletcher has been with the Duke. If I find that out, won't I expose them both?"

CHAPTER V.

"WHAT BUSINESS IS IT OF YOURS?"

THINGS had not gone altogether smoothly with the Duchess herself since the breaking up of the party at Gatherum Castle,—nor perhaps quite smoothly with the Duke. It was now March. The House was again sitting, and they were both in London,—but till they came to town they had remained at the Castle, and that huge mansion had not been found to be more comfortable by either of them as it became empty. For a time the Duchess had been cowed by her husband's stern decision; but as he again became gentle to her, —almost seeming by his manner to apologise for his unwonted roughness,—she plucked up her spirit and declared to herself that she would not give up the battle. All that she did,—was it not for his sake? And why should she not have her ambition in life as well as he his? And had she not succeeded in all that she had done? Could it be right that she should be asked to abandon everything, to own herself to have been defeated, to be shown to have failed before all the world, because such a one as Major Pountney had made a fool of himself? She attributed it all to Major Pountney;— very wrongly. When a man's mind is veering towards some decision, some conclusion which he has been perhaps slow in reaching, it is probably a little thing which at last fixes his mind and clenches his thoughts. The

Duke had been gradually teaching himself to hate the crowd around him and to reprobate his wife's strategy, before he had known that there was a Major Pountney under his roof. Others had offended him, and first and foremost among them his own colleague, Sir Orlando. The Duchess hardly read his character aright, and certainly did not understand his present motives, when she thought that all might be forgotten as soon as the disagreeable savour of the major should have passed away.

But in nothing, as she thought, had her husband been so silly as in his abandonment of Silverbridge. When she heard that the day was fixed for declaring the vacancy, she ventured to ask him a question. His manner to her lately had been more than urbane, more than affectionate;—it had almost been that of a lover. He had petted her and caressed her when they met, and once even said that nothing should really trouble him as long as he had her with him. Such a speech as that never in his life had he made before to her! So she plucked up her courage and asked her question, —not exactly on that occasion, but soon afterwards; " May not I say a word to Sprugeon about the election?"

" Not a word!" And he looked at her as he had looked on that day when he had told her of the major's sins. She tossed her head and pouted her lips and walked on without speaking. If it was to be so, then indeed would she have failed. And, therefore, though in his general manner he was loving to her, things were not going smooth with her.

And things were not going smooth with him because there had reached him a most troublous despatch from

Sir Orlando Drought only two days before the Cabinet meeting at which the points to be made in the Queen's speech were to be decided. It had been already agreed that a proposition should be made to Parliament by the Government, for an extension of the county suffrage, with some slight redistribution of seats. The towns with less than 20,000 inhabitants were to take in some increased portions of the country parishes around. But there was not enough of a policy in this to satisfy Sir Orlando, nor was the conduct of the bill through the House to be placed in his hands. That was to be intrusted to Mr. Monk, and Mr. Monk would be, if not nominally the leader, yet the chief man of the Government in the House of Commons. This was displeasing to Sir Orlando, and he had, therefore, demanded from the Prime Minister more of a "policy." Sir Orlando's present idea of a policy was the building four bigger ships of war than had ever been built before,—with larger guns, and more men, and thicker iron plates, and, above all, with a greater expenditure of money. He had even gone so far as to say, though not in his semi-official letter to the Prime Minister, that he thought that "The Salvation of the Empire" should be the cry of the Coalition party. "After all," he said, "what the people care about is the Salvation of the Empire!" Sir Orlando was at the head of the Admiralty; and if glory was to be achieved by the four ships, it would rest first on the head of Sir Orlando.

Now the Duke thought that the Empire was safe, and had been throughout his political life averse to increasing the army and navy estimates. He regarded the four ships as altogether unnecessary,—and when reminded that he might in this way consolidate the

Coalition, said that he would rather do without the Coalition and the four ships than have to do with both of them together,—an opinion which was thought by some to be almost traitorous to the party as now organised. The secrets of Cabinets are not to be disclosed lightly, but it came to be understood,—as what is done at Cabinet meetings generally does come to be understood,—that there was something like a disagreement. The Prime Minister, the Duke of St. Bungay, and Mr. Monk were altogether against the four ships. Sir Orlando was supported by Lord Drummond and another of his old friends. At the advice of the elder Duke, a paragraph was hatched, in which it was declared that her Majesty, "having regard to the safety of the nation and the possible, though happily not probable, chances of war, thought that the present strength of the navy should be considered." "It will give him scope for a new gun-boat on an altered principle," said the Duke of St. Bungay. But the Prime Minister, could he have had his own way, would have given Sir Orlando no scope whatever. He would have let the Coalition have gone to the dogs and have fallen himself into infinite political ruin, but that he did not dare that men should hereafter say of him that this attempt at government had failed because he was stubborn, imperious, and self-confident. He had known when he took his present place that he must yield to others; but he had not known how terrible it is to have to yield when a principle is in question,—how great is the suffering when a man finds himself compelled to do that which he thinks should not be done! Therefore, though he had been strangely loving to his wife, the time had not gone smoothly with him.

In direct disobedience to her husband the Duchess did speak a word to Mr. Sprugeon. When at the Castle she was frequently driven through Silverbridge, and on one occasion had her carriage stopped at the ironmonger's door. Out came Mr. Sprugeon, and there were at first half-a-dozen standing by who could hear what she said. Millepois, the cook, wanted to have some new kind of iron plate erected in the kitchen. Of course she had provided herself beforehand with her excuse. As a rule, when the cook wanted anything done, he did not send word to the tradesman by the Duchess. But on this occasion the Duchess was personally most anxious. She wanted to see how the iron plate would work. It was to be a particular kind of iron plate. Then, having watched her opportunity, she said her word, "I suppose we shall be safe with Mr. Lopez." When Mr. Sprugeon was about to reply, she shook her head and went on about the iron plate. This would be quite enough to let Mr. Sprugeon understand that she was still anxious about the borough. Mr. Sprugeon was an intelligent man, and possessed of discretion to a certain extent. As soon as he saw the little frown and the shake of the head, he understood it all. He and the Duchess had a secret together. Would not everything about the Castle in which a morsel of iron was employed want renewing? And would not the Duchess take care that it should all be renewed by Sprugeon? But then he must be active, and his activity would be of no avail unless others helped him. So he whispered a word to Sprout, and it soon became known that the Castle interest was all alive.

But unfortunately the Duke was also on the alert.

The Duke had been very much in earnest when he made up his mind that the old custom should be abandoned at Silverbridge and had endeavoured to impress that determination of his upon his wife. The Duke knew more about his property and was better acquainted with its details than his wife or others believed. He heard that in spite of all his orders the Castle interest was being maintained, and a word was said to him which seemed to imply that this was his wife's doings. It was then about the middle of February, and arrangements were in process for the removal of the family to London. The Duke had already been up to London for the meeting of Parliament, and had now come back to Gatherum, purporting to return to London with his wife. Then it was that it was hinted to him that her Grace was still anxious as to the election,—and had manifested her anxiety. The rumour hurt him, though he did not in the least believe it. It showed to him, as he thought, not that his wife had been false to him, —as in truth she had been,—but that even her name could not be kept free from slander. And when he spoke to her on the subject, he did so rather with the view of proving to her how necessary it was that she should keep herself altogether aloof from such matters, than with any wish to make further inquiry. But he elicited the whole truth. "It is so hard to kill an old-established evil," he said.

"What evil have you failed to kill now?"

"Those people at Silverbridge still say that I want to return a member for them."

"Oh; that's the evil! You know I think that instead of killing an evil, you have murdered an excellent institution." This at any rate was very imprudent on the part of the Duchess. After that disobedient word spoken to Mr. Sprugeon, she should have been more on her guard.

"As to that, Glencora, I must judge for myself."

"Oh yes,—you have been jury, and judge, and executioner."

"I have done as I thought right to do. I am sorry that I should fail to carry you with me in such a matter, but even failing in that I must do my duty. You will at any rate agree with me that when I say the thing should be done, it should be done."

"If you wanted to destroy the house, and cut down all the trees, and turn the place into a wilderness, I suppose you would only have to speak. Of course I know it would be wrong that I should have an opinion. As 'man' you are of course to have your own way." She was in one of her most aggravating moods. Though he might compel her to obey, he could not compel her to hold her tongue.

"Glencora, I don't think you know how much you add to my troubles, or you would not speak to me like that."

"What am I to say? It seems to me that any more suicidal thing than throwing away the borough never was done. Who will thank you? What additional support will you get? How will it increase your power? It's like King Lear throwing off his clothes in the storm because his daughters turned him out. And you did n't do it because you thought it right."

"Yes, I did," he said, scowling.

"You did it because Major Pountney disgusted you. You kicked him out. Why would n't that satisfy you without sacrificing the borough? It is n't what I think or say about it, but that everybody is thinking and saying the same thing."

"I choose that it shall be so."

"Very well."

"And I don't choose that your name shall be mixed up in it. They say in Silverbridge that you are canvassing for Mr. Lopez."

"Who says so?"

"I presume it's not true."

"Who says so, Plantagenet?"

"It matters not who has said so, if it be untrue. I presume it to be false."

"Of course it is false." Then the Duchess remembered her word to Mr. Sprugeon, and the cowardice of the lie was heavy on her. I doubt whether she would have been so shocked by the idea of a falsehood as to have been kept back from it had she before resolved that it would save her; but she was not in her practice a false woman, her courage being too high for falsehood. It now seemed to her that by this lie she was owning herself to be quelled and brought into absolute subjection by her husband. So she burst out into truth. "Now I think of it I did say a word to Mr. Sprugeon. I told him that — that I hoped Mr. Lopez would be returned. I don't know whether you call that canvassing."

"I desired you not to speak to Mr. Sprugeon," he thundered forth.

"That's all very well, Plantagenet, but if you desire me to hold my tongue altogether, what am I to do?"

"What business is this of yours?"

"I suppose I may have my political sympathies as

well as another. Really you are becoming so autocratic that I shall have to go in for women's rights."

"You mean me to understand then that you intend to put yourself in opposition to me."

"What a fuss you make about it all!" she said. "Nothing that one can do is right! You make me wish that I was a milkmaid or a farmer's wife." So saying she bounced out of the room, leaving the Duke sick at heart, low in spirit, and doubtful whether he were right or wrong in his attempts to manage his wife. Surely he must be right in feeling that in his high office a clearer conduct and cleaner way of walking was expected from him than from other men! Noblesse oblige! To his uncle the privilege of returning a member to Parliament had been a thing of course; and when the radical newspapers of the day abused his uncle, his uncle took that abuse as a thing of course. The old Duke acted after his kind, and did not care what others said of him. And he himself, when he first came to his dukedom, was not as he was now. Duties, though they were heavy enough, were lighter then. Serious matters were less serious. There was this and that matter of public policy on which he was intent, but, thinking humbly of himself, he had not yet learned to conceive that he must fit his public conduct in all things to a straight rule of patriotic justice. Now it was different with him, and though the change was painful, he felt it to be imperative. He would fain have been as other men, but he could not. But in this change it was so needful to him that he should carry with him the full sympathies of one person;—that she who was the nearest to him of all should act with him! And now she had not only disobeyed him, but had told him, as some grocer's wife might tell her husband, that he was "making a fuss about it all!"

And then, as he thought of the scene which has been described, he could not quite approve of himself. He knew that he was too self-conscious,—that he was thinking too much about his own conduct and the conduct of others to him. The phrase had been odious to him, but still he could not acquit himself of "making a fuss." Of one thing only was he sure,—that a grievous calamity had befallen him when circumstances compelled him to become the Queen's Prime Minister.

He said nothing further to his wife till they were in London together, and then he was tempted to caress her again, to be loving to her, and to show her that he had forgiven her. But she was brusque to him, as though she did not wish to be forgiven. "Cora," he said, "do not separate yourself from me."

"Separate myself! What on earth do you mean? I have not dreamed of such a thing." The Duchess answered him as though he had alluded to some actual separation.

"I do not mean that. God forbid that a misfortune such as that should ever happen! Do not disjoin yourself from me in all these troubles."

"What am I to do when you scold me? You must know pretty well by this time that I don't like to be scolded. 'I desired you not to speak to Mr. Sprugeon!'" As she repeated his words she imitated his manner and voice closely. "I should n't dream of addressing the children with such magnificence of anger. 'What business is it of yours!' No woman likes that sort of thing, and I'm not sure that I am acquainted with any woman who likes it much less than—Glencora, Duchess of Omnium." As she said these last words in a low whisper, she curtseyed down to the ground.

"You know how anxious I am," he began, "that you should share everything with me,—even in politics. But in all things there must at last be one voice that shall be the ruling voice."

"And that is to be yours,—of course."

"In such a matter as this it must be."

"And, therefore, I like to do a little business of my own behind your back. It's human nature, and you've got to put up with it. I wish you had a better wife. I dare say there are many who would be better. There's the Duchess of St. Bungay who never troubles her husband about politics, but only scolds him because the wind blows from the east. It is just possible there might be worse."

"Oh, Glencora!"

"You had better make the best you can of your bargain and not expect too much from her. And don't ride over her with a very high horse. And let her have her own way a little if you really believe that she has your interest at heart."

After this he was quite aware that she had got the better of him altogether. On that occasion he smiled and kissed her, and went his way. But he was by no means satisfied. That he should be thwarted by her, ate into his very heart;—and it was a wretched thing to him that he could not make her understand his feeling in this respect. If it were to go on he must throw up everything. Ruat cælum, fiat—proper subordination from his wife in regard to public matters! No wife had a fuller allowance of privilege, or more complete power in her hands, as to things fit for women's management. But it was intolerable to him that she should seek to interfere with him in matters of a public nature. And she was constantly doing so. She had always this or that aspirant for office on hand;—this or that job to be carried, though the jobs were not perhaps much in themselves;—this or that affair to be managed by her own political allies, such as Barrington Erle and Phineas Finn. And in his heart he suspected her of a design of managing the Government in her own way, with her own particular friend, Mrs. Finn, for her Prime Minister. If he could in no other way put an end to such evils as these, he must put an end to his own political life. Ruat cælum, fiat justitia. Now "justitia" to him was not compatible with feminine interference in his own special work.

It may therefore be understood that things were not going very smoothly with the Duke and Duchess; and it may also be understood why the Duchess had had very little to say to Mr. Lopez about the election. She was aware that she owed something to Mr. Lopez, whom she had certainly encouraged to stand for the borough, and she had therefore sent her card to his wife and was prepared to invite them both to her parties;—but just at present she was a little tired of Ferdinand Lopez, and perhaps unjustly disposed to couple him with that unfortunate wretch, Major Pountney.

CHAPTER VI.

SHOWING THAT A MAN SHOULD NOT HOWL.

ARTHUR FLETCHER, in his letter to Mrs. Lopez, had told her that when he found out who was to be his antagonist at Silverbridge, it was too late for him to give up the contest. He was, he said, bound in faith to continue it by what had passed between himself and others. But in truth he had not reached this conclusion without some persuasion from others. He had been at Longbarns with his brother when he first heard that Lopez intended to stand, and he at once signified his desire to give way. The information reached him from Mr. Frank Gresham, of Greshamsbury, a gentleman connected with the De Courcys who was now supposed to represent the De Courcy interest in the county, and who had first suggested to Arthur that he should come forward. It was held at Longbarns that Arthur was bound in honour to Mr. Gresham and to Mr. Gresham's friends, and to this opinion he had yielded.

Since Emily Wharton's marriage her name had never been mentioned at Longbarns in Arthur's presence. When he was away,—and of course his life was chiefly passed in London,—old Mrs. Fletcher was free enough in her abuse of the silly creature who had allowed herself to be taken out of her own rank by a Portuguese Jew. But she had been made to understand by her elder son, the lord of Longbarns, that not a word was to be said when Arthur was there. "I think he ought to be taught to forget her," Mrs. Fletcher had said. But John, in his own quiet but imperious way, had declared that there were some men to whom such lessons could not be taught, and that Arthur was one of them. "Is he never to get a wife, then?" Mrs. Fletcher had asked. John would n't pretend to answer that question, but was quite sure that his brother would not be tempted into other matrimonial arrangements by anything that could be said against Emily Lopez. When Mrs. Fletcher declared in her extreme anger that Arthur was a fool for his trouble, John did not contradict her, but declared that the folly was of a nature to require tender treatment.

Matters were in this condition at Longbarns when Arthur communicated to his brother the contents of Mr. Gresham's letter, and expressed his own purpose of giving up Silverbridge. "I don't quite see that," said John.

"No;—and it is impossible that you should be expected to see it. I don't quite know how to talk about it even to you, though I think you are about the softest-hearted fellow out."

"I don't acknowledge the soft heart;—but go on."

"I don't want to interfere with that man. I have a sort of feeling that as he has got her he might as well have the seat too."

"The seat, as you call it, is not there for his gratification or for yours. The seat is there in order that the people of Silverbridge may be represented in Parliament."

"Let them get somebody else. I don't want to put

myself in opposition to him, and I certainly do not want to oppose her."

"They can't change their candidate in that way at a day's notice. You would be throwing Gresham over, and, if you ask me, I think that is a thing you have no right to do. This objection of yours is sentimental, and there is nothing of which a man should be so much in dread as sentimentalism. It is not your fault that you oppose Mr. Lopez. You were in the field first, and you must go on with it." John Fletcher, when he spoke in this way, was, at Longbarns, always supposed to be right; and on the present occasion he, as usual, prevailed. Then Arthur Fletcher wrote his letter to the lady. He would not have liked to have had it known that the composition and copying of that little note had cost him an hour. He had wished that she should understand his feelings, and yet it was necessary that he should address her in words that should be perfectly free from affection or emotion. He must let her know that, though he wrote to her, the letter was for her husband as well as for herself, and he must do this in a manner which would not imply any fear that his writing to her would be taken amiss. The letter when completed was at any rate simple and true; and yet, as we know, it was taken very much amiss.

Arthur Fletcher had by no means recovered from the blow he had received that day when Emily had told him everything down by the river side; but then, it must be said of him that he had no intention of recovery. He was as a man who, having taken a burden on his back, declares to himself that he will, for certain reasons, carry it throughout his life. The man knows that with the burden he cannot walk as men walk who are unencumbered, but for those reasons of his he has chosen to laden himself, and having done so he abandons regret and submits to his circumstances. So had it been with him. He would make no attempt to throw off the load. It was now far back in his life, as much at least as three years, since he had first assured himself of his desire to make Emily Wharton the companion of his life. From that day she had been the pivot on which his whole existence had moved. She had refused his offers more than once, but had done so with so much tender kindness, that, though he had found himself to be wounded and bruised, he had never abandoned his object. Her father and all his own friends encouraged him. He was continually told that her coldness was due to the simple fact that she had not yet learned to give her heart away. And so he had persevered, being ever thoroughly intent on his purpose, till he was told by herself that her love was given to this other man.

Then he knew that it behoved him to set some altered course of life before him. He could not shoot his rival or knock him over the head, nor could he carry off his girl, as used to be done in rougher times. There was nothing now for a man in such a catastrophe as this but submission. But he might submit and shake off his burden, or submit and carry it hopelessly. He told himself that he would do the latter. She had been his goddess, and he would not now worship at another shrine. And then ideas came into his head,—not hopes, or purposes, or a belief even in any possibility, —but vague ideas, mere castles in the air, that a time might come in which it might be in his power to serve her, and to prove to her beyond doubting what had

SHOWING THAT A MAN SHOULD NOT HOWL. 61

been the nature of his love. Like others of his family, he thought ill of Lopez, believing the man to be an adventurer, one who would too probably fall into misfortune, however high he might now seem to hold his head. He was certainly a man not standing on the solid basis of land, or of Three per Cents,—those solidities to which such as the Whartons and Fletchers are wont to trust. No doubt, should there be such fall, the man's wife would have other help than that of her rejected lover. She had a father, brother, and cousins, who would also be there to aid her. The idea was, therefore, but a castle in the air. And yet it was dear to him. At any rate he resolved that he would live for it, and that the woman should still be his goddess, though she was the wife of another man, and might now perhaps never even be seen by him. Then there came upon him, immediately almost after her marriage, the necessity of writing to her. The task was one which, of course, he did not perform lightly.

He never said a word of this to anybody else;—but his brother understood it all, and in a somewhat silent fashion fully sympathised with him. John could not talk to him about love, or mark passages of poetry for him to read, or deal with him at all romantically; but he could take care that his brother had the best horses to ride, and the warmest corner out shooting, and that everything in the house should be done for his brother's comfort. As the squire looked and spoke at Longbarns, others looked and spoke,—so that everybody knew that Mr. Arthur was to be contradicted in nothing. Had he, just at this period, ordered a tree in the park to be cut down, it would, I think, have been cut down, without reference to the master! But, perhaps,

John's power was most felt in the way in which he repressed the expressions of his mother's high indignation. "Mean slut!" she once said, speaking of Emily in her eldest son's hearing. For the girl, to her thinking, had been mean and had been a slut. She had not known,—so Mrs. Fletcher thought,—what birth and blood required of her.

"Mother," John Fletcher had said, "you would break Arthur's heart if he heard you speak in that way, and I am sure you would drive him from Longbarns. Keep it to yourself." The old woman had shaken her head angrily, but she had endeavoured to do as she had been bid.

"Isn't your brother riding that horse a little rashly?" Reginald Cotgrave said to John Fletcher in the hunting-field one day.

"I didn't observe," said John; "but whatever horse he's on, he always rides rashly." Arthur was mounted on a long, raking thoroughbred black animal, which he had bought himself about a month ago, and which, having been run at steeplechases, rushed at every fence as though he were going to swallow it. His brother had begged him to put some rough-rider up till the horse could be got to go quietly, but Arthur had persevered. And during the whole of this day the squire had been in a tremor, lest there should be some accident.

"He used to have a little more judgment, I think," said Cotgrave. "He went at that double just now as hard as the brute could tear. If the horse hadn't done it all, where would he have been?"

"In the further ditch, I suppose. But you see the horse did do it all."

This was all very well as an answer to Reginald

SHOWING THAT A MAN SHOULD NOT HOWL. 63

Cotgrave,—to whom it was not necessary that Fletcher should explain the circumstances. But the squire had known as well as Cotgrave that his brother had been riding rashly, and he had understood the reason why. "I don't think a man ought to break his neck," he said, "because he can't get everything that he wishes." The two brothers were standing then together before the fire in the squire's own room, having just come in from hunting.

"Who is going to break his neck?"

"They tell me that you tried to to-day."

"Because I was riding a pulling horse. I'll back him to be the biggest leaper and the quickest horse in Herefordshire."

"I dare say,—though for the matter of that the chances are very much against it. But a man should n't ride so as to have those things said of him."

"What is a fellow to do if he can't hold a horse?"

"Get off him."

"That 's nonsense, John!"

"No, it 's not. You know what I mean very well. If I were to lose half my property to-morrow, don't you think it would cut me up a good deal?"

"It would me, I know."

"But what would you think of me if I howled about it?"

"Do I howl?" asked Arthur angrily.

"Every man howls who is driven out of his ordinary course by any trouble. A man howls if he goes about frowning always."

"Do I frown?"

"Or laughing."

"Do I laugh?"

"Or galloping over the country like a mad devil who wants to get rid of his debts by breaking his neck. Æquam memento—— You remember all that, don't you?"

"I remember it; but it is n't so easy to do it."

"Try. There are other things to be done in life except getting married. You are going into Parliament."

"I don't know that."

"Gresham tells me there is n't a doubt about it. Think of that. Fix your mind upon it. Don't take it only as an accident, but as the thing you 're to live for. If you 'll do that,—if you 'll so manage that there shall be something to be done in Parliament which only you can do, you won't ride a runaway horse as you did that brute to-day." Arthur looked up into his brother's face almost weeping. "We expect much of you, you know. I 'm not a man to do anything except be a good steward for the family property, and keep the old house from falling down. You 're a clever fellow,—so that between us, if we both do our duty, the Fletchers may still thrive in the land. My house shall be your house, and my wife your wife, and my children your children. And then the honour you win shall be my honour. Hold up your head,—and sell that beast." Arthur Fletcher squeezed his brother's hand and went away to dress.

CHAPTER VII.

THE SILVERBRIDGE ELECTION.

ABOUT a month after this affair with the runaway horse Arthur Fletcher went to Greshamsbury, preparatory to his final sojourn at Silverbridge, for the week previous to his election. Greshamsbury, the seat of Francis Gresham, Esq., who was a great man in these parts, was about twenty miles from Silverbridge, and the tedious work of canvassing the electors could not therefore be done from thence;—but he spent a couple of pleasant days with his old friend, and learned what was being said and what was being done in and about the borough. Mr. Gresham was a man not as yet quite forty years of age, very popular, with a large family, of great wealth, and master of the county hounds. His father had been an embarrassed man, with a large estate; but this Gresham had married a lady with immense wealth, and had prospered in the world. He was not an active politician. He did not himself care for Parliament, or for the good things which political power can give; and was on this account averse to the Coalition. He thought that Sir Orlando Drought and the others were touching pitch and had defiled themselves. But he was conscious that in so thinking he was one of but a small minority; and, bad as the world around him certainly was, terrible as had been the fall of the glory of old England, he was nevertheless content to live without loud grumbling as long as the farmers paid him their rent, and the labourers in his part of the country did not strike for wages, and the land when sold would fetch thirty years' purchase. He had not therefore been careful to ascertain that Arthur Fletcher would pledge himself to oppose the Coalition before he proffered his assistance in this matter of the borough. It would not be easy to find such a candidate, or perhaps possible to bring him in when found. The Fletchers had always been good conservatives, and were proper people to be in Parliament. A conservative in Parliament is, of course, obliged to promote a great many things which he does not really approve. Mr. Gresham quite understood that. You can't have tests and qualifications, rotten boroughs and the divine right of kings, back again. But as the glorious institutions of the country are made to perish, one after the other, it is better that they should receive the coup de grace tenderly from loving hands than be roughly throttled by radicals. Mr. Gresham would thank his stars that he could still preserve foxes down in his own country, instead of doing any of this dirty work,—for let the best be made of such work, still it was dirty,—and was willing, now as always, to give his assistance, and if necessary to spend a little money, to put a Fletcher into Parliament and to keep a Lopez out.

There was to be a third candidate. That was the first news that Fletcher heard. "It will do us all the good in the world," said Mr. Gresham. "The rads in the borough are not satisfied with Mr. Lopez. They say they don't know him. As long as a certain set could make it be believed that he was the Duke's nominee they were content to accept him;—even though he was not proposed directly by the Duke's people in the usual way. But the Duke has made himself understood at last. You have seen the Duke's letter?" Arthur had not seen the Duke's letter, which had only been published in the Silverbridge Gazette of that week, and he now read it, sitting in Mr. Gresham's magistrate's-room, as a certain chamber in the house had been called since the days of the present squire's great-grandfather.

The Duke's letter was addressed to his recognised man of business in those parts, and was as follows:—

"Carlton Terrace, March, 187—.

"My dear Mr. Moreton." (Mr. Moreton was the successor of one Mr. Fothergill, who had reigned supreme in those parts under the old Duke.)

"I am afraid that my wishes with regard to the borough and the forthcoming election there of a member of Parliament are not yet clearly understood, although I endeavoured to declare them when I was at Gatherum Castle. I trust that no elector will vote for this or that gentleman with an idea that the return of any special candidate will please me. The ballot will of course prevent me or any other man from knowing how an elector may vote;—but I beg to assure the electors generally that should they think fit to return a member pledged to oppose the Government of which I form a part, it would not in any way change my cordial feelings towards the town. I may perhaps be allowed to add that, in my opinion, no elector can do his duty except by voting for the candidate whom he thinks best qualified to serve the country. In regard to the gentlemen who are now before the constituency,

I have no feeling for one rather than for the other; and had I any such feeling I should not wish it to actuate the vote of a single elector. I should be glad if this letter could be published so as to be brought under the eyes of the electors generally.

"Yours faithfully,
"Omnium."

When the Duke said that he feared that his wishes were not understood, and spoke of the inefficacy of his former declaration, he was alluding of course to the Duchess and to Mr. Sprugeon. Mr. Sprugeon guessed that it might be so, and, still wishing to have the Duchess for his good friend, was at once assiduous in explaining to his friends in the borough that even this letter did not mean anything. A Prime Minister was bound to say that kind of thing! But the borough, if it wished to please the Duke, must return Lopez in spite of the Duke's letter. Such was Mr. Sprugeon's doctrine. But he did not carry Mr. Sprout with him. Mr. Sprout at once saw his opportunity, and suggested to Mr. Du Boung, the local brewer, that he should come forward. Du Boung was a man rapidly growing into provincial eminence, and jumped at the offer. Consequently there were three candidates. Du Boung came forward as a conservative prepared to give a cautious, but very cautious, support to the Coalition. Mr. Du Boung, in his printed address, said very sweet things of the Duke generally. The borough was blessed by the vicinity of the Duke. But, looking at the present perhaps unprecedented crisis in affairs, Mr. Du Boung was prepared to give no more than a very cautious support to the Duke's Government. Arthur

Fletcher read Mr. Du Boung's address immediately after the Duke's letter.

"The more the merrier," said Arthur.

"Just so. Du Boung will not rob you of a vote, but he will cut the ground altogether from under the other man's feet. You see that as far as actual political programme goes there is n't much to choose between any of you. You are all Government men."

"With a difference."

"One man in these days is so like another," continued Gresham sarcastically, "that it requires good eyes to see the shades of the colours."

"Then you 'd better support Du Boung," said Arthur.

"I think you 've just a turn in your favour. Besides, I could n't really carry a vote myself. As for Du Boung, I 'd sooner have him than a foreign cad like Lopez." Then Arthur Fletcher frowned and Mr. Gresham became confused, remembering the catastrophe about the young lady whose story he had heard. "Du Boung used to be plain English as Bung before he got rich and made his name beautiful," continued Gresham, "but I suppose Mr. Lopez does come of foreign extraction."

"I don't know what he comes from," said Arthur moodily. "They tell me he 's a gentleman. However, as we are to have a contest, I hope he may n't win."

"Of course you do. And he shan't win. Nor shall the great Du Boung. You shall win, and become Prime Minister, and make me a peer. Would you like papa to be Lord Greshamsbury?" he said to a little girl who then rushed into the room.

"No, I would n't. I 'd like papa to give me the pony which the man wants to sell out in the yard."

"She 's quite right, Fletcher," said the squire. "I 'm much more likely to be able to buy them ponies as simple Frank Gresham than I should be if I had a lord's coronet to pay for."

This was on a Saturday, and on the following Monday Mr. Gresham drove the candidate over to Silverbridge and started him on his work of canvassing. Mr. Du Boung had been busy ever since Mr. Sprout's brilliant suggestion had been made, and Lopez had been in the field even before him. Each one of the candidates called at the house of every elector in the borough,—and every man in the borough was an elector. When they had been at work for four or five days each candidate assured the borough that he had already received promises of votes sufficient to insure his success, and each candidate was as anxious as ever, —nay, was more rabidly anxious than ever,—to secure the promise of a single vote. Hints were made by honest citizens of the pleasure they would have in supporting this or that gentleman,—for the honest citizens assured one gentleman after the other of the satisfaction they had in seeing so all-sufficient a candidate in the borough,—if the smallest pecuniary help were given them, even a day's pay, so that their poor children might not be injured by their going to the poll. But the candidates and their agents were stern in their replies to such temptations. "That 's a dodge of that rascal Sprout," said Sprugeon to Mr. Lopez. "That 's one of Sprout's men. If he could get half-a-crown from you it would be all up with us." But though Sprugeon called Sprout a rascal, he laid the same bait both for Du Boung and for Fletcher;—but laid it in vain. Everybody said that it was a very clean election. "A brewer standing, and devil a glass of beer!" said one old elector who had remembered better things when the borough never heard of a contest.

On the third day of his canvass Arthur Fletcher with his gang of agents and followers behind him met Lopez with his gang in the street. It was probable that they would so meet, and Fletcher had resolved what he would do when such a meeting took place. He walked up to Lopez, and with a kindly smile offered his hand. The two men, though they had never been intimate, had known each other, and Fletcher was determined to show that he would not quarrel with a man because that man had been his favoured rival. In comparison with that other matter this affair of the candidature was of course trivial. But Lopez, who had, as the reader may remember, made some threat about a horsewhip, had come to a resolution of a very different nature. He put his arms akimbo, resting his hands on his hips, and altogether declined the proffered civility. "You had better walk on," he said, and then stood, scowling, on the spot till the other should pass by. Fletcher looked at him for a moment, then bowed and passed on. At least a dozen men saw what had taken place, and were aware that Mr. Lopez had expressed his determination to quarrel personally with Mr. Fletcher, in opposition to Mr. Fletcher's expressed wish for amity. And before they had gone to bed that night all the dozen knew the reason why. Of course there was some one then at Silverbridge clever enough to find out that Arthur Fletcher had been in love with Miss Wharton, but that Miss Wharton had lately been married to Mr. Lopez. No doubt the incident added a pleasurable emotion to the excitement caused by the election at Silverbridge generally. A personal quarrel is attractive everywhere. The expectation of such an occurrence will bring together the whole House of Commons. And of course this quarrel was very attractive in Silverbridge. There were some Fletcherites and Lopezites in the quarrel; as there were also Du Boungites, who maintained that when gentlemen could not canvass without quarrelling in the streets they were manifestly unfit to represent such a borough as Silverbridge in Parliament;—and that therefore Mr. Du Boung should be returned.

Mr. Gresham was in the town that day, though not till after the occurrence, and Fletcher could not avoid speaking of it. "The man must be a cur," said Gresham.

"It would make no difference in the world to me," said Arthur, struggling hard to prevent signs of emotion from showing themselves in his face, "were it not that he has married a lady whom I have long known and whom I greatly esteem." He felt that he could hardly avoid all mention of the marriage, and yet was determined that he would say no word that his brother would call "howling."

"There has been no previous quarrel, or offence?" asked Gresham.

"None in the least." When Arthur so spoke he forgot altogether the letter he had written; nor, had he then remembered it, would he have thought it possible that that letter should have given offence. He had been the sufferer, not Lopez. This man had robbed him of his happiness; and, though it would have been foolish in him to make a quarrel for a grievance such as that, there might have been some excuse had he done so. It had taken him some time to perceive that greatly as this man had injured him, there had been no injustice done to him, and that therefore there should be no complaint made by him. But that this other man should complain was to him unintelligible.

"He is not worth your notice," said Mr. Gresham. "He is simply not a gentleman, and does not know how to behave himself. I am very sorry for the young lady;—that's all." At this allusion to Emily Arthur felt that his face became red with the rising blood; and he felt also that his friend should not have spoken thus openly,—thus irreverently,—on so sacred a subject. But at the moment he said nothing further. As far as his canvass was concerned it had been successful, and he was beginning to feel sure that he would be the new member. He endeavoured therefore to drown his sorrow in this coming triumph.

But Lopez had been by no means gratified with his canvass or with the conduct of the borough generally. He had already begun to feel that the Duchess and Mr. Sprugeon and the borough had thrown him over shamefully. Immediately on his arrival in Silverbridge a local attorney had with the blandest possible smile asked him for a cheque for £500. Of course there must be money spent at once, and of course the money must come out of the candidate's pocket. He had known all this beforehand, and yet the demand for the money had come upon him as an injury. He gave the cheque, but showed clearly by his manner that he resented the application. This did not tend to bind to him more closely the services of those who were present when the demand was made. And then, as he began his canvass, he found that he could not conjure at all with the name of the Duke, or even with that of the Duchess; and was told on the second day by Mr. Sprugeon himself that he had better fight the battle "on his own hook." Now his own hook in Silverbridge was certainly not a strong hook. Mr. Sprugeon was still of opinion that a good deal might be done by judicious manipulation, and went so far as to suggest that another cheque for £500 in the hands of Mr. Wise, the lawyer, would be effective. But Lopez did not give the other cheque, and Sprugeon whispered to him that the Duke had been too many for the Duchess. Still he had persevered, and a set of understrappers around him, who would make nothing out of the election without his candidature, assured him from time to time that he would even yet come out all right at the ballot. With such a hope still existing he had not scrupled to affirm in his speeches that the success of his canvass had been complete. But, on the morning of the day on which he met Fletcher in the street, Mr. Du Boung had called upon him accompanied by two of the Du Boung agents and by Mr. Sprugeon himself,—and had suggested that he, Lopez, should withdraw from the contest, so that Du Boung might be returned, and that the "liberal interests" of the borough might not be sacrificed.

This was a heavy blow, and one which Ferdinand Lopez was not the man to bear with equanimity. From the moment in which the Duchess had mentioned the borough to him, he had regarded the thing as certain. After a while he had understood that his return must be accompanied by more trouble and greater expense than he had at first anticipated;—but still he had thought that it was all but sure. He had altogether misunderstood the nature of the influence exercised by the Duchess, and the nature also of the Duke's resolution. Mr. Sprugeon had of course wished to have a candidate, and had allured him. Perhaps he had in some degree been ill-treated by the borough. But he was a man whom the feeling of injustice to himself would drive almost to frenzy, though he never measured the amount of his own injustice to others. When the proposition was made to him, he scowled at them all, and declared that he would fight the borough to the last. "Then you'll let Mr. Fletcher in to a certainty," said Mr. Sprout. Now there was an idea in the borough that, although all the candidates were ready to support the Duke's government, Mr. Du Boung and Mr. Lopez were the two liberals. Mr. Du Boung was sitting in the room when the appeal was made, and declared that he feared that such would be the result. "I'll tell you what I'll do," said Lopez; "I'll toss up which of us retires." Mr. Sprout, on behalf of Mr. Du Boung, protested against that proposition. Mr. Du Boung, who was a gentleman of great local influence, was in possession of four-fifths of the liberal interests of the borough. Even were he to retire Mr. Lopez could not get in. Mr. Sprout declared that this was known to all the borough at large. He, Sprout, was sorry that a gentleman like Mr. Lopez should have been brought down there under false ideas. He had all through told Mr. Sprugeon that the Duke had been in earnest, but Mr. Sprugeon had not comprehended the position. It had been a pity. But anybody who understood the borough could see with one eye that Mr. Lopez had not a chance. If Mr. Lopez would retire Mr. Du Boung would no doubt be returned. If Mr. Lopez went to the poll, Mr. Fletcher would probably be the new member. This was the picture as it was painted by Mr. Sprout,—who had, even then, heard something of the loves of the two candidates, and who had thought that Lopez would be glad to injure Arthur Fletcher's chances of success. So far he was not wrong;—but the sense of the injury done to himself oppressed Lopez so much that he could not guide himself by reason. The idea of retiring was very painful to him, and he did not believe these men. He thought it to be quite possible that they were there to facilitate the return of Arthur Fletcher. He had never even heard of Du Boung till he had come to Silverbridge two or three days ago. He still could not believe that Du Boung would be returned. He thought over it all for a moment, and then he gave his answer. "I've been brought down here to fight, and I'll fight it to the last," he said. "Then you'll hand over the borough to Mr. Fletcher," said Sprout, getting up and ushering Mr. Du Boung out of the room.

It was after that, but on the same day, that Lopez and Fletcher met each other in the street. The affair did not take a minute, and then they parted, each on his own way. In the course of that evening Mr. Sprugeon told his candidate that he, Sprugeon, could not concern himself any further in that election. He was very sorry for what had occurred;—very sorry indeed. It was no doubt a pity that the Duke had been so firm,

"But,"—and Mr. Sprugeon shrugged his shoulders as he spoke,—"when a nobleman like the Duke chooses to have a way of his own, he must have it." Mr. Sprugeon went on to declare that any further candidature would be waste of money, waste of time, and waste of energy, and then signified his intention of retiring, as far as this election went, into private life. When asked, he acknowledged that they who had been acting with him had come to the same resolve. Mr. Lopez had in fact come there as the Duke's nominee, and as the Duke had no nominee, Mr. Lopez was in fact "nowhere."

"I don't suppose that any man was ever so treated before, since members were first returned to Parliament," said Lopez.

"Well, sir;—yes, sir; it is a little hard. But, you see, sir, her Grace meant the best. Her Grace did mean the best, no doubt. It may be, sir, there was a little misunderstanding;—a little misunderstanding at the Castle, sir." Then Mr. Sprugeon retired, and Lopez understood that he was to see nothing more of the ironmonger.

Of course there was nothing for him now but to retire;—to shake the dust off his feet and get out of Silverbridge as quickly as he could. But his friends had all deserted him and he did not know how to retire. He had paid £500, and he had a strong opinion that a portion at least of the money should be returned to him. He had a keen sense of ill-usage, and at the same time a feeling that he ought not to run out of the borough like a whipt dog, without showing his face to any one. But his strongest sensation at this moment was one of hatred against Arthur Fletcher.

He was sure that Arthur Fletcher would be the new member. He did not put the least trust in Mr. Du Boung. He had taught himself really to think that Fletcher had insulted him by writing to his wife, and that a further insult had been offered to him by that meeting in the street. He had told his wife that he would ask Fletcher to give up the borough, and that he would make that request with a horsewhip in his hand. It was too late now to say anything of the borough, but it might not be too late for the horsewhip. He had a great desire to make good that threat as far as the horsewhip was concerned,—having an idea that he would thus lower Fletcher in his wife's eyes. It was not that he was jealous,—not jealous according to the ordinary meaning of the word. His wife's love to himself had been too recently given and too warmly maintained for such a feeling as that. But there was a rancorous hatred in his heart against the man, and a conviction that his wife at any rate esteemed the man whom he hated. And then would he not make his retreat from the borough with more honour if before he left he could horsewhip his successful antagonist? We, who know the feeling of Englishmen generally better than Mr. Lopez did, would say—certainly not. We would think that such an incident would by no means redound to the credit of Mr. Lopez. And he himself, probably, at cooler moments, would have seen the folly of such an idea. But anger about the borough had driven him mad, and now in his wretchedness the suggestion had for him a certain charm. The man had outraged all propriety by writing to his wife. Of course he would be justified in horsewhipping him. But there were difficulties. A man is not horsewhipped simply because you wish to horsewhip him.

In the evening, as he was sitting alone, he got a note from Mr. Sprugeon. "Mr. Sprugeon's compliments. Does n't Mr. Lopez think an address to the electors should appear in to-morrow's Gazette,—very short and easy;—something like the following." Then Mr. Sprugeon added a very "short and easy letter" to the electors of the borough of Silverbridge, in which Mr. Lopez was supposed to tell them that although his canvass promised to him every success, he felt that he owed it to the borough to retire lest he should injure the borough by splitting the liberal interest with their much respected fellow-townsman, Mr. Du Boung. In the course of the evening he did copy that letter, and sent it out to the newspaper office. He must retire, and it was better for him that he should retire after some recognised fashion. But he wrote another letter also, and sent it over to the Opposition hotel. The other letter was as follows:—

"Sir,—Before this election began you were guilty of gross impertinence in writing a letter to my wife,— to her extreme annoyance and to my most justifiable anger. Any gentleman would think that the treatment you had already received at her hands would have served to save her from such insult, but there are men who will never take a lesson without a beating. And now, since you have been here, you have presumed to offer to shake hands with me in the street, though you ought to have known that I should not choose to meet you on friendly terms after what has taken place. I now write to tell you that I shall carry a horsewhip while I am here, and that if I meet you in the streets again before I leave the town I shall use it.

"FERDINAND LOPEZ.

"Mr. Arthur Fletcher."

This letter he sent at once to his enemy, and then sat late into the night thinking of his threat and of the manner in which he would follow it up. If he could only get one fair blow at Fletcher his purpose, he thought, would be achieved. In any matter of horse-whipping the truth hardly ever gets itself correctly known. The man who has given the first blow is generally supposed to have thrashed the other. What might follow, though it might be inconvenient, must be borne. The man had insulted him by writing to his wife, and the sympathies of the world, he thought, would be with him. To give him his due, it must be owned that he had no personal fear as to the encounter.

That night Arthur Fletcher had gone over to Greshamsbury, and on the following morning he returned with Mr. Gresham. "For Heaven's sake look at that!" he said, handing the letter to his friend.

"Did you ever write to his wife?" asked Gresham, when he read it.

"Yes;—I did. All this is dreadful to me;—dreadful. Well;—you know how it used to be with me. I need not go into all that; need I?"

"Don't say a word more than you think necessary."

"When you asked me to stand for the place I had not heard that he thought of being a candidate. I wrote and told her so, and told her also that had I known it before I would not have come here."

"I don't quite see that," said Gresham.

"Perhaps not;—perhaps I was a fool. But we need n't go into that. At any rate there was no insult to him. I wrote in the simplest language."

"Looking at it all round I think you had better not have written."

"You would n't say so if you saw the letter. I 'm sure you would n't. I had known her all my life. My brother is married to her cousin. Oh heavens! we had been all but engaged. I would have done anything for her. Was it not natural that I should tell her? As far as the language was concerned the letter was one to be read at Charing Cross."

"He says that she was annoyed and insulted."

"Impossible! It was a letter that any man might have written to any woman."

"Well;—you have got to take care of yourself at any rate. What will you do?"

"What ought I to do?"

"Go to the police." Mr. Gresham had himself once, when young, thrashed a man who had offended him, and had then thought himself much aggrieved because the police had been called in. But that had been twenty years ago, and Mr. Gresham's opinions had been matured and, perhaps, corrected by age.

"No; I won't do that," said Arthur Fletcher.

"That's what you ought to do."

"I could n't do that."

"Then take no notice of the letter and carry a fairly big stick. It should be big enough to hurt him a good deal, but not to do him any serious damage." At that moment an agent came in with news of the man's retirement from the contest. "Has he left the town?" asked Gresham. No;—he had not left the town, nor had he been seen by any one that morning. "You had better let me go out and get the stick, before you show yourself," said Gresham. And so the stick was selected.

As the two walked down the street together, almost the first thing they saw was Lopez standing at his hotel door with a cutting whip in his hand. He was at that moment quite alone, but on the opposite side of the street there was a policeman,—one of the borough constables,—very slowly making his way along the pavement. His movement, indeed, was so slow that any one watching him would have come to the conclusion that that particular part of the High Street had some attraction for him at that special moment. Alas, alas! How age will alter the spirit of a man! Twenty years since Frank Gresham would have thought any one to be a mean miscreant who would have interposed a policeman between him and his foe. But it is to be feared that while selecting that stick he had said a word which was causing the constable to loiter on the pavement!

But Gresham turned no eye to the policeman as he walked on with his friend, and Fletcher did not see the man. "What an ass he is!" said Fletcher,—as he got the handle of the stick well into his hand. Then Lopez advanced to them with his whip raised; but as he did so the policeman came across the street quickly, but very quietly, and stood right before him. The man was so thoroughly in the way of the aggrieved wretch that it was out of the question that he should touch Fletcher with his whip.

"Do you usually walk about attended by a policeman?" said Lopez, with all the scorn which he knew how to throw into his voice.

"I did n't know that the man was here," said Fletcher.

"You may tell that to the marines. All the borough shall know what a coward you are." Then he turned round and addressed the street, but still under the shadow, as it were, of the policeman's helmet. "This man who presumes to offer himself as a candidate to represent Silverbridge in Parliament has insulted my wife. And now, because he fears that I shall horsewhip him, he goes about the street under the care of a policeman."

"This is intolerable," said Fletcher, turning to his friend.

"Mr. Lopez," said Gresham, "I am sorry to say that I must give you in charge;—unless you will undertake to leave the town without interfering further with Mr. Fletcher either by word or deed."

"I will undertake nothing," said Lopez. "The man has insulted my wife, and is a coward."

About two o'clock on the afternoon of that day Mr. Lopez appeared before the Silverbridge bench of magistrates, and was there sworn to keep the peace to Mr. Fletcher for the next six months. After that he was allowed to leave the town, and was back in London, with his wife in Belgrave Mansion, to dinner that evening.

On the day but one after this the ballot was taken, and at eight o'clock on the evening of that day Arthur Fletcher was declared to be duly elected. But Mr. Du Boung ran him very hard.

The numbers were—

> FLETCHER . . . 315
> DU BOUNG . . . 308

Mr. Du Boung's friends during these two last days had not hesitated to make what use they could on behalf of their own candidate of the Lopez and Fletcher quarrel. If Mr. Fletcher had insulted the other man's wife, surely he could not be a proper member for Silverbridge. And then the row was declared to have been altogether discreditable. Two strangers had come into this peaceful town and had absolutely quarrelled with sticks and whips in the street, calling each other opprobrious names. Would it not be better that they should elect their own respectable townsman? All this was nearly effective. But, in spite of all, Arthur Fletcher was at last returned.

CHAPTER VIII.

LOPEZ BACK IN LONDON.

LOPEZ, as he returned to town, recovered something of his senses, though he still fancied that Arthur Fletcher had done him a positive injury by writing to his wife. But something of that madness left him which had come from his deep sense of injury, both as to the letter and as to the borough, and he began to feel that he had been wrong about the horsewhip. He was very low in spirits on this return journey. The money which he had spent had been material to him, and the loss of it for the moment left him nearly bare. While he had had before his eyes the hope of being a member of Parliament he had been able to buoy himself up. The position itself would have gone very far with Sexty Parker, and would, he thought, have had some effect even with his father-in-law. But now he was returning a beaten man. Who is there that has not felt that fall from high hope to utter despair which comes from some single failure? As he thought of this he was conscious that his anger had led him into great imprudence at Silverbridge. He had not been circumspect as it specially behoved a man to be surrounded by such difficulties as his. All his life he had been schooling his temper so as to keep it under control,—sometimes with great difficulty, but always with a consciousness that in his life everything might depend on it. Now he had, alas, allowed it to get the better of him. No doubt he had been insulted;—but, nevertheless, he had been wrong to speak of a horsewhip.

His one great object must now be to conciliate his father-in-law, and he had certainly increased his difficulty in doing this by his squabble down at Silverbridge. Of course the whole thing would be reported in the London papers, and of course the story would be told against him, as the respectabilities of the town had been opposed to him. But he knew himself to be clever, and he still hoped that he might overcome these difficulties. Then it occurred to him that in doing this he must take care to have his wife entirely on his side. He did not doubt her love; he did not in the least doubt her rectitude;—but there was the lamentable fact that she thought well of Arthur Fletcher. It might be that he had been a little too imperious with his wife. It suited his disposition to be imperious within his own household;—to be imperious out of it, if that were possible;—but he was conscious of having had a fall at Silverbridge, and he must for a while take in some sail.

He had telegraphed to her, acquainting her with his defeat, and telling her to expect his return. "Oh, Ferdinand," she said, "I am so unhappy about this. It has made me so wretched!"

"Better luck next time," he said with his sweetest smile. "It is no good groaning over spilt milk. They have n't treated me really well,—have they?"

"I suppose not,—though I do not quite understand it all."

He was burning to abuse Arthur Fletcher, but he abstained. He would abstain at any rate for the present moment. "Dukes and Duchesses are no doubt very grand people," he said, "but it is a pity they should not know how to behave honestly, as they expect others to behave to them. The Duchess has thrown me over in the most infernal way. I really can't understand it. When I think of it I am lost in wonder. The truth, I suppose, is, that there has been some quarrel between him and her."

"Who will get in?"

"Oh, Du Boung, no doubt." He did not think so, but he could not bring himself to declare the success of his enemy to her. "The people there know him. Your old friend is as much a stranger there as I am. By-the-way he and I had a little row in the place."

"A row, Ferdinand!"

"You need n't look like that, my pet. I have n't killed him. But he came up to speak to me in the street, and I told him what I thought about his writing to you." On hearing this Emily looked very wretched. "I could not restrain myself from doing that. Come;—you must admit that he should n't have written."

"He meant it in kindness."

"Then he should n't have meant it. Just think of it. Suppose that I had been making up to any girl,—which by-the-bye I never did but to one in my life,"—then he put his arm round her waist and kissed her, "and she were to have married some one else. What would have been said of me if I had begun to correspond with her immediately? Don't suppose I am blaming you, dear."

"Certainly I do not suppose that," said Emily.

"But you must admit that it were rather strong." He paused, but she said nothing. "Only I suppose you can bring yourself to admit nothing against him. However, so it was. There was a row, and a policeman came up, and they made me give a promise that I did n't mean to shoot him or anything of that kind." As she heard this she turned pale, but said nothing. "Of course I did n't want to shoot him. I wished him to know what I thought about it, and I told him. I hate to trouble you with all this, but I could n't bear that you should n't know it all."

"It is very sad!"

"Sad enough! I have had plenty to bear, I can tell you. Everybody seemed to turn away from me there. Everybody deserted me." As he said this he could perceive that he must obtain her sympathy by recounting his own miseries and not Arthur Fletcher's sins. "I was all alone and hardly knew how to hold up my head against so much wretchedness. And then I found myself called upon to pay an enormous sum for my expenses."

"Oh, Ferdinand!"

"Think of their demanding £500!"

"Did you pay it?"

"Yes, indeed. I had no alternative. Of course they took care to come for that before they talked of my resigning. I believe it was all planned beforehand. The whole thing seems to me to have been a swindle from the beginning to the end. By Heaven, I 'm almost inclined to think that the Duchess knew all about it herself!"

"About the £500!"

"Perhaps not the exact sum, but the way in which the thing was to be done. In these days one does n't know whom to trust. Men, and women too, have become so dishonest that nobody is safe anywhere. It has been awfully hard upon me,—awfully hard. I don't suppose that there was ever a moment in my life when the loss of £500 would have been so much to me as it is now. The question is, what will your father do for us?" Emily could not but remember her husband's intense desire to obtain money from her father not yet three months since, as though all the world depended on his getting it,—and his subsequent elation, as though all his sorrows were over forever, because the money had been promised. And now,—almost immediately,—he was again in the same position. She endeavoured to judge him kindly, but a feeling of insecurity in reference to his affairs struck her at once and made her heart cold. Everything had been achieved, then, by a gift of £3,000,—surely a small sum to effect such a result with a man living as her husband lived. And now the whole £3,000 was gone;—surely a large sum to have vanished in so short a time! Something of the uncertainty of business she could understand, but a business must be perilously uncertain if subject to such vicissitudes as these! But as ideas of this nature crowded themselves into her mind she told herself again and again that she had taken him for better and for worse. If the worse were already coming she would still be true to her promise. "You had better tell papa everything," she said.

"Had it not better come from you?"

"No, Ferdinand. Of course I will do as you bid me. I will do anything that I can do. But you had better tell him. His nature is such that he will respect you more if it come from yourself. And then it is so necessary that he should know all;—all." She put whatever emphasis she knew how to use upon this word.

"You could tell him—all, as well as I."

"You would not bring yourself to tell it to me, nor could I understand it. He will understand everything, and if he thinks that you have told him everything, he will at any rate respect you."

He sat silent for a while meditating, feeling always and most acutely that he had been ill-used,—never thinking for an instant that he had ill-used others. "Three thousand pounds, you know, was no fortune for your father to give you!" She had no answer to make, but she groaned in spirit as she heard the accusation. "Don't you feel that yourself?"

"I know nothing about money, Ferdinand. If you had told me to speak to him about it before we were married I would have done so."

"He ought to have spoken to me. It is marvellous how close-fisted an old man can be. He can't take it with him." Then he sat for half an hour in moody silence, during which she was busy with her needle. After that he jumped up, with a manner altogether altered,—gay, only that the attempt was too visible to deceive even her,—and shook himself, as though he were ridding himself of his trouble. "You are right, old girl. You are always right,—almost. I will go to your father to-morrow, and tell him everything. It is n't so very much that I want him to do. Things will all come right again. I'm ashamed that you should have seen me in this way;—but I have been disappointed about the election, and troubled about that

Mr. Fletcher. You shall not see me give way again like this. Give me a kiss, old girl."

She kissed him, but she could not even pretend to recover herself as he had done. "Had we not better give up the brougham?" she said.

"Certainly not. For Heaven's sake do not speak in that way! You do not understand things.".

"No; certainly I do not."

"It is n't that I have n't the means of living, but that in my business money is so often required for instant use. And situated as I am at present an addition to my capital would enable me to do so much!" She certainly did not understand it, but she had sufficient knowledge of the world and sufficient common sense to be aware that their present rate of expenditure ought to be matter of importance to a man who felt the loss of £500 as he felt that loss at Silverbridge.

On the next morning Lopez was at Mr. Wharton's chambers early,—so early that the lawyer had not yet reached them. He had resolved,—not that he would tell everything, for such men never even intend to tell everything,—but that he would tell a good deal. He must, if possible, affect the mind of the old man in two ways. He must ingratiate himself;—and at the same time make it understood that Emily's comfort in life would depend very much on her father's generosity. The first must be first accomplished, if possible,—and then the second, as to which he could certainly produce at any rate belief. He had not married a rich man's daughter without an intention of getting the rich man's money! Mr. Wharton could understand that. If the worst came to the worst, Mr. Wharton must of course maintain his daughter,—and his daughter's husband!

But things had not come to the worst as yet, and he did not intend on the present occasion to represent that view of his affairs to his father-in-law.

Mr. Wharton when he entered his chambers found Lopez seated there. He was himself at this moment very unhappy. He had renewed his quarrel with Everett,—or Everett rather had renewed the quarrel with him. There had been words between them about money lost at cards. Hard words had been used, and Everett had told his father that if either of them were a gambler it was not he. Mr. Wharton had resented this bitterly and had driven his son from his presence, —and now the quarrel made him very wretched. He certainly was sorry that he had called his son a gambler, but his son had been, as he thought, inexcusable in the retort which he had made. He was a man to whom his friends gave credit for much sternness;—but still he was one who certainly had no happiness in the world independent of his children. His daughter had left him, not as he thought under happy auspices,—and he was now, at this moment, soft-hearted and tender in his regards as to her. What was there in the world for him but his children? And now he felt himself to be alone and destitute. He was already tired of whist at the Eldon. That which had been a delight to him once or twice a week, became almost loathsome when it was renewed from day to day;—and not the less when his son told him that he also was a gambler. "So you have come back from Silverbridge?" he said.

"Yes, sir; I have come back, not exactly triumphant. A man should not expect to win always." Lopez had resolved to pluck up his spirit and carry himself like a man.

"You seem to have got into some scrape down there, besides losing your election."

"Oh; you have seen that in the papers already. I have come to tell you of it. As Emily is concerned in it you ought to know."

"Emily concerned! How is she concerned?"

Then Lopez told the whole story,—after his own fashion, and yet with no palpable lie. Fletcher had written to her a letter which he had thought to be very offensive. On hearing this, Mr. Wharton looked very grave, and asked for the letter. Lopez said that he had destroyed it, not thinking that such a document should be preserved. Then he went on to explain that it had had reference to the election, and that he had thought it to be highly improper that Fletcher should write to his wife on that or on any other subject. "It depends very much on the letter," said the old man.

"But on any subject,—after what has passed."

"They were very old friends."

"Of course I will not argue with you, Mr. Wharton; but I own that it angered me. It angered me very much,—very much indeed. I took it to be an insult to her, and when he accosted me in the street down at Silverbridge I told him so. I may not have been very wise, but I did it on her behalf. Surely you can understand that such a letter might make a man angry."

"What did he say?"

"That he would do anything for her sake,—even retire from Silverbridge if his friends would let him." Mr. Wharton scratched his head, and Lopez saw that he was perplexed. "Should he have offered to do anything for her sake, after what had passed?"

"I know the man so well," said Mr. Wharton, "that

I cannot and do not believe him to have harboured an improper thought in reference to my child."

"Perhaps it was an indiscretion only."

"Perhaps so. I cannot say. And then they took you before the magistrates?"

"Yes;—in my anger I had threatened him. Then there was a policeman and a row. And I had to swear that I would not hurt him. Of course I have no wish to hurt him."

"I suppose it ruined your chance at Silverbridge?"

"I suppose it did." This was a lie, as Lopez had retired before the row took place. "What I care for most now is that you should not think that I have misbehaved myself."

The story had been told very well, and Mr. Wharton was almost disposed to sympathise with his son-in-law. That Arthur Fletcher had meant nothing that could be regarded as offensive to his daughter he was quite sure;—but it might be that in making an offer intended to be generous he had used language which the condition of the persons concerned made indiscreet. "I suppose," he said, "that you spent a lot of money at Silverbridge?" This gave Lopez the opening that he wanted, and he described the manner in which the £500 had been extracted from him. "You can't play that game for nothing," said Mr. Wharton.

"And just at present I could very ill afford it. I should not have done it had I not felt it a pity to neglect such a chance of rising in the world. After all, a seat in the British House of Commons is an honour."

"Yes;—yes;—yes."

"And the Duchess, when she spoke to me about it, was so certain."

"I will pay the £500," said Mr. Wharton.

"Oh, sir, that is generous!" Then he got up and took the old man's hands. "Some day, when you are at liberty, I hope that you will allow me to explain to you the exact state of my affairs. When I wrote to you from Como I told you that I would wish to do so. You do not object?"

"No," said the lawyer,—but with infinite hesitation in his voice. "No; I don't object. But I do not know how I could serve them. I shall be busy just now, but I will give you the cheque. And if you and Emily have nothing better to do, come and dine to-morrow." Lopez with real tears in his eyes took the cheque, and promised to come on the morrow. "And in the meantime I wish you would see Everett." Of course he promised that he would see Everett.

Again he was exalted, on this occasion not so much by the acquisition of the money as by the growing conviction that his father-in-law was a cow capable of being milked. And the quarrel between Everett and his father might clearly be useful to him. He might either serve the old man by reducing Everett to proper submission, or he might manage to creep into the empty space which the son's defection would make in the father's heart and the father's life. He might at any rate make himself necessary to the old man, and become such a part of the household in Manchester Square as to be indispensable. Then the old man would every day become older and more in want of assistance. He thought that he saw the way to worm himself into confidence, and, so on, into possession. The old man was not a man of iron as he had feared, but quite human, and if properly managed, soft and malleable.

He saw Sexty Parker in the City that day, and used his cheque for £500 in some triumphant way, partly cajoling and partly bullying his poor victim. To Sexty also he had to tell his own story about the row down at Silverbridge. He had threatened to thrash the fellow in the street, and the fellow had not dared to come out of his house without a policeman. Yes;—he had lost his election. The swindling of those fellows at Silverbridge had been too much for him. But he flattered himself that he had got the better of Master Fletcher. That was the tone in which he told the story to his friend in the City.

Then, before dinner, he found Everett at the club. Everett Wharton was to be found there now almost every day. His excuse to himself lay in the political character of the institution. The club intended to do great things,—to find liberal candidates for all the boroughs and counties in England which were not hitherto furnished, and then to supply the candidates with money. Such was the great purpose of the Progress. It had not as yet sent out many candidates or collected much money. As yet it was, politically, almost quiescent. And therefore Everett Wharton, whose sense of duty took him there, spent his afternoons either in the whist-room or at the billiard-table.

The story of the Silverbridge row had to be told again, and was told nearly with the same incidents as had been narrated to the father. He could of course abuse Arthur Fletcher more roundly, and be more confident in his assertion that Fletcher had insulted his wife. But he came as quickly as he could to the task which he had on hand. "What's all this between you and your father?"

"Simply this. I sometimes play a game of whist, and therefore he called me a gambler. Then I reminded him that he also sometimes played a game of whist, and I asked him what deduction was to be drawn."

"He is awfully angry with you."

"Of course I was a fool. My father has the whip-hand of me, because he has money and I have none, and it was simply kicking against the pricks to speak as I did. And then too there is n't a fellow in London has a higher respect for his father than I have, nor yet a warmer affection. But it is hard to be driven in that way. Gambler is a nasty word."

"Yes, it is; very nasty. But I suppose a man does gamble when he loses so much money that he has to ask his father to pay it for him."

"If he does so often, he gambles. I never asked him for money to pay what I had lost before in my life."

"I wonder you told him."

"I never lie to him, and he ought to know that. But he is just the man to be harder to his own son than to anybody else in the world. What does he want me to do now?"

"I don't know that he wants you to do anything," said Lopez.

"Did he send you to me?"

"Well;—no; I can't say that he did. I told him I should see you as a matter of course, and he said something rough,—about your being an ass."

"I dare say he did."

"But if you ask me," said Lopez, "I think he would take it kindly of you if you were to go and see him. Come and dine to-day, just as if nothing had happened."

"I could not do that,—unless he asked me."

"I can't say that he asked you, Everett. I would say so, in spite of its being a lie, if I did n't fear that your father might say something unkind, so that the lie would be detected by both of you."

"And yet you ask me to go and dine there!"

"Yes, I do. It's only going away if he does cut up rough. And if he takes it well,—why then,—the whole thing is done."

"If he wants me, he can ask me."

"You talk about it, my boy, just as if a father were the same as anybody else. If I had a father with a lot of money, by George he should knock me about with his stick if he liked, and I would be just the same the next day."

"Unfortunately I am of a stiffer nature," said Everett, taking some pride to himself for his stiffness, and being perhaps as little "stiff" as any young man of his day.

That evening, after dinner in Manchester Square, the conversation between the father-in-law and the son-in-law turned almost exclusively on the son and brother-in-law. Little or nothing was said about the election, and the name of Arthur Fletcher was not mentioned. But out of his full heart the father spoke. He was wretched about Everett. Did Everett mean to cut him? "He wants you to withdraw some name you called him," said Lopez.

"Withdraw some name,—as he might ask some hot-headed fellow to do, of his own age, like himself; some fellow that he had quarrelled with! Does he expect his father to send him a written apology? He had been gambling, and I told him that he was a gambler.

Is that too much for a father to say?" Lopez shrugged his shoulders, and declared that it was a pity. "He will break my heart if he goes on like this," said the old man.

"I asked him to come and dine to-day, but he did n't seem to like it."

"Like it! No. He likes nothing but that infernal club."

When the evening was over Lopez felt that he had done a good stroke of work. He had not exactly made up his mind to keep the father and son apart. That was not a part of his strategy,—at any rate as yet. But he did intend to make himself necessary to the old man,—to become the old man's son, and if possible the favourite son. And now he thought that he had already done much towards the achievement of his object.

CHAPTER IX.

THE JOLLY BLACKBIRD.

There was great triumph at Longbarns when the news of Arthur's victory reached the place;—and when he arrived there himself with his friend, Mr. Gresham, he was received as a conquering hero. But of course the tidings of "the row" had gone before him, and it was necessary that both he and Mr. Gresham should tell the story;—nor could it be told privately. Sir Alured Wharton was there, and Mrs. Fletcher. The old lady had heard of the row, and of course required to be told all the particulars. This was not pleasant to the hero, as in talking of the man it was impossible for them not to talk of the man's wife. "What a terrible misfortune for poor Mr. Wharton," said the old lady, nodding her head at Sir Alured. Sir Alured sighed and said nothing. Certainly a terrible misfortune, and one which affected more or less the whole family of Whartons!

"Do you mean to say that he was going to attack Arthur with a whip?" asked John Fletcher.

"I only know that he was standing there with a whip in his hand," said Mr. Gresham.

"I think he would have had the worst of that."

"You would have laughed," said Arthur, "to see me walking majestically along the High Street with a cudgel which Gresham had just bought for me as being of the proper medium size. I don't doubt he meant to have a fight. And then you should have seen the policeman sloping over and putting himself in the way. I never quite understood where that policeman came from."

"They are very well off for policemen in Silverbridge," said Gresham. "They've always got them going about."

"He must be mad," said John.

"Poor unfortunate young woman!" said Mrs. Fletcher, holding up both her hands. "I must say that I cannot but blame Mr. Wharton. If he had been firm, it never would have come to that. I wonder whether he ever sees him."

"Of course he does," said John. "Why shouldn't he see him? You'd see him if he'd married a daughter of yours."

"Never!" exclaimed the old woman. "If I had had a child so lost to all respect as that, I do not say that I would not have seen her. Human nature might have prevailed. But I would never willingly have put myself into contact with one who had so degraded me and mine."

"I shall be very anxious to know what Mr. Wharton does about his money," said John.

Arthur allowed himself but a couple of days among his friends, and then hurried up to London to take his seat. When there he was astonished to find how many questions were asked him about "the row," and how much was known about it,—and at the same time how little was really known. Everybody had heard that there had been a row, and everybody knew that there had been a lady in the case. But there seemed to be a general idea that the lady had been in some way misused, and that Arthur Fletcher had come forward like a Paladin to protect her. A letter had been written, and the husband, ogre-like, had intercepted the letter. The lady was the most unfortunate of human beings,—or would have been but for that consolation which she must have in the constancy of her old lover. As to all these matters the stories varied; but everybody was agreed on one point. All the world knew that Arthur Fletcher had gone to Silverbridge, had stood for the borough, and had taken the seat away from his rival,—because that rival had robbed him of his bride. How the robbery had been effected the world could not quite say. The world was still of opinion that the lady was violently attached to the man she had not married. But Captain Gunner explained it all clearly to Major Pountney by asserting that the poor girl had been coerced into the marriage by her father. And thus Arthur Fletcher found himself almost as much a hero in London as at Longbarns.

Fletcher had not been above a week in town, and had become heartily sick of the rumours which in various shapes made their way round to his own ears, when he received an invitation from Mr. Wharton to go and dine with him at a tavern called the Jolly Blackbird. The invitation surprised him,—that he should be asked by such a man to dine at such a place,—but he accepted it as a matter of course. He was indeed much interested in a bill for the drainage of common lands which was to be discussed in the House that night; there was a good deal of common land round Silverbridge, and he had some idea of making his first speech,—but he calculated that he might get his dinner and yet be back in time for the debate. So he went to the Jolly Blackbird,—a very quaint, old-fashioned law dining-house in the neighbourhood of Portugal Street, which had managed not to get itself pulled down a dozen years ago on behalf of the Law Courts which are to bless some coming generation. Arthur had never been there before and was surprised at the black wainscoting, the black tables, the old-fashioned grate, the two candles on the table, and the silent waiter. "I wanted to see you, Arthur," said the old man, pressing his hand in a melancholy way, "but I could n't ask you to Manchester Square. They come in sometimes in the evening, and it might have been unpleasant. At your young men's clubs they let strangers dine. We have n't anything of that kind at the Eldon. You 'll find they 'll give you a very good bit of fish here, and a fairish steak." Arthur declared that he thought it a capital place,—the best fun in the world. "And they 've a very good bottle of claret;—better than we get at the Eldon, I think. I don't know that I can say much for their champagne. We 'll try it. You young fellows always drink champagne."

"I hardly ever touch it," said Arthur. "Sherry and claret are my wines."

"Very well;—very well. I did want to see you, my boy. Things have n't turned out just as we wished; —have they?"

"Not exactly, sir."

"No, indeed. You know the old saying, 'God disposes it all.' I have to make the best of it,—and so no doubt do you."

"There 's no doubt about it, sir," said Arthur, speaking in a low but almost angry voice. They were not in a room by themselves, but in a recess which separated them from the room. "I don't know that I want to talk about it, but to me it is one of those things for which there is no remedy. When a man loses his leg, he hobbles on, and sometimes has a good time of it at last;—but there he is, without a leg."

"It was n't my fault, Arthur."

"There has been no fault, but my own. I went in for the running and got distanced. That's simply all about it, and there's no more to be said."

"You ain't surprised that I should wish to see you."

"I'm ever so much obliged. I think it's very kind of you."

"I can't go in for a new life as you can. I can't take up politics and Parliament. It's too late for me."

"I'm going to. There's a bill coming on this very night that I'm interested about. You must n't be angry if I rush off a little before ten. We are going to lend money to the parishes on the security of the rates for draining bits of common land. Then we shall sell the land and endow the unions so as to lessen the poor rates, and increase the cereal products of the country. We think we can bring 300,000 acres under the plough in three years, which now produce almost nothing, and in five years would pay all the expenses. Putting the value of the land at £25 an acre, which is low, we shall have created property to the value of seven millions and a half. That's something, you know."

"Oh yes," said Mr. Wharton, who felt himself quite unable to follow with any interest the aspirations of the young legislator.

"Of course it's complicated," continued Arthur, "but when you come to look into it it comes out clear enough. It is one of the instances of the omnipotence of capital. Parliament can do such a thing, not because it has any creative power of its own, but because it has the command of unlimited capital." Mr. Wharton looked at him, sighing inwardly as he reflected that unrequited love should have brought a clear-headed young barrister into mists so thick and labyrinths so mazy as these. "A very good beef-steak indeed," said Arthur. "I don't know when I ate a better one. Thank you, no;—I 'll stick to the claret." Mr. Wharton had offered him Madeira. " Claret and brown meat always go well together. Pancake! I don't object to a pancake. A pancake 's a very good thing. Now would you believe it, sir; they can't make a pancake at the House."

" And yet they sometimes fall very flat too," said the lawyer, making a real lawyer's joke.

" It 's all in the mixing, sir," said Arthur, carrying it on. " We 've mixture enough just at present, but it is n't of the proper sort;—too much of the flour, and not enough of the egg."

But Mr. Wharton had still something to say, though he hardly knew how to say it. " You must come and see us in the Square after a bit."

" Oh;—of course."

" I would n't ask you to dine there to-day, because I thought we should be less melancholy here;—but you must n't cut us altogether. You have n't seen Everett since you 've been in town?"

" No, sir. I believe he lives a good deal,—a good deal with—Mr. Lopez. There was a little row down at Silverbridge. Of course it will wear off, but just at present his lines and my lines don't converge."

" I 'm very unhappy about him, Arthur."

"There's nothing the matter!"

"My girl has married that man. I've nothing to say against him;—but of course it was n't to my taste; and I feel it as a separation. And now Everett has quarrelled with me."

"Quarrelled with you!"

Then the father told the story as well as he knew how. His son had lost some money, and he had called his son a gambler;—and consequently his son would not come near him. "It is bad to lose them both, Arthur."

"That is so unlike Everett."

"It seems to me that everybody has changed,—except myself. Who would have dreamed that she would have married that man? Not that I have anything to say against him except that he was not of our sort. He has been very good about Everett, and is very good about him. But Everett will not come to me unless I—withdraw the word;—say that I was wrong to call him a gambler. That is a proposition that no son should make to a father."

"It is very unlike Everett," repeated the other. "Has he written to that effect?"

"He has not written a word."

"Why don't you see him yourself, and have it out with him?"

"Am I to go to that club after him?" said the father.

"Write to him and bid him come to you. I'll give up my seat if he don't come to you. Everett was always a quaint fellow, a little idle, you know,—mooning about after ideas——"

"He's no fool, you know," said the father.

"Not at all;—only vague. But he's the last man

in the world to have nasty vulgar ideas of his own importance as distinguished from yours."

"Lopez says———"

"I would n't quite trust Lopez."

"He is n't a bad fellow in his way, Arthur. Of course he is not what I would have liked for a son-in-law. I need n't tell you that. But he is kind and gentle-mannered, and has always been attached to Everett. You know he saved Everett's life at the risk of his own." Arthur could not but smile as he perceived how the old man was being won round by the son-in-law, whom he had treated so violently before the man had become his son-in-law. "By-the-way, what was all that about a letter you wrote to him?"

"Emily,—I mean Mrs. Lopez,—will tell you if you ask her."

"I don't want to ask her. I don't want to appear to set the wife against the husband. I am sure, my boy, you would write nothing that could affront her."

"I think not, Mr. Wharton. If I know myself at all, or my own nature, it is not probable that I should affront your daughter."

"No; no; no. I know that, my dear boy. I was always sure of that. Take some more wine."

"No more, thank you. I must be off because I 'm so anxious about this bill."

"I could n't ask Emily about this letter. Now that they are married I have to make the best of it,—for her sake. I could n't bring myself to say anything to her which might seem to accuse him."

"I thought it right, sir, to explain to her that were I not in the hands of other people I would not do anything to interfere with her happiness by opposing her husband. My language was most guarded."

"He destroyed the letter."

"I have a copy of it if it comes to that," said Arthur.

"It will be best, perhaps, to say nothing further about it. Well;—good night, my boy, if you must go." Then Fletcher went off to the House, wondering as he went at the change which had apparently come over the character of his old friend. Mr. Wharton had always been a strong man, and now he seemed to be as weak as water. As to Everett, Fletcher was sure that there was something wrong, but he could not see his way to interfere himself. For the present he was divided from the family. Nevertheless he told himself again and again that that division should not be permanent. Of all the world she must always be to him the dearest.

CHAPTER X.

THE HORNS.

The first months of the session went on very much as the last session had gone. The ministry did nothing brilliant. As far as the outer world could see, they seemed to be firm enough. There was no opposing party in the House strong enough to get a vote against them on any subject. Outsiders, who only studied politics in the columns of their newspapers, imagined the Coalition to be very strong. But they who were inside, members themselves, and the club quid-nuncs who were always rubbing their shoulders against members, knew better. The opposition to the Coalition was within the Coalition itself. Sir Orlando Drought had not been allowed to build his four ships, and was consequently eager in his fears that the country would be invaded by the combined forces of Germany and France, that India would be sold by those powers to Russia, that Canada would be annexed to the States, that a great independent Roman Catholic hierarchy would be established in Ireland, and that Malta and Gibraltar would be taken away from us;—all which evils would be averted by the building of four big ships. A wet blanket of so terrible a size was in itself pernicious to the Cabinet, and heartrending to the poor Duke. But Sir Orlando could do worse even than this. As he was not to build his four ships, neither should Mr. Monk be allowed to readjust the county suffrage.

When the skeleton of Mr. Monk's scheme was discussed in the Cabinet, Sir Orlando would not agree to it. The gentlemen, he said, who had joined the present Government with him, would never consent to a measure which would be so utterly destructive of the county interest. If Mr. Monk insisted on his measure in its proposed form, he must, with very great regret, place his resignation in the Duke's hands, and he believed that his friends would find themselves compelled to follow the same course. Then our Duke consulted the old Duke. The old Duke's advice was the same as ever. The Queen's Government was the main object. The present ministry enjoyed the support of the country, and he considered it the duty of the First Lord of the Treasury to remain at his post. The country was in no hurry, and the question of suffrages in the counties might be well delayed. Then he added a little counsel which might be called quite private, as it was certainly intended for no other ears than those of his younger friend. "Give Sir Orlando rope enough and he'll hang himself. His own party are becoming tired of him. If you quarrel with him this session, Drummond, and Ramsden, and Beeswax would go out with him, and the Government would be broken up; but next session you may get rid of him safely."

"I wish it were broken up," said the Prime Minister.

"You have your duty to do by the country and by the Queen, and you must n't regard your own wishes. Next session let Monk be ready with his bill again,— the same measure exactly. Let Sir Orlando resign then if he will. Should he do so I doubt whether any one would go with him. Drummond does not like him much better than you and I do." The poor Prime

Minister was forced to obey. The old Duke was his only trusted counsellor, and he found himself constrained by his conscience to do as that counsellor counselled him. When, however, Sir Orlando, in his place as Leader of the House, in answer to some question from a hot and disappointed radical, averred that the whole of her Majesty's Government had been quite in unison on this question of the county suffrage, he was hardly able to restrain himself. "If there be differences of opinion they must be kept in the background," said the Duke of St. Bungay. "Nothing can justify a direct falsehood," said the Duke of Omnium. Thus it came to pass that the only real measure which the Government had in hand was one by which Phineas Finn hoped so to increase the power of Irish municipalities as to make the Home Rulers believe that a certain amount of Home Rule was being conceded to them. It was not a great measure, and poor Phineas himself hardly believed in it. And thus the Duke's ministry came to be called the Faineants.

But the Duchess, though she had been much snubbed, still persevered. Now and again she would declare herself to be broken-hearted, and would say that things might go their own way, that she would send in her resignation, that she would retire into private life and milk cows, that she would shake hands with no more parliamentary cads and "caddesses,"—a word which her Grace condescended to coin for her own use; that she would spend the next three years in travelling about the world; and lastly that, let there come of it whatever might, Sir Orlando Drought should never again be invited into any house of which she was the mistress. This last threat, which was perhaps the most indiscreet of them all, she absolutely made good,—thereby adding very greatly to her husband's difficulties.

But by the middle of June the parties at the house in Carlton Terrace were as frequent and as large as ever. Indeed it was all party with her. The Duchess possessed a pretty little villa down at Richmond, on the river, called The Horns, and gave parties there when there were none in London. She had picnics, and flower parties, and tea parties, and afternoons, and evenings, on the lawn,—till half London was always on its way to Richmond or back again. How she worked! And yet from day to day she swore that the world was ungrateful, and that she would work no more! I think that the world was ungrateful. Everybody went. She was so far successful that nobody thought of despising her parties. It was quite the thing to go to the Duchess's, whether at Richmond or in London. But people abused her and laughed at her. They said that she intrigued to get political support for her husband,—and, worse than that, they said that she failed. She did not fail altogether. The world was not taken captive as she had intended. Young members of Parliament did not become hotly enthusiastic in support of her and her husband as she had hoped that they would do. She had not become an institution of granite as her dreams had fondly told her might be possible;—for there had been moments in which she had almost thought that she could rule England by giving dinner and supper parties, by ices and champagne. But in a dull, phlegmatic way, they who ate the ices and drank the champagne were true to her. There was a feeling abroad that "Glencora" was a "good sort of fellow" and ought to be supported. And when the ridicule became too strong, or the abuse too sharp, men would take up the cudgels for her, and fight her battles;—a little too openly, perhaps, as they would do it under her eyes, and in her hearing, and would tell what they had done, mistaking on such occasions her good-humour for sympathy. There was just enough of success to prevent that abandonment of her project which she so often threatened, but not enough to make her triumphant. She was too clever not to see that she was ridiculed. She knew that men called her Glencora among themselves. She was herself quite alive to the fact that she herself was wanting in dignity, and that with all the means at her disposal, with all her courage and all her talent, she did not quite play the part of the really great lady. But she did not fail to tell herself that labour continued would at last be successful, and she was strong to bear the buffets of the ill-natured. She did not think that she brought first-class materials to her work, but she believed,—a belief as erroneous as, alas, it is common, —that first-rate results might be achieved by second-rate means. "We had such a battle about your Grace last night," Captain Gunner said to her.

"And were you my knight?"

"Indeed I was. I never heard such nonsense."

"What were they saying?"

"Oh, the old story;—that you were like Martha, busying yourself about many things."

"Why shouldn't I busy myself about many things? It is a pity, Captain Gunner, that some of you men have not got something to busy yourselves about." All this was unpleasant. She could on such an occasion make up her mind to drop any Captain Gunner who had ventured to take too much upon himself; but she felt that in the efforts which she had made after popularity, she had submitted herself to unpleasant familiarities;—and though persistent in her course, she was still angry with herself.

When she had begun her campaign as the Prime Minister's wife, one of her difficulties had been with regard to money. An abnormal expenditure became necessary, for which her husband's express sanction must be obtained, and steps taken in which his personal assistance would be necessary;—but this had been done, and there was now no further impediment in that direction. It seemed to be understood that she was to spend what money she pleased. There had been various contests between them, but in every contest she had gained something. He had been majestically indignant with her in reference to the candidature at Silverbridge,—but, as is usual with many of us, had been unable to maintain his anger about two things at the same time. Or, rather, in the majesty of his anger about her interference, he had disdained to descend to the smaller faults of her extravagance. He had seemed to concede everything else to her, on condition that he should be allowed to be imperious in reference to the borough. In that matter she had given way, never having opened her mouth about it after that one unfortunate word to Mr. Sprugeon. But, having done so, she was entitled to squander her thousands without remorse,—and she squandered them. "It is your five-and-twenty thousand pounds, my dear," she once said to Mrs. Finn, who often took upon herself to question the prudence of all this expenditure. This referred to a certain sum of money which had been left by the old Duke to Madame Goesler, as she was then called,—a legacy which that lady had repudiated. The money had, in truth, been given away to a relation of the Duke's by the joint consent of the lady and of the Duke himself, but the Duchess was pleased to refer to it occasionally as a still existing property.

"My five-and-twenty thousand pounds, as you call it, would not go very far."

"What's the use of money if you don't spend it? The Duke would go on collecting it and buying more property,—which always means more trouble,—not because he is avaricious, but because for the time that comes easier than spending. Supposing he had married a woman without a shilling, he would still have been a rich man. As it is, my property was more even than his own. If we can do any good by spending the money, why should n't it be spent?"

"If you can do any good!"

"It all comes round to that. It is n't because I like always to live in a windmill! I have come to hate it. At this moment I would give worlds to be down at Matching with no one but the children, and to go about in a straw hat and a muslin gown. I have a fancy that I could sit under a tree and read a sermon, and think it the sweetest recreation. But I 've made the attempt to do all this, and it is so mean to fail!"

"But where is to be the end of it?"

"There shall be no end as long as he is Prime Minister. He is the first man in England. Some people would say the first in Europe,—or in the world. A Prince should entertain like a Prince."

"He need not be always entertaining."

"Hospitality should run from a man with his wealth and his position, like water from a fountain. As his hand is known to be full, so it should be known to be open. When the delight of his friends is in question he should know nothing of cost. Pearls should drop from him as from a fairy. But I don't think you understand me."

"Not when the pearls are to be picked up by Captain Gunners, Lady Glen."

"I can't make the men any better,—nor yet the women. They are poor mean creatures. The world is made up of such. I don't know that Captain Gunner is worse than Sir Orlando Drought or Sir Timothy Beeswax. People seen by the mind are exactly different to things seen by the eye. They grow smaller and smaller as you come nearer down to them, whereas things become bigger. I remember when I used to think that members of the Cabinet were almost gods, and now they seem to be no bigger than the shoeblacks,—only less picturesque. He told me the other day of the time when he gave up going into power for the sake of taking me abroad. Ah me! how much was happening then,—and how much has happened since that! We did n't know you then."

"He has been a good husband to you."

"And I have been a good wife to him! I have never had him for an hour out of my heart since that, or ever for a moment forgotten his interest. I can't live with him because he shuts himself up reading blue books, and is always at his office or in the House;— but I would if I could. Am I not doing it all for him? You don't think that the Captain Gunners are particularly pleasant to me! Think of your life and of mine. You have had lovers."

"One in my life,—when I was quite entitled to have one."

"Well; I am Duchess of Omnium, and I am the wife of the Prime Minister, and I had a larger property of my own than any other young woman that ever was born; and I am myself, too,—Glencora M'Cluskie that was, and I 've made for myself a character that I 'm not ashamed of. But I 'd be the curate's wife to-morrow, and make puddings, if I could only have my own husband and my own children with me. What 's the use of it all? I like you better than anybody else, but you do nothing but scold me." Still the parties went on, and the Duchess laboured hard among her guests, and wore her jewels, and stood on her feet all the night, night after night, being civil to one person, bright to a second, confidential to a third, and sarcastic to an unfortunate fourth;—and in the morning she would work hard with her lists, seeing who had come to her and who had stayed away, and arranging who should be asked and who should be omitted.

In the meantime the Duke altogether avoided these things. At first he had been content to show himself, and escape as soon as possible;—but now he was never seen at all in his own house, except at certain heavy dinners. To Richmond he never went at all, and in his own house in town very rarely even passed through the door that led into the reception-rooms. He had not time for ordinary society. So said the Duchess. And many, perhaps the majority of those who frequented the house, really believed that his official duties were too onerous to leave him time for conversation. But in truth the hours went heavily with him as he sat alone in his study, sighing for some sweet parliamentary task, and regretting the days in which he was privileged to sit in the House of Commons till two o'clock in the morning, in the hope that he might get a clause or two passed in his bill for decimal coinage.

It was at The Horns at an afternoon party, given there in the gardens by the Duchess, early in July, that Arthur Fletcher first saw Emily after her marriage, and Lopez after the occurrence in Silverbridge. As it happened he came out upon the lawn close after them, and found them speaking to the Duchess as they passed on. She had put herself out of the way to be civil to Mr. and Mrs. Lopez, feeling that she had in some degree injured him in reference to the election, and had therefore invited both him and his wife on more than one occasion. Arthur Fletcher was there as a young man well known in the world, and as a supporter of the Duke's Government. The Duchess had taken up Arthur Fletcher,—as she was wont to take up new men, and had personally become tired of Lopez. Of course she had heard of the election, and had been told that Lopez had behaved badly. Of Mr. Lopez she did not know enough to care anything, one way or the other;—but she still encouraged him because she had caused him disappointment. She had now detained them a minute on the terrace before the windows while she said a word, and Arthur Fletcher became one of the little party before he knew whom he was meeting. "I am delighted," she said, "that you two Silverbridge heroes should meet together here as friends." It was almost incumbent on her to say something, though it would have been better for her not to have alluded to their heroism. Mrs. Lopez put out her hand, and Arthur Fletcher of course took it. Then the two men bowed slightly to each other, raising their hats. Arthur paused a moment with them, as they passed on from the Duchess, thinking that he would say something in a friendly tone. But he was silenced by the frown on the husband's face, and was almost constrained to go away without a word. It was very difficult for him even to be silent, as her greeting had been kind. But yet it was impossible for him to ignore the displeasure displayed in the man's countenance. So he touched his hat, and asking her to remember him affectionately to her father, turned off the path and went away.

"Why did you shake hands with that man?" said Lopez. It was the first time since their marriage that his voice had been that of an angry man and an offended husband.

"Why not, Ferdinand? He and I are very old friends, and we have not quarrelled."

"You must take up your husband's friendships and your husband's quarrels. Did I not tell you that he had insulted you?"

"He never insulted me."

"Emily, you must allow me to be the judge of that. He insulted you, and then he behaved like a poltroon down at Silverbridge, and I will not have you know him any more. When I say so I suppose that will be enough." He waited for a reply, but she said nothing. "I ask you to tell me that you will obey me in this."

"Of course he will not come to my house, nor should I think of going to his, if you disapproved."

"Going to his house! He is unmarried."

"Supposing he had a wife! Ferdinand, perhaps it will be better that you and I should not talk about him."

"By G——," said Lopez, "there shall be no subject on which I will be afraid to talk to my own wife. I insist on your assuring me that you will never speak to him again."

He had taken her along one of the upper walks because it was desolate, and he could there speak to her, as he thought, without being heard. She had, almost unconsciously, made a faint attempt to lead him down upon the lawn, no doubt feeling averse to private conversation at the moment; but he had persevered, and had resented the little effort. The idea in his mind that she was unwilling to hear him abuse Arthur Fletcher, unwilling to renounce the man, anxious to escape his order for such renunciation, added fuel to his jealousy. It was not enough for him that she had rejected this man and had accepted him. The man had been her lover, and she should be made to denounce the man. It might be necessary for him to control his feelings before old Wharton;—but he knew enough of his wife to be sure that she would not speak evil of him or betray him to her father. Her loyalty to him, which he could understand though not appreciate, enabled him to be a tyrant to her. So now he repeated his order to her, pausing in the path, with a voice unintentionally loud, and frowning down upon her as he spoke. "You must tell me, Emily, that you will never speak to him again."

She was silent, looking up into his face, not with tremulous eyes, but with infinite woe written in them, had he been able to read the writing. She knew that he was disgracing himself, and yet he was the man whom she loved! "If you bid me not to speak to him, I will not;—but he must know the reason why."

"He shall know nothing from you. You do not mean to say that you would write to him?"

"Papa must tell him."

"I will not have it so. In this matter, Emily, I will be master,—as it is fit that I should be. I will not have you talk to your father about Mr. Fletcher."

"Why not, Ferdinand?"

"Because I have so decided. He is an old family friend. I can understand that, and do not therefore wish to interfere between him and your father. But he has taken upon himself to write an insolent letter to you as my wife, and to interfere in my affairs. As to what should be done between you and him I must be the judge, and not your father."

"And must I not speak to papa about it?"

"No!"

"Ferdinand, you make too little, I think, of the associations and affections of a whole life."

"I will hear nothing about affection," he said angrily.

"You cannot mean that,—that—you doubt me?"

"Certainly not. I think too much of myself and too little of him." It did not occur to him to tell her that he thought too well of her for that. "But the man who has offended me must be held to have offended you also."

"You might say the same if it were my father."

He paused at this, but only for a moment. "Certainly I might. It is not probable, but no doubt I might do so. If your father were to quarrel with me, you would not, I suppose, hesitate between us?"

"Nothing on earth could divide me from you."

"Nor me from you. In this very matter I am only taking your part, if you did but know it." They had now passed on, and had met other persons, having made their way through a little shrubbery on to a further lawn; and she had hoped, as they were surrounded by people, that he would allow the matter to drop. She had been unable as yet to make up her mind as to what she would say if he pressed her hard. But if it could be passed by,—if nothing more were demanded from her,—she would endeavour to forget it all, saying to herself that it had come from sudden passion. But he was too resolute for such a termination as that, and too keenly alive to the expediency of making her thoroughly subject to him. So he turned her round and took her back through the shrubbery, and in the middle of it stopped her again and renewed his demand. "Promise me that you will not speak again to Mr. Fletcher."

"Then I must tell papa."

"No;—you shall tell him nothing."

"Ferdinand, if you exact a promise from me that I will not speak to Mr. Fletcher or bow to him should circumstances bring us together as they did just now, I must explain to my father why I have done so."

"You will wilfully disobey me?"

"In that I must." He glared at her, almost as though he were going to strike her, but she bore his look without flinching. "I have left all my old friends, Ferdinand, and have given myself heart and soul to you. No woman did so with a truer love or more devoted intention of doing her duty to her husband. Your affairs shall be my affairs."

"Well; yes; rather."

She was endeavouring to assure him of her truth, but could understand the sneer which was conveyed in his acknowledgment. "But you cannot, nor can I for your sake, abolish the things which have been."

"I wish to abolish nothing that has been. I speak of the future."

"Between our family and that of Mr. Fletcher there has been old friendship which is still very dear to my father,—the memory of which is still very dear to me. At your request I am willing to put all that aside from me. There is no reason why I should ever see any of the Fletchers again. Our lives will be apart. Should we meet our greeting would be very slight. The separation can be effected without words. But if you demand an absolute promise,—I must tell my father."

"We will go home at once," he said instantly, and aloud. And home they went, back to London, without exchanging a word on the journey. He was absolutely black with rage, and she was content to remain silent. The promise was not given, nor, indeed, was it exacted under the conditions which the wife had imposed upon it. He was most desirous to make her subject to his will in all things, and quite prepared to exercise tyranny over her to any extent,—so that her father should know nothing of it. He could not afford to quarrel with Mr. Wharton. "You had better go to bed," he said, when he got her back to town;—and she went, if not to bed, at any rate into her own room.

CHAPTER XI.

SIR ORLANDO RETIRES.

"HE is a horrid man. He came here and quarrelled with the other man in my house, or rather down at Richmond, and made a fool of himself, and then quarrelled with his wife and took her away. What fools, what asses, what horrors men are! How impossible it is to be civil and gracious without getting into a mess. I am tempted to say that I will never know anybody any more." Such was the complaint made by the Duchess to Mrs. Finn a few days after the Richmond party, and from this it was evident that the latter affair had not passed without notice.

"Did he make a noise about it?" asked Mrs. Finn.

"There was not a row, but there was enough of a quarrel to be visible and audible. He walked about and talked loud to the poor woman. Of course it was my own fault. But the man was clever and I liked him, and people told me that he was of the right sort."

"The Duke heard of it?"

"No;—and I hope he won't. It would be such a triumph for him, after all the fuss at Silverbridge. But he never hears of anything. If two men fought a duel in his own dining-room he would be the last man in London to know it."

"Then say nothing about it, and don't ask the men any more."

"You may be sure I won't ask the man with the

wife any more. The other man is in Parliament and can't be thrown over so easily—and it was n't his fault. But I 'm getting so sick of it all! I 'm told that Sir Orlando has complained to Plantagenet that he is n't asked to the dinners."

"Impossible!"

"Don't you mention it, but he has. Warburton has told me so." Warburton was one of the Duke's private secretaries.

"What did the Duke say?"

"I don't quite know. Warburton is one of my familiars, but I did n't like to ask him for more than he chose to tell me. Warburton suggested that I should invite Sir Orlando at once; but there I was obdurate. Of course if Plantagenet tells me I 'll ask the man to come every day of the week;—but it is one of those things that I shall need to be told directly. My idea is, you know, that they had better get rid of Sir Orlando,—and that if Sir Orlando chooses to kick over the traces, he may be turned loose without any danger. One has little birds that give one all manner of information, and one little bird has told me that Sir Orlando and Mr. Roby don't speak. Mr. Roby is not very much himself, but he is a good straw to show which way the wind blows. Plantagenet certainly sent no message about Sir Orlando, and I 'm afraid the gentleman must look for his dinners elsewhere."

The Duke had in truth expressed himself very plainly to Mr. Warburton; but with so much indiscreet fretfulness that the discreet private secretary had not told it even to the Duchess. "This kind of thing argues a want of cordiality that may be fatal to us," Sir Orlando had said somewhat grandiloquently to the Duke, and the Duke had made—almost no reply. "I suppose I may ask my own guests in my own house," he had said afterwards to Mr. Warburton, "though in public life I am everybody's slave." Mr. Warburton, anxious of course to maintain the unity of the party, had told the Duchess so much as would, he thought, induce her to give way; but he had not repeated the Duke's own observations, which were, Mr. Warburton thought, hostile to the interests of the party. The Duchess had only smiled and made a little grimace, with which the private secretary was already well acquainted. And Sir Orlando received no invitation.

In those days Sir Orlando was unhappy and irritable, doubtful of further success as regarded the Coalition, but quite resolved to pull the house down about the ears of the inhabitants rather than to leave it with gentle resignation. To him it seemed to be impossible that the Coalition should exist without him. He too had had moments of high-vaulting ambition, in which he had almost felt himself to be the great man required by the country, the one ruler who could gather together in his grasp the reins of government and drive the State coach single-handed safe through its difficulties for the next half-dozen years. There are men who cannot conceive of themselves that anything should be difficult for them, and again others who cannot bring themselves so to trust themselves as to think that they can ever achieve anything great. Samples of each sort from time to time rise high in political life, carried thither apparently by Epicurean concourse of atoms; and it often happens that the more confident samples are by no means the most capable. The concourse of atoms had carried Sir Orlando so high that he could not but think himself intended for something higher. But the Duke, who had really been wafted to the very top, had always doubted himself, believing himself capable of doing some one thing by dint of industry, but with no further confidence in his own powers. Sir Orlando had perceived something of his leader's weakness, and had thought that he might profit by it. He was not only a distinguished member of the Cabinet, but even the recognised Leader of the House of Commons. He looked out the facts and found that for five-and-twenty years out of the last thirty the Leader of the House of Commons had been the Head of the Government. He felt that he would be mean not to stretch out his hand and take the prize destined for him. The Duke was a poor timid man who had very little to say for himself. Then came the little episode about the dinners. It had become very evident to all the world that the Duchess of Omnium had cut Sir Orlando Drought,—that the Prime Minister's wife, who was great in hospitality, would not admit the First Lord of the Admiralty into her house. The doings at Gatherum Castle, and in Carlton Terrace, and at The Horns were watched much too closely by the world at large to allow such omissions to be otherwise than conspicuous. Since the commencement of the session there had been a series of articles in the People's Banner violently abusive of the Prime Minister, and in one or two of these the indecency of these exclusions had been exposed with great strength of language. And the Editor of ·the People's Banner had discovered that Sir Orlando Drought was the one man in Parliament fit to rule the nation. Till Parliament should discover this fact, or at least acknowledge it,—the discovery having been happily made by the People's Banner,—the Editor of the People's Banner thought that there could be no hope for the country. Sir Orlando of course saw all these articles, and in his very heart believed that a man had at length sprung up among them fit to conduct a newspaper. The Duke also unfortunately saw the People's Banner. In his old happy days two papers a day, one in the morning and the other before dinner, sufficed to tell him all that he wanted to know. Now he felt it necessary to see almost every rag that was published. And he would skim through them all till he found the lines in which he himself was maligned, and then, with sore heart and irritated nerves, would pause over every contumelious word. He would have bitten his tongue out rather than have spoken of the tortures he endured, but he was tortured and did endure. He knew the cause of the bitter personal attacks made on him,—of the abuse with which he was loaded, and of the ridicule, infinitely more painful to him, with which his wife's social splendour was bespattered. He remembered well the attempt which Mr. Quintus Slide had made to obtain an entrance into his house, and his own scornful rejection of that gentleman's overtures. He knew,—no man knew better,—the real value of that able Editor's opinion. And yet every word of it was gall and wormwood to him. In every paragraph there was a scourge which hit him on the raw and opened wounds which he could show to no kind surgeon, for which he could find solace in no friendly treatment. Not even to his wife could he condescend to say that Mr. Quintus Slide had hurt him.

Then Sir Orlando had come himself. Sir Orlando explained himself gracefully. He of course could understand that no gentleman had a right to complain because he was not asked to another gentleman's house. But the affairs of the country were above private considerations; and he, actuated by public feelings, would condescend to do that which under other circumstances would be impossible. The public press, which was ever vigilant, had suggested that there was some official estrangement, because he, Sir Orlando, had not been included in the list of guests invited by his Grace. Did not his Grace think that there might be seeds of,—he would not quite say decay for the Coalition, in such a state of things? The Duke paused a moment, and then said that he thought there were no such seeds. Sir Orlando bowed haughtily and withdrew,—swearing at the moment that the Coalition should be made to fall into a thousand shivers. This had all taken place a fortnight before the party at The Horns from which poor Mrs. Lopez had been withdrawn so hastily.

But Sir Orlando, when he commenced the proceedings consequent on this resolution, did not find all that support which he had expected. Unfortunately there had been an uncomfortable word or two between him and Mr. Roby, the political Secretary at the Admiralty. Mr. Roby had never quite seconded Sir Orlando's ardour in that matter of the four ships, and Sir Orlando in his pride of place had ventured to snub Mr. Roby. Now Mr. Roby could bear a snubbing perhaps as well as any other official subordinate,—but he was one who would study the question and assure himself that it was, or that it was not, worth his while to bear it. He, too, had discussed with his friends the condition of the Coalition, and had come to conclusions rather adverse to Sir Orlando than otherwise. When, therefore, the First Secretary sounded him as to the expediency of some step in the direction of a firmer political combination than that at present existing,—by which of course was meant the dethronement of the present Prime Minister,—Mr. Roby had snubbed him! Then there had been slight official criminations and recriminations, till a state of things had come to pass which almost justified the statement made by the Duchess to Mrs. Finn.

The Coalition had many component parts, some coalescing without difficulty, but with no special cordiality. Such was the condition of things between the very conservative Lord-Lieutenant of Ireland and his somewhat radical Chief Secretary, Mr. Finn,—between probably the larger number of those who were contented with the duties of their own offices and the pleasures and profits arising therefrom. Some by this time hardly coalesced at all, as was the case with Sir Gregory Grogram and Sir Timothy Beeswax, the Attorney-General and Solicitor-General;—and was especially the case with the Prime Minister and Sir Orlando Drought. But in one or two happy cases the Coalition was sincere and loyal,—and in no case was this more so than with regard to Mr. Rattler and Mr. Roby. Mr. Rattler and Mr. Roby had throughout their long parliamentary lives belonged to opposite parties, and had been accustomed to regard each other with mutual jealousy and almost with mutual hatred. But now they had come to see how equal, how alike, and how sympathetic were their tastes, and how well each might help the other. As long as Mr. Rattler could keep his old place at the Treasury,—and his ambition never stirred him to aught higher,—he was quite contented that his old rival should be happy at the Admiralty. And that old rival, when he looked about him and felt his present comfort, when he remembered how short-lived had been the good things which had hitherto come in his way, and how little probable it was that long-lived good things should be his when the Coalition was broken up, manfully determined that loyalty to the present Head of the Government was his duty. He had sat for too many years on the same bench with Sir Orlando to believe much in his power of governing the country. Therefore, when Sir Orlando dropped his hint Mr. Roby did not take it.

"I wonder whether it's true that Sir Orlando complained to the Duke that he was not asked to dinner?" said Mr. Roby to Mr. Rattler.

"I should hardly think so. I can't fancy that he would have the pluck," said Mr. Rattler. "The Duke is n't the easiest man in the world to speak to about such a thing as that."

"It would be a monstrous thing for a man to do! But Drought's head is quite turned. You can see that."

"We never thought very much about him, you know, on our side."

"It was what your side thought about him," rejoined Roby, "that put him where he is now."

"It was the fate of accidents, Roby, which puts so many of us in our places, and arranges our work for us, and makes us little men or big men. There are other men besides Drought who have been tossed up in a blanket till they don't know whether their heads or their heels are highest."

"I quite believe in the Duke," said Mr. Roby, almost alarmed by the suggestion which his new friend had seemed to make.

"So do I, Roby. He has not the obduracy of Lord Brock, nor the ineffable manner of Mr. Mildmay, nor the brilliant intellect of Mr. Gresham."

"Nor the picturesque imagination of Mr. Daubeny," said Mr. Roby, feeling himself bound to support the character of his late chief.

"Nor his audacity," said Mr. Rattler. "But he has peculiar gifts of his own, and gifts fitted for the peculiar combination of circumstances, if he will only be content to use them. He is a just, unambitious, intelligent man, in whom after a while the country would come to have implicit confidence. But he is thin-skinned and ungenial."

"I have got into his boat," said Roby enthusiastically, "and he will find that I shall be true to him."

"There is no better boat to be in at present," said the slightly sarcastic Rattler. "As to the Drought pinnace, it will be more difficult to get it afloat than the four ships themselves. To tell the truth honestly, Roby, we have to rid ourselves of Sir Orlando. I have a great regard for the man."

"I can't say I ever liked him," said Roby.

"I don't talk about liking,—but he has achieved success, and is to be regarded. Now he has lost his head, and he is bound to get a fall. The question is, —who shall fall with him?"

"I do not feel myself at all bound to sacrifice myself."

"I don't know who does. Sir Timothy Beeswax, I suppose, will resent the injury done him. But I can hardly think that a strong government can be formed by Sir Orlando Drought and Sir Timothy Beeswax. Any secession is a weakness,—of course; but I think we may survive it." And so Mr. Rattler and Mr. Roby made up their minds that the First Lord of the Admiralty might be thrown overboard without much danger to the Queen's ship.

Sir Orlando, however, was quite in earnest. The man had spirit enough to feel that no alternative was left to him after he had condescended to suggest that he should be asked to dinner and had been refused. He tried Mr. Roby, and found that Mr. Roby was a mean fellow, wedded, as he told himself, to his salary. Then he sounded Lord Drummond, urging various reasons. The country was not safe without more ships. Mr. Monk was altogether wrong about revenue. Mr. Finn's ideas about Ireland were revolutionary. But Lord Drummond thought that, upon the whole, the present ministry served the country well, and considered himself bound to adhere to it. "He cannot bear the idea of being out of power," said Sir Orlando to himself. He next said a word to Sir Timothy; but Sir Timothy was not the man to be led by the nose by Sir Orlando. Sir Timothy had his grievances and meant to have his revenge, but he knew how to choose his own time. "The Duke's not a bad fellow," said Sir Timothy,—"perhaps a little weak, but well-meaning. I think we ought to stand by him a little longer. As for Finn's Irish bill, I have n't troubled myself about it." Then Sir Orlando declared to himself that Sir Timothy was a coward, and resolved that he would act alone.

About the middle of July he went to the Duke at the Treasury, was closeted with him, and in a very long narration of his own differences, difficulties, opinions, and grievances, explained to the Duke that his conscience called upon him to resign. The Duke listened and bowed his head, and with one or two very gently uttered words expressed his regret. Then Sir Orlando, in another long speech, laid bare his bosom to the Chief whom he was leaving, declaring the inexpressible sorrow with which he had found himself called upon to take a step which he feared might be prejudicial to the political status of a man whom he honoured so much as he did the Duke of Omnium. Then the Duke bowed again, but said nothing. The man had been guilty of the impropriety of questioning the way in which the Duke's private hospitality was exercised, and the Duke could not bring himself to be genially civil to such an offender. Sir Orlando went on to say that he would of course explain his views in the Cabinet, but that he had thought it right to make them known to the Duke as soon as they were formed. "The best friends must part, Duke," he said as he took his leave. "I hope not, Sir Orlando; I hope not," said the Duke. But Sir Orlando had been too full of himself and of the words he was to speak, and of the thing he was about to do, to understand either the Duke's words or his silence.

And so Sir Orlando resigned, and thus supplied the only morsel of political interest which the session produced. "Take no more notice of him than if your footman was going," had been the advice of the old Duke. Of course there was a Cabinet meeting on the occasion, but even there the commotion was very slight, as every member knew before entering the room what it was that Sir Orlando intended to do. Lord Drummond said that the step was one to be much lamented. "Very much, indeed," said the Duke of St. Bungay. His words themselves were false and hypocritical, but the tone of his voice took away all the deceit. "I am afraid," said the Prime Minister, "from what Sir Orlando has said to me privately, that we cannot hope that he will change his mind. "That I certainly cannot do," said Sir Orlando, with all the dignified courage of a modern martyr.

On the next morning the papers were full of the political fact, and were blessed with a subject on which they could exercise their prophetical sagacity. The remarks made were generally favourable to the Government. Three or four of the morning papers were of opinion that though Sir Orlando had been a strong man, and a good public servant, the ministry might exist without him. But the People's Banner was able to expound to the people at large that the only grain of salt by which the ministry had been kept from putrefaction had been now cast out, and that mortification, death, and corruption must ensue. It was one of Mr. Quintus Slide's greatest efforts.

CHAPTER XII.

"GET ROUND HIM."

FERDINAND LOPEZ maintained his anger against his wife for more than a week after the scene at Richmond, feeding it with reflections on what he called her disobedience. Nor was it a make-believe anger. She had declared her intention to act in opposition to his expressed orders. He felt that his present condition was prejudicial to his interests, and that he must take his wife back into favour, in order that he might make progress with her father, but could hardly bring himself to swallow his wrath. He thought that it was her duty to obey him in everything,—and that disobedience on a matter touching her old lover was an abominable offence, to be visited with severest marital displeasure, and with a succession of scowls that should make her miserable for a month at least. Nor on her behalf would he have hesitated, though the misery might have continued for three months. But then the old man was the main hope of his life, and must be made its mainstay. Brilliant prospects were before him. He had used to think that Mr. Wharton was a hale man, with some terribly vexatious term of life before him. But now, now that he was seen more closely, he appeared to be very old. He would sit half bent in the arm-chair in Stone Buildings, and look as though he were near a hundred. And from day to day he seemed to lean more upon his son-in-law, whose visits to him were continued, and always well taken. The constant subject of discourse between them was Everett Wharton, who had not yet seen his father since the misfortune of their quarrel. Everett had declared to Lopez a dozen times that he would go to his father if his father wished it, and Lopez as often reported to the father that Everett would not go to him unless the father expressed such a wish. And so they had been kept apart. Lopez did not suppose that the old man would disinherit his son altogether,—did not, perhaps, wish it. But he thought that the condition of the old man's mind would affect the partition of his property, and that the old man would surely make some new will in the present state of his affairs. The old man always asked after his daughter, begging that she would come to him, and at last it was necessary that an evening should be fixed. "We shall be delighted to come to-day or to-morrow," Lopez said.

"We had better say to-morrow. There would be nothing to eat to-day. The house is n't now what it used to be." It was therefore expedient that Lopez should drop his anger when he got home, and prepare his wife to dine in Manchester Square in a proper frame of mind.

Her misery had been extreme;—very much more bitter than he had imagined. It was not only that his displeasure made her life for the time wearisome, and robbed the only society she had of all its charms. It was not only that her heart was wounded by his anger. Those evils might have been short-lived. But she had seen,—she could not fail to see,—that his conduct was unworthy of her and of her deep love. Though she struggled hard against the feeling, she could not but despise the meanness of his jealousy. She knew thoroughly well that there had been no grain of offence in that letter from Arthur Fletcher,—and she knew that no man, no true man, would have taken offence at it. She tried to quench her judgment, and to silence the verdict which her intellect gave against him, but her intellect was too strong even for her heart. She was beginning to learn that the god of her idolatry was but a little human creature, and that she should not have worshipped at so poor a shrine. But nevertheless the love should be continued, and, if possible, the worship, though the idol had been already found to have feet of clay. He was her husband, and she would be true to him. As morning after morning he left her, still with that harsh, unmanly frown upon his face, she would look up at him with entreating eyes, and when he returned would receive him with her fondest smile.

At length he, too, smiled. He came to her after that interview with Mr. Wharton and told her, speaking with the soft yet incisive voice which she used to love so well, that they were to dine in the Square on the following day. "Let there be an end of all this," he said, taking her in his arms and kissing her. Of course she did not tell him that "all this" had sprung from his ill-humour and not from hers. "I own I have been angry," he continued. "I will say nothing more about it now; but that man did vex me."

"I have been so sorry that you should have been vexed."

"Well;—let it pass away. I don't think your father is looking very well."

"He is not ill?"

"Oh no. He feels the loss of your society. He is so much alone. You must be more with him."

"Has he not seen Everett yet?"

"No. Everett is not behaving altogether well." Emily was made unhappy by this and showed it. "He is the best fellow in the world. I may safely say there is no other man whom I regard so warmly as I do your brother. But he takes wrong ideas into his head, and nothing will knock them out. I wonder what your father has done about his will."

"I have not an idea. Nothing, you may be sure, will make him unjust to Everett."

"Ah!—You don't happen to know whether he ever made a will?"

"Not at all. He would be sure to say nothing about it to me,—or to anybody."

"That is a kind of secrecy which I think wrong. It leads to so much uncertainty. You would'n't like to ask him?"

"No;—certainly."

"It is astonishing to me how afraid you are of your father. He has n't any land; has he?"

"Land!"

"Real estate. You know what I mean. He could n't well have landed property without your knowing it." She shook her head. "It might make an immense difference to us, you know."

"Why so?"

"If he were to die without a will, any land,—houses and that kind of property,—would go to Everett. I never knew a man who told his children so little. I want to make you understand these things. You and I will be badly off if he does n't do something for us."

"You don't think he is really ill?"

"No;—not ill. Men above seventy are apt to die, you know."

"Oh, Ferdinand,—what a way to talk of it!"

"Well, my love, the thing is so seriously matter-of-fact, that it is better to look at it in a matter-of-fact way. I don't want your father to die."

"I hope not. I hope not."

"But I should be very glad to learn what he means to do while he lives. I want to get you into sympathy with me in this matter;—but it is so difficult."

"Indeed I sympathise with you."

"The truth is he has taken an aversion to Everett."

"God forbid!"

"I am doing all I can to prevent it. But if he does throw Everett over we ought to have the advantage of it. There is no harm in saying as much as that. Think what it would be if he should take it into his head to leave his money to hospitals. My G——! fancy what my condition would be if I were to hear of such a will as that! If he destroyed an old will, partly because he did n't like our marriage, and partly in anger against Everett, and then die without making another, the property would be divided,—unless he had bought land. You see how many dangers there are. Oh dear! I can look forward and see myself mad,—or else see myself so proudly triumphant!" All this horrified her, but he did not see her horror. He knew that she disliked it, but thought that she disliked the trouble, and that she dreaded her father. "Now I do think that you could help me a little," he continued.

"What can I do?"

"Get round him when he's a little down in the mouth. That is the way in which old men are conquered." How utterly ignorant he was of the very nature of her mind and disposition! To be told by her husband that she was to "get round" her father! "You should see him every day. He would be delighted if you would go to him at his chambers. Or you could take care to be in the Square when he comes home. I don't know whether we had not better leave this and go and live near him. Would you mind that?"

"I would do anything you would suggest as to living anywhere."

"But you won't do anything I suggest as to your father."

"As to being with him, if I thought he wished it,— though I had to walk my feet off, I would go to him."

"There's no need of hurting your feet. There's the brougham."

"I do so wish, Ferdinand, you would discontinue the brougham. I don't at all want it. I don't at all dislike cabs. And I was only joking about walking. I walk very well."

"Certainly not. You fail altogether to understand my ideas about things. If things were going bad with us, I would infinitely prefer getting a pair of horses for you to putting down the one you have." She certainly did not understand his ideas. "Whatever we do we must hold our heads up. I think he is coming round to cotton to me. He is very close, but I can see that he likes my going to him. Of course, as he grows older from day to day, he'll constantly want some one to lean on more than heretofore."

"I would go and stay with him if he wanted me."

"I have thought of that too. Now that would be a saving,—without any fall. And if we were both there we could hardly fail to know what he was doing. You could offer that, could n't you? You could say as much as that?"

"I could ask him if he wished it."

"Just so. Say that it occurs to you that he is lonely by himself, and that we will both go to the Square at a moment's notice if he thinks it will make him comfortable. I feel sure that that will be the best step to take. I have already had an offer for these rooms, and could get rid of the things we have bought to advantage."

This, too, was terrible to her, and at the same time altogether unintelligible. She had been invited to buy little treasures to make their home comfortable, and had already learned to take that delight in her belongings which is one of the greatest pleasures of a young married woman's life. A girl in her old home, before she is given up to a husband, has many sources of interest, and probably from day to day sees many people. And the man just married goes out to his work, and occupies his time, and has his thickly peopled world around him. But the bride, when the bridal honours of the honeymoon are over, when the sweet care of the first cradle has not yet come to her, is apt to be lonely and to be driven to the contemplation of the pretty things with which her husband and her friends have surrounded her. It had certainly been so with this young bride, whose husband left her in the morning and only returned for their late dinner. And now she was told that her household gods had

had a price put upon them and that they were to be sold. She had intended to suggest that she would pay her father a visit, and her husband immediately proposed that they should quarter themselves permanently on the old man! She was ready to give up her brougham, though she liked the comfort of it well enough; but to that he would not consent because the possession of it gave him an air of wealth; but without a moment's hesitation he could catch at the idea of throwing upon her father the burden of maintaining both her and himself! She understood the meaning of this. She could read his mind so far. She endeavoured not to read the book too closely,— but there it was, opened to her wider day by day, and she knew that the lessons which it taught were vulgar and damnable.

And yet she had to hide from him her own perception of himself! She had to sympathise with his desires and yet to abstain from doing that which his desires demanded from her. Alas, poor girl! She soon knew that her marriage had been a mistake. There was probably no one moment in which she made the confession to herself. But the conviction was there, in her mind, as though the confession had been made. Then there would come upon her unbidden, unwelcome reminiscences of Arthur Fletcher,—thoughts that she would struggle to banish, accusing herself of some heinous crime because the thoughts would come back to her. She remembered his light wavy hair, which she had loved as one loves the beauty of a dog, which had seemed to her young imagination, to her in the ignorance of her early years, to lack something of a dreamed-of manliness. She remembered his eager, boyish, honest entreaties to herself, which to her had been without that dignity of a superior being which a husband should possess. She became aware that she had thought the less of him because he had thought the more of her. She had worshipped this other man because he had assumed superiority and had told her that he was big enough to be her master. But now,—now that it was all too late,—the veil had fallen from her eyes. She could now see the difference between manliness and "deportment." Ah,—that she should ever have been so blind, she who had given herself credit for seeing so much clearer than they who were her elders! And now, though at last she did see clearly, she could not have the consolation of telling any one what she had seen. She must bear it all in silence, and live with it, and still love this god of clay that she had chosen. And, above all, she must never allow herself even to think of that other man with the wavy light hair,—that man who was rising in the world, of whom all people said all good things, who was showing himself to be a man by the work he did, and whose true tenderness she could never doubt.

Her father was left to her. She could still love her father. It might be that it would be best for him that she should go back to her old home, and take care of his old age. If he should wish it, she would make no difficulty of parting with the things around her. Of what concern were the prettinesses of life to one whose inner soul was hampered with such ugliness? It might be better that they should live in Manchester Square,—if her father wished it. It was clear to her now that her husband was in urgent want of money, though of his affairs, even of his way of making money, she knew nothing. As that was the case, of course she would consent to any practicable retrenchment which he would propose. And then she thought of other coming joys and coming troubles,—of how in future years she might have to teach a girl falsely to believe that her father was a good man, and to train a boy to honest purposes, whatever parental lessons might come from the other side.

But the mistake she had made was acknowledged. The man who could enjoin her to "get round" her father could never have been worthy of the love she had given him.

CHAPTER XIII.

"COME AND TRY IT."

THE husband was almost jovial when he came home just in time to take his young wife to dine with their father. "I 've had such a day in the City," he said, laughing. " I wish I could introduce you to my friend, Mr. Sextus Parker."

" Cannot you do so?"

"Well, no; not exactly. Of course you 'd like him because he is such a wonderful character, but he 'd hardly do for your drawing-room. He 's the vulgarest little creature you ever put your eyes on; and yet in a certain way he 's my partner."

"Then I suppose you trust him?"

"Indeed I don't;—but I make him useful. Poor little Sexty! I do trust him to a degree, because he believes in me and thinks he can do best by sticking to me. The old saying of 'honour among thieves' is n't without a dash of truth in it. When two men are in a boat together they must be true to each other, else neither will get to the shore."

"You don't attribute high motives to your friend."

"I 'm afraid there are not very many high motives in the world, my girl, especially in the City;—nor yet at Westminster. It can hardly be from high motives when a lot of men, thinking differently on every possible subject, come together for the sake of pay and power. I don't know whether, after all, Sextus Parker may n't have as high motives as the Duke of Omnium. I don't suppose any one ever had lower motives than the Duchess when she chiselled me about Silverbridge. Never mind;—it 'll all be one a hundred years hence. Get ready, for I want you to be with your father a little before dinner."

Then, when they were in the brougham together, he began a course of very plain instructions. "Look here, dear; you had better get him to talk to you before dinner. I dare say Mrs. Roby will be there, and I will get her on one side. At any rate you can manage it because we shall be early, and I 'll take up a book while you are talking to him."

"What do you wish me to say to him, Ferdinand?"

"I have been thinking of your own proposal, and I am quite sure that we had better join him in the Square. The thing is, I am in a little mess about the rooms, and can't stay on without paying very dearly for them."

"I thought you had paid for them."

"Well;—yes; in one sense I had; but you don't understand about business. You had better not interrupt me now, as I have got a good deal to say before we get to the Square. It will suit me to give up the rooms. I don't like them, and they are very dear. As you yourself said, it will be a capital thing for us to go and stay with your father."

"I meant only for a visit."

"It will be for a visit,—and we 'll make it a long visit." It was odd that the man should have been so devoid of right feeling himself as not to have known that the ideas which he expressed were revolting! "You can sound him. Begin by saying that you are afraid he is desolate. He told me himself that he was desolate, and you can refer to that. Then tell him that we are both of us prepared to do anything that we can to relieve him. Put your arm over him, and kiss him, and all that sort of thing." She shrunk from him into the corner of the brougham, and yet he did not perceive it. "Then say that you think he would be happier if we were to join him here for a time. You can make him understand that there would be no difficulty about the apartments. But don't say it all in a set speech, as though it were prepared,—though of course you can let him know that you have suggested it to me and that I am willing. Be sure to let him understand that the idea began with you."

"But it did not."

"You proposed to go and stay with him. Tell him just that. And you should explain to him that he can dine at the club just as much as he likes. When you were alone with him here of course he had to come home; but he need n't do that now unless he chooses. Of course the brougham would be my affair. And if he should say anything about sharing the house expenses, you can tell him that I would do anything he might propose." Her father to share the household expenses in his own house, and with his own children! "You say as much as you can of all this before dinner, so that when we are sitting below he may suggest it if he pleases. It would suit me to get in there next week if possible."

And so the lesson had been given. She had said little or nothing in reply, and he had only finished as they entered the Square. She had hardly a minute allowed her to think how far she might follow, and in what she must ignore, her husband's instructions. If she might use her own judgment she would tell her father at once that a residence for a time beneath his roof would be a service to them pecuniarily. But this she might not do. She understood that her duty to her husband did forbid her to proclaim his poverty in opposition to his wishes. She would tell nothing that he did not wish her to tell,—but then no duty could require her to say what was false. She would make the suggestion about their change of residence, and would make it with proper affection;—but as regarded themselves she would simply say that it would suit their views to give up their rooms if it suited him.

Mr. Wharton was all alone when they entered the drawing-room,—but, as Lopez had surmised, had asked his sister-in-law round the corner to come to dinner. "Roby always likes an excuse to get to his club," said the old man, "and Harriet likes an excuse to go anywhere." It was not long before Lopez began to play his part by seating himself close to the open window and looking out into the Square; and Emily when she found herself close to her father, with her hand in his, could hardly divest herself of a feeling that she also was playing her part. "I see so very little of you," said the old man plaintively.

"I 'd come up oftener if I thought you 'd like it."

"It is n't liking, my dear. Of course you have to live with your husband. Is n't this sad about Everett?"

"Very sad. But Everett has n't lived here for ever so long."

"I don't know why he should n't. He was a fool to go away when he did. Does he go to you?"

"Yes;—sometimes."

"And what does he say?"

"I 'm sure he would be with you at once if you would ask him."

"I have asked him. I 've sent word by Lopez over and over again. If he means that I am to write to him and say that I 'm sorry for offending him, I won't. Don't talk of him any more. It makes me so angry that I sometimes feel inclined to do things which I know I should repent when dying."

"Not anything to injure Everett, papa!"

"I wonder whether he ever thinks that I am an old man and all alone, and that his brother-in-law is daily with me. But he 's a fool, and thinks of nothing. I know it is very sad being here night after night by myself." Mr. Wharton forgot, no doubt, at the moment, that he passed the majority of his evenings at the Eldon,—though, had he been reminded of it, he might have declared with perfect truth that the delights of his club were not satisfactory.

"Papa," said Emily, "would you like us to come and live here?"

"What,—you and Lopez;—here, in the Square?"

"Yes;—for a time. He is thinking of giving up the place in Belgrave Mansion."

"I thought he had them for—for ever so many months."

"He does not like them, and they are expensive, and he can give them up. If you would wish it, we would come here,—for a time." He turned round and looked at her almost suspiciously; and she,—she blushed as she remembered how accurately she was obeying her husband's orders. "It would be such a joy to me to be near you again."

There was something in her voice which instantly reassured him. "Well——," he said; "come and try it if it will suit him. The house is big enough. It will ease his pocket and be a comfort to me. Come and try it."

It astonished her that the thing should be done so easily. Here was all that her husband had proposed to arrange by deep diplomacy settled in three words. And yet she felt ashamed of herself,—as though she had taken her father in. That terrible behest to "get round him" still grated on her ears. Had she got round him? Had she cheated him into this? "Papa," she said, "do not do this unless you feel sure that you will like it."

"How is anybody to feel sure of anything, my dear?"

"But if you doubt, do not do it."

"I feel sure of one thing, that it will be a great saving to your husband, and I am nearly sure that that ought not to be a matter of indifference to him. There is plenty of room here, and it will at any rate be a comfort to me to see you sometimes." Just at this moment Mrs. Roby came in, and the old man began to tell his news aloud. "Emily has not gone away for long. She's coming back like a bad shilling."

"Not to live in the Square?" said Mrs. Roby, looking round at Lopez.

"Why not? There's room here for them, and it will be just as well to save expense. When will you come, my dear?"

"Whenever the house may be ready, papa."

"It's ready now. You ought to know that. I am not going to refurnish the rooms for you, or anything of that kind. Lopez can come in and hang up his hat whenever it pleases him."

During this time Lopez had hardly known how to speak or what to say. He had been very anxious that his wife should pave the way, as he would have called it. He had been urgent with her to break the ice to her father. But it had not occurred to him that the matter would be settled without any reference to himself. Of course he had heard every word that had been spoken, and was aware that his own poverty had been suggested as the cause for such a proceeding. It was a great thing for him in every way. He would live for nothing, and would also have almost unlimited power of being with Mr. Wharton as old age grew on him. This ready compliance with his wishes was a benefit far too precious to be lost. But yet he felt that his own dignity required some reference to himself. It was distasteful to him that his father-in-law should regard him,—or, at any rate, that he should speak of him,—as a pauper, unable to provide a home for his own wife. "Emily's notion in suggesting it, sir," he said, "has been her care for your comfort." The barrister turned round and looked at him, and Lopez did not quite like the look. "It was she thought of it first, and she certainly had no other idea than that. When she mentioned it to me I was delighted to agree."

Emily heard it all and blushed. It was not absolutely untrue in words,—this assertion of her husband's, —but altogether false in spirit. And yet she could not contradict him. "I don't see why it should not do very well, indeed," said Mrs. Roby.

"I hope it may," said the barrister. "Come, Emily,

I must take you down to dinner to-day. You are not at home yet, you know. As you are to come, the sooner the better."

During dinner not a word was said on the subject. Lopez exerted himself to be pleasant, and told all that he had heard as to the difficulties of the Cabinet. Sir Orlando had resigned, and the general opinion was that the Coalition was going to pieces. Had Mr. Wharton seen the last article in the People's Banner about the Duke? Lopez was strongly of opinion that Mr. Wharton ought to see that article. "I never had the People's Banner within my fingers in my life," said the barrister angrily, "and I certainly never will."

"Ah, sir; this is an exception. You should see this. When Slide really means to cut a fellow up, he can do it. There's no one like him. And the Duke has deserved it. He's a poor, vacillating creature, led by the Duchess; and she,—according to all that one hears,—she isn't much better than she should be."

"I thought the Duchess was a great friend of yours," said Mr. Wharton.

"I don't care much for such friendship. She threw me over most shamefully."

"And therefore, of course, you are justified in taking away her character. I never saw the Duchess of Omnium in my life, and should probably be very uncomfortable if I found myself in her society; but I believe her to be a good sort of woman in her way." Emily sat perfectly silent, knowing that her husband had been rebuked, but feeling that he had deserved it. He, however, was not abashed; but changed the conversation, dashing into City rumours, and legal reforms. The old man from time to time said sharp little things, showing that his intellect was not senile, all of which his son-in-law bore imperturbably. It was not that he liked it, or was indifferent, but that he knew that he could not get the good things which Mr. Wharton could do for him without making some kind of payment. He must take the sharp words of the old man, —and take all that he could get besides.

When the two men were alone together after dinner, Mr. Wharton used a different tone. "If you are to come," he said, "you might as well do it as soon as possible."

"A day or two will be enough for us."

"There are one or two things you should understand. I shall be very happy to see your friends at any time, but I shall like to know when they are coming before they come."

"Of course, sir."

"I dine out a good deal."

"At the club," suggested Lopez.

"Well;—at the club or elsewhere. It does n't matter. There will always be dinner here for you and Emily, just as though I were at home. I say this, so that there need be no questionings or doubts about it hereafter. And don't let there ever be any question of money between us."

"Certainly not."

"Everett has an allowance, and this will be tantamount to an allowance to Emily. You have also had £3,500. I hope it has been well expended;—except the £500 at that election, which has, of course, been thrown away."

"The other was brought into the business."

"I don't know what the business is. But you and

Emily must understand that the money has been given as her fortune."

"Oh, quite so;—part of it, you mean."

"I mean just what I say."

"I call it part of it, because, as you observed just now, our living here will be the same as though you made Emily an allowance."

"Ah;—well; you can look at it in that light if you please. John has the key of the cellar. He's a man I can trust. As a rule I have port and sherry at table every day. If you like claret I will get some a little cheaper than what I use when friends are here."

"What wine I have is quite indifferent to me."

"I like it good, and I have it good. I always breakfast at 9.30. You can have yours earlier if you please. I don't know that there's anything else to be said. I hope we shall get into the way of understanding each other, and being mutually comfortable. Shall we go upstairs to Emily and Mrs. Roby?" And so it was determined that Emily was to come back to her old house about eight months after her marriage.

Mr. Wharton himself sat late into the night, all alone, thinking about it. What he had done, he had done in a morose way, and he was aware that it was so. He had not beamed with smiles, and opened his arms lovingly, and, bidding God bless his dearest children, told them that if they would only come and sit round his hearth he should be the happiest old man in London. He had said little or nothing of his own affection even for his daughter, but had spoken of the matter as one of which the pecuniary aspect alone was important. He had found out that the saving so effected would be material to Lopez, and had resolved that there should be no shirking of the truth in what he was prepared to do. He had been almost asked to take the young married couple in, and feed them,—so that they might live free of expense. He was willing to do it,—but was not willing that there should be any soft-worded, high-toned false pretension. He almost read Lopez to the bottom, —not, however, giving the man credit for dishonesty so deep or cleverness so great as he possessed. But as regarded Emily, he was also actuated by a personal desire to have her back again as an element of happiness to himself. He had pined for her since he had been left alone, hardly knowing what it was that he had wanted. And now as he thought of it all, he was angry with himself that he had not been more loving and softer in his manner to her. She at any rate was honest. No doubt of that crossed his mind. And now he had been bitter to her,—bitter in his manner,—simply because he had not wished to appear to have been taken in by her husband. Thinking of all this, he got up, and went to his desk, and wrote her a note, which she would receive on the following morning after her husband had left her. It was very short.

"Dearest E.,—I am so overjoyed that you are coming back to me.   A. W."

He had judged her quite rightly. The manner in which the thing had been arranged had made her very wretched. There had been no love in it;—nothing apparently but assertions on one side that much was being given, and on the other acknowledgments that much was to be received. She was aware that in this her father had condemned her husband. She also had condemned him;—and felt, alas, that she also had been condemned. But this little letter took away that sting. She could read in her father's note all the action of his mind. He had known that he was bound to acquit her, and he had done so with one of the old long-valued expressions of his love.

CHAPTER XIV.

THE VALUE OF A THICK SKIN.

Sir Orlando Drought must have felt bitterly the quiescence with which he sank into obscurity on the second bench on the opposite side of the House. One great occasion he had on which it was his privilege to explain to four or five hundred gentlemen the insuperable reasons which caused him to break away from those right honourable friends to act with whom had been his comfort and his duty, his great joy and his unalloyed satisfaction. Then he occupied the best part of an hour in abusing those friends and all their measures. This no doubt had been a pleasure, as practice had made the manipulation of words easy to him,—and he was able to revel in that absence of responsibility which must be as a fresh perfumed bath to a Minister just freed from the trammels of office. But the pleasure was surely followed by much suffering when Mr. Monk, —Mr. Monk who was to assume his place as Leader of the House,—only took five minutes to answer him, saying that he and his colleagues regretted much the loss of the Right Honourable Baronet's services, but that it would hardly be necessary for him to defend the ministry on all those points on which it had been attacked, as, were he to do so, he would have to repeat the arguments by which every measure brought forward by the present ministry had been supported. Then Mr. Monk sat down, and the business of the House went on just as if Sir Orlando Drought had not moved his seat at all.

"What makes everybody and everything so dead?" said Sir Orlando to his old friend Mr. Boffin as they walked home together from the House that night. They had in former days been staunch friends, sitting night after night close together, united in opposition, and sometimes, for a few halcyon months, in the happier bonds of office. But when Sir Orlando had joined the Coalition, and when the sterner spirit of Mr. Boffin had preferred principles to place,—to use the language in which he was wont to speak to himself and to his wife and family of his own abnegation,—there had come a coolness between them. Mr. Boffin, who was not a rich man, nor by any means indifferent to the comforts of office, had felt keenly the injury done to him when he was left hopelessly in the cold by the desertion of his old friends. It had come to pass that there had been no salt left in the opposition. Mr. Boffin in all his parliamentary experience had known nothing like it. Mr. Boffin had been sure that British honour was going to the dogs and that British greatness was at an end. But the secession of Sir Orlando gave a little fillip to his life. At any rate he could walk home with his old friend and talk of the horrors of the present day.

"Well, Drought, if you ask me, you know, I can only speak as I feel. Everything must be dead when men holding different opinions on every subject under the sun come together in order that they may carry on a government as they would a trade business. The work may be done, but it must be done without spirit."

"But it may be all important that the work should

be done," said the baronet, apologising for his past misconduct.

"No doubt;—and I am very far from judging those who make the attempt. It has been made more than once before, and has, I think, always failed. I don't believe in it myself, and I think that the death-like torpor of which you speak is one of its worst consequences." After that Mr. Boffin admitted Sir Orlando back into his heart of hearts.

Then the end of the session came, very quietly and very early. By the end of July there was nothing left to be done, and the world of London was allowed to go down into the country almost a fortnight before its usual time.

With many men, both in and out of Parliament, it became a question whether all this was for good or evil. The Boffinites had of course much to say for themselves. Everything was torpid. There was no interest in the newspapers,—except when Mr. Slide took the tomahawk into his hands. A member of Parliament this session had not been by half so much bigger than another man as in times of hot political warfare. One of the most moving sources of our national excitement seemed to have vanished from life. We all know what happens to stagnant waters. So said the Boffinites, and so also now said Sir Orlando. But the Government was carried on and the country was prosperous. A few useful measures had been passed by unambitious men, and the Duke of St. Bungay declared that he had never known a session of Parliament more thoroughly satisfactory to the ministers.

But the old Duke in so saying had spoken as it were

his public opinion,—giving, truly enough, to a few of his colleagues, such as Lord Drummond, Sir Gregory Grogram and others, the results of his general experience; but in his own bosom and with a private friend he was compelled to confess that there was a cloud in the heavens. The Prime Minister had become so moody, so irritable, and so unhappy, that the old Duke was forced to doubt whether things could go on much longer as they were. He was wont to talk of these things to his friend Lord Cantrip, who was not a member of the Government, but who had been a colleague of both the Dukes, and whom the old Duke regarded with peculiar confidence. "I cannot explain it to you," he said to Lord Cantrip. "There is nothing that ought to give him a moment's uneasiness. Since he took office there has n't once been a majority against him in either House on any question that the Government has made its own. I don't remember such a state of things,—so easy for the Prime Minister, —since the days of Lord Liverpool. He had one thorn in his side, our friend who was at the Admiralty, and that thorn like other thorns has worked itself out. Yet at this moment it is impossible to get him to consent to the nomination of a successor to Sir Orlando." This was said a week before the session had closed.

"I suppose it is his health," said Lord Cantrip.

"He's well enough as far as I can see;—though he will be ill unless he can relieve himself from the strain on his nerves."

"Do you mean by resigning?"

"Not necessarily. The fault is that he takes things too seriously. If he could be got to believe that he might eat, and sleep, and go to bed, and amuse himself like other men, he might be a very good Prime Minister. He is over troubled by his conscience. I have seen a good many Prime Ministers, Cantrip, and I 've taught myself to think that they are not very different from other men. One wants in a Prime Minister a good many things, but not very great things. He should be clever but need not be a genius; he should be conscientious but by no means strait-laced; he should be cautious but never timid, bold but never venturesome; he should have a good digestion, genial manners, and, above all, a thick skin. These are the gifts we want, but we can't always get them, and have to do without them. For my own part, I find that though Smith be a very good Minister, the best perhaps to be had at the time, when he breaks down Jones does nearly as well."

"There will be a Jones, then, if your Smith does break down?"

"No doubt. England would n't come to an end because the Duke of Omnium shut himself up at Matching. But I love the man, and, with some few exceptions, am contented with the party. We can't do better, and it cuts me to the heart when I see him suffering, knowing how much I did myself to make him undertake the work."

"Is he going to Gatherum Castle?"

"No;—to Matching. There is some discomfort about that."

"I suppose," said Lord Cantrip,—speaking almost in a whisper, although they were closeted together, " I suppose the Duchess is a little troublesome."

"She 's the dearest woman in the world," said the Duke of St. Bungay. " I love her almost as I do my own daughter. And she is most zealous to serve him."

"I fancy she overdoes it."

"No doubt."

"And that he suffers from perceiving it," said Lord Cantrip.

"But a man has n't a right to suppose that he shall have no annoyances. The best horse in the world has some fault. He pulls, or he shies, or is slow at his fences, or does n't like heavy ground. He has no right to expect that his wife shall know everything and do everything without a mistake. And then he has such faults of his own! His skin is so thin. Do you remember dear old Brock? By heavens;—there was a covering, a hide impervious to fire or steel! He would n't have gone into tantrums because his wife asked too many people to the house. Nevertheless, I won't give up all hope."

"A man's skin may be thickened, I suppose."

"No doubt;—as a blacksmith's arm."

But the Duke of St. Bungay, though he declared that he would n't give up hope, was very uneasy on the matter. "Why won't you let me go?" the other Duke had said to him.

"What;—because such a man as Sir Orlando Drought throws up his office?"

But in truth the Duke of Omnium had not been instigated to ask the question by the resignation of Sir Orlando. At that very moment the People's Banner had been put out of sight at the bottom of a heap of other newspapers behind the Prime Minister's chair, and his present misery had been produced by Mr. Quintus Slide. To have a festering wound and to be able to show the wound to no surgeon, is wretchedness indeed! "It's not Sir Orlando, but a sense of general failure," said the Prime Minister. Then his old friend had made use of that argument of the ever-recurring majorities to prove that there had been no failure. "There seems to have come a lethargy upon the country," said the poor victim. Then the Duke of St. Bungay knew that his friend had read that pernicious article in the People's Banner, for the Duke had also read it and remembered that phrase of a "lethargy on the country," and understood at once how the poison had rankled.

It was a week before he would consent to ask any man to fill the vacancy made by Sir Orlando. He would not allow suggestions to be made to him and yet would name no one himself. The old Duke, indeed, did make a suggestion, and anything coming from him was of course borne with patience. Barrington Erle, he thought, would do for the Admiralty. But the Prime Minister shook his head. "In the first place he would refuse, and that would be a great blow to me."

"I could sound him," said the old Duke. But the Prime Minister again shook his head and turned the subject. With all his timidity he was becoming autocratic and peevishly imperious. Then he went to Lord Cantrip, and when Lord Cantrip, with all the kindness which he could throw into his words, stated the reasons which induced him at present to decline office, he was again in despair. At last he asked Phineas Finn to move to the Admiralty, and, when our old friend somewhat reluctantly obeyed, of course he had the same difficulty in filling the office Finn had held. Other changes and other complications became necessary, and Mr. Quintus Slide, who hated Phineas Finn even worse than the poor Duke, found ample scope for his patriotic indignation.

This all took place in the closing week of the session, filling our poor Prime Minister with trouble and dismay, just when other people were complaining that there was nothing to think of and nothing to do. Men do not really like leaving London before the grouse calls them,—the grouse, or rather the fashion of the grouse. And some ladies were very angry at being separated so soon from their swains in the City. The tradesmen too were displeased,—so that there were voices to re-echo the abuse of the People's Banner. The Duchess had done her best to prolong the session by another week, telling her husband of the evil consequences above suggested, but he had thrown wide his arms and asked her with affected dismay whether he was to keep Parliament sitting in order that more ribbons might be sold! "There is nothing to be done," said the Duke almost angrily.

"Then you should make something to be done," said the Duchess, mimicking him.

CHAPTER XV.

RETRIBUTION.

THE Duchess had been at work with her husband for the last two months in the hope of renewing her autumnal festivities, but had been lamentably unsuccessful. The Duke had declared that there should be no more rural crowds, no repetition of what he called London turned loose on his own grounds. He could not forget the necessity which had been imposed upon him of turning Major Pountney out of his house, or the change that had been made in his gardens, or his wife's attempt to conquer him at Silverbridge. "Do you mean," she said, "that we are to have nobody?" He replied that he thought it would be best to go to Matching. "And live a Darby and Joan life?" said the Duchess.

"I said nothing of Darby and Joan. Whatever may be my feelings I hardly think that you are fitted for that kind of thing. Matching is not so big as Gatherum, but it is not a cottage. Of course you can ask your own friends."

"I don't know what you mean by my own friends. I endeavour always to ask yours."

"I don't know that Major Pountney, and Captain Gunner, and Mr. Lopez were ever among the number of my friends."

"I suppose you mean Lady Rosina?" said the Duchess. "I shall be happy to have her at Matching if you wish it."

"I should like to see Lady Rosina De Courcy at Matching very much."

"And is there to be nobody else? I'm afraid I should find it rather dull while you two were opening your hearts to each other." Here he looked at her angrily. "Can you think of anybody besides Lady Rosina?"

"I suppose you will wish to have Mrs. Finn?"

"What an arrangement! Lady Rosina for you to flirt with, and Mrs. Finn for me to grumble to."

"That is an odious word," said the Prime Minister.

"What;—flirting? I don't see anything bad about the word. The thing is dangerous. But you are quite at liberty if you don't go beyond Lady Rosina. I should like to know whether you would wish anybody else to come?" Of course he made no becoming answer to this question, and of course no becoming answer was expected. He knew that she was trying to provoke him because he would not let her do this year as she had done last. The house, he had no doubt, would be full to overflowing when he got there. He could not help that. But as compared with Gatherum Castle the house at Matching was small, and his domestic authority sufficed at any rate for shutting up Gatherum for the time.

I do not know whether at times her sufferings were not as acute as his own. He, at any rate, was Prime Minister, and it seemed to her that she was to be reduced to nothing. At the beginning of it all he had, with unwonted tenderness, asked her for her sympathy in his undertaking, and, according to her powers, she

had given it to him with her whole heart. She had
thought that she had seen a way by which she might
assist him in his great employment, and she had worked
at it like a slave. Every day she told herself that she
did not, herself, love the Captain Gunners and Major
Pountneys, nor the Sir Orlandos, nor, indeed, the Lady
Rosinas. She had not followed the bent of her own
inclination when she had descended to sheets and
towels, and busied herself to establish an archery-
ground. She had not shot an arrow during the whole
season, nor had she cared who had won and who had
lost. It had not been for her own personal delight that
she had kept open house for forty persons throughout
four months of the year, in doing which he had never
taken an ounce of the labour off her shoulders by any
single word or deed! It had all been done for his sake,
—that his reign might be long and triumphant, that
the world might say that his hospitality was noble and
full, that his name might be in men's mouths, and that
he might prosper as a British Minister. Such, at least,
were the assertions which she made to herself, when
she thought of her own grievances and her own troubles.
And now she was angry with her husband. It was
very well for him to ask for her sympathy, but he had
none to give her in return! He could not pity her failures,—even though he had himself caused them! If
he had a grain of intelligence about him he must, she
thought, understand well enough how sore it must be
for her to descend from her princely entertainments to
solitude at Matching, and thus to own before all the
world that she was beaten. Then when she asked him
for advice, when she was really anxious to know how
far she might go in filling her house without offending

him, he told her to ask Lady Rosina De Courcy! If he chose to be ridiculous he might. She would ask Lady Rosina De Courcy. In her active anger she did write to Lady Rosina De Courcy a formal letter, in which she said that the Duke hoped to have the pleasure of her ladyship's company at Matching Park on the 1st of August. It was an absurd letter, somewhat long, written very much in the Duke's name, with overwhelming expressions of affection, instigated in the writer's mind partly by the fun of the supposition that such a man as her husband should flirt with such a woman as Lady Rosina. There was something too of anger in what she wrote, some touch of revenge. She sent off this invitation, and she sent no other. Lady Rosina took it all in good part, and replied saying that she should have the greatest pleasure in going to Matching. She had declared to herself that she would ask none but those he had named, and in accordance with her resolution she sent out no other written invitations.

He had also told her to ask Mrs. Finn. Now this had become almost a matter of course. There had grown up from accidental circumstances so strong a bond between these two women, that it was taken for granted by both their husbands that they should be nearly always within reach of one another. And the two husbands were also on kindly, if not affectionate terms with each other. The nature of the Duke's character was such that, with a most loving heart, he was hardly capable of that opening out of himself to another which is necessary for positive friendship. There was a stiff reserve about him, of which he was himself only too conscious, which almost prohibited friendship. But he liked Mr. Finn both as a man and a member of his party, and was always satisfied to have him as a guest. The Duchess, therefore, had taken it for granted that Mrs. Finn would come to her,—and that Mr. Finn would come also during any time that he might be able to escape from Ireland. But, when the invitation was verbally conveyed, Mr. Finn had gone to the Admiralty, and had already made his arrangements for going to sea, as a gallant sailor should. "We are going away in the 'Black Watch' for a couple of months," said Mrs. Finn. Now the "Black Watch" was the Admiralty yacht.

"Heavens and earth!" ejaculated the Duchess.

"It is always done. The First Lord would have his epaulets stripped if he did n't go to sea in August."

"And must you go with him?"

"I have promised."

"I think it very unkind,—very hard upon me. Of course you knew that I should want you."

"But if my husband wants me too?"

"Bother your husband! I wish with all my heart I had never helped to make up the match."

"It would have been made up just the same, Lady Glen."

"You know that I cannot get on without you. And he ought to know it too. There is n't another person in the world that I can really say a thing to."

"Why don't you have Mrs. Grey?"

"She's going to Persia after her husband. And then she is not wicked enough. She always lectured me, and she does it still. What do you think is going to happen?"

"Nothing terrible, I hope," said Mrs. Finn, mindful

of her husband's new honours at the Admiralty, and hoping that the Duke might not have repeated his threat of resigning.

"We are going to Matching."

"So I supposed."

"And whom do you think we are going to have?"

"Not Major Pountney?"

"No;—not at my asking."

"Nor Mr. Lopez?"

"Nor yet Mr. Lopez. Guess again."

"I suppose there will be a dozen to guess."

"No," shrieked the Duchess. "There will only be one. I have asked one,—at his special desire,—and as you won't come I shall ask nobody else. When I pressed him to name a second he named you. I'll obey him to the letter. Now, my dear, who do you think is the chosen one,—the one person who is to solace the perturbed spirit of the Prime Minister for the three months of the autumn?"

"Mr. Warburton, I should say."

"Oh, Mr. Warburton! No doubt Mr. Warburton will come as a part of his luggage, and possibly half-a-dozen Treasury clerks. He declares, however, that there is nothing to do, and therefore Mr. Warburton's strength may alone suffice to help him to do it. There is to be one unnecessary guest,—unnecessary, that is, for official purpose; though,—oh,—so much needed for his social happiness. Guess once more."

"Knowing the spirit of mischief that is in you,—perhaps it is Lady Rosina."

"Of course it is Lady Rosina," said the Duchess, clapping her hands together. "And I should like to know what you mean by a spirit of mischief! I asked him, and he himself said that he particularly wished to have Lady Rosina at Matching. Now, I 'm not a jealous woman,—am I?"

"Not of Lady Rosina."

"I don't think they 'll do any harm together, but it is particular, you know. However, she is to come. And nobody else is to come. I did count upon you." Then Mrs. Finn counselled her very seriously as to the bad taste of such a joke, explaining to her that the Duke had certainly not intended that her invitations should be confined to Lady Rosina. But it was not all joke with the Duchess. She had been driven almost to despair, and was very angry with her husband. He had brought the thing upon himself, and must now make the best of it. She would ask nobody else. She declared that there was nobody whom she could ask with propriety. She was tired of asking. Let her ask whom she would he was dissatisfied. The only two people he cared to see were Lady Rosina and the old Duke. She had asked Lady Rosina for his sake. Let him ask his old friend himself if he pleased.

The Duke and Duchess with all the family went down together, and Mr. Warburton went with them. The Duchess had said not a word more to her husband about his guests, nor had he alluded to the subject. But each was labouring under a conviction that the other was misbehaving, and with that feeling it was impossible that there should be confidence between them. He busied himself with books and papers,— always turning over those piles of newspapers to see what evil was said of himself,—and speaking only now and again to his private secretary. She engaged herself with the children or pretended to read a novel.

Her heart was sore within her. She had wished to punish him, but in truth she was punishing herself.

On the day of their arrival, the father and mother, with Lord Silverbridge, the eldest son, who was home from Eton, and the private secretary dined together. As the Duke sat at table, he began to think how long it was since such a state of things had happened to him before, and his heart softened towards her. Instead of being made angry by the strangeness of her proceeding, he took delight in it, and in the course of the evening spoke a word to signify his satisfaction. "I 'm afraid it won't last long," she said, "for Lady Rosina comes to-morrow."

"Oh, indeed."

"You bid me ask her yourself."

Then he perceived it all;—how she had taken advantage of his former answer to her and had acted upon it in a spirit of contradictory petulance. But he resolved that he would forgive it and endeavour to bring her back to him. "I thought we were both joking," he said good-humouredly.

"Oh no! I never suspected you of a joke. At any rate she is coming."

"She will do neither of us any harm. And Mrs. Finn?"

"You have sent her to sea."

"She may be at sea,—and he too; but it is without my sending. The First Lord I believe usually does go a cruise. Is there nobody else?"

"Nobody else,—unless you have asked any one."

"Not a creature. Well;—so much the better. I dare say Lady Rosina will get on very well."

"You will have to talk to her," said the Duchess.

"I will do my best," said the Duke.

Lady Rosina came and no doubt did think it odd. But she did not say so, and it really did seem to the Duchess as though all her vengeance had been blown away by the winds. And she too laughed at the matter—to herself, and began to feel less cross and less perverse. The world did not come to an end because she and her husband with Lady Rosina and her boy and the private secretary sat down to dinner every day together. The parish clergyman with the neighbouring squire and his wife and daughter did come one day,—to the relief of M. Millepois, who had begun to feel that the world had collapsed. And every day at a certain hour the Duke and Lady Rosina walked together for an hour and a half in the park. The Duchess would have enjoyed it, instead of suffering, could she only have had her friend, Mrs. Finn, to hear her jokes. "Now, Plantagenet," she said, "do tell me one thing. What does she talk about?"

"The troubles of her family generally, I think."

"That can't last forever."

"She wears cork soles to her boots and she thinks a good deal about them."

"And you listen to her?"

"Why not? I can talk about cork soles as well as anything else. Anything that may do material good to the world at large, or even to yourself privately, is a fit subject for conversation to rational people."

"I suppose I never was one of them."

"But I can talk upon anything," continued the Duke, "as long as the talker talks in good faith and does not say things that should not be said, or deal with matters that are offensive. I could talk for an hour about bankers' accounts, but I should not expect a stranger to ask me the state of my own. She has almost persuaded me to send to Mr. Sprout of Silverbridge and get some cork soles myself."

"Don't do anything of the kind," said the Duchess with animation;—as though she had secret knowledge that cork soles were specially fatal to the family of the Pallisers.

"Why not, my dear?"

"He was the man who especially, above all others, threw me over at Silverbridge." Then again there came upon his brow that angry frown which during the last few days had been dissipated by the innocence of Lady Rosina's conversation. "Of course I don't mean to ask you to take any interest in the borough again. You have said that you would n't, and you are always as good as your word."

"I hope so."

"But I certainly would not employ a tradesman just at your elbow who has directly opposed what was generally understood in the town to be your interests."

"What did Mr. Sprout do? This is the first I have heard of it."

"He got Mr. Du Boung to stand against Mr. Lopez."

"I am very glad for the sake of the borough that Mr. Lopez did not get in."

"So am I. But that is nothing to do with it. Mr. Sprout knew at any rate what my wishes were, and went directly against them."

"You were not entitled to have wishes in the matter, Glencora."

"That's all very well;—but I had, and he knew it. As for the future, of course the thing is over. But you have done everything for the borough."

"You mean that the borough has done much for me."

"I know what I mean very well;—and I shall take it very ill if a shilling out of the Castle ever goes into Mr. Sprout's pocket again."

It is needless to trouble the reader at length with the sermon which he preached her on the occasion,—showing the utter corruption which must come from the mixing up of politics with trade, or with the scorn which she threw into the few words with which she interrupted him from time to time. "Whether a man makes good shoes, and at a reasonable price, and charges for them honestly,—that is what you have to consider," said the Duke impressively.

"I'd rather pay double for bad shoes to a man who did not thwart me."

"You should not condescend to be thwarted in such a matter. You lower yourself by admitting such a feeling." And yet he writhed himself under the lashes of Mr. Slide!

"I know an enemy when I see him," said the Duchess, "and as long as I live I'll treat an enemy as an enemy."

There was ever so much of it, in the course of which the Duke declared his purpose of sending at once to Mr. Sprout for ever so many cork soles, and the Duchess,—most imprudently,—declared her purpose of ruining Mr. Sprout. There was something in this threat which grated terribly against the Duke's sense of honour;—that his wife should threaten to ruin a poor tradesman, that she should do so in reference to the political affairs of the borough which he all but owned,—that she should do so in declared opposition to him! Of course he ought to have known that her sin consisted simply in her determination to vex him at the moment. A more good-natured woman did not live;—or one less prone to ruin any one. But any reference to the Silverbridge election brought back upon him the remembrance of the cruel attacks which had been made upon him and rendered him for the time moody, morose, and wretched. So they again parted ill friends, and hardly spoke when they met at dinner.

The next morning there reached Matching a letter which greatly added to his bitterness of spirit against the world in general and against her in particular. The letter, though marked "private," had been opened, as were all his letters, by Mr. Warburton, but the private secretary thought it necessary to show the letter to the Prime Minister. He, when he had read it, told Warburton that it did not signify, and maintained for half an hour an attitude of quiescence. Then he walked forth, having the letter hidden in his hand, and finding his wife alone, gave it her to read. "See what you have brought upon me," he said, "by your interference and disobedience." The letter was as follows:—

"Manchester Square, August 3, 187—.

"My Lord Duke,—I consider myself entitled to complain to your Grace of the conduct with which I was treated at the last election at Silverbridge, whereby I was led into very heavy expenditure without the least chance of being returned for the borough. I am aware that I had no direct conversation with your Grace on the subject, and that your Grace can plead that as between man and man, I had no authority from yourself for supposing that I should receive your Grace's support. But I was distinctly asked by the Duchess to stand, and was assured by her that if I did so I should have all the assistance that your Grace's influence could procure for me;—and it was also explained to me that your Grace's official position made it inexpedient that your Grace on this special occasion should have any personal conference with your own candidate. Under these circumstances I submit to your Grace that I am entitled to complain of the hardship I have suffered.

"I had not been long in the borough before I found that my position was hopeless. Influential men in the town who had been represented to me as being altogether devoted to your Grace's interests started a third candidate,—a liberal as myself,—and the natural consequence was that neither of us succeeded, though my return as your Grace's candidate would have been certain had not this been done. That all this was preconcerted there can be no doubt, but, before the mine was sprung on me,—immediately, indeed, on my arrival, if I remember rightly,—an application was made to me for £500, so that the money might be exacted before the truth was known to me. Of course I should not have paid the £500 had I known that your Grace's usual agents in the town,—I may name Mr. Sprout especially,—were prepared to act against me. But I did pay the money, and I think your Grace will agree with me that a very opprobrious term might be applied without injustice to the transaction.

"My Lord Duke, I am a poor man;—ambitious I will own, whether that be a sin or a virtue,—and willing perhaps to incur expenditure which can hardly be justified in pursuit of certain public objects. But I must say, with the most lively respect for your Grace personally, that I do not feel inclined to sit down tamely under such a loss as this. I should not have dreamed of interfering in the election at Silverbridge had not the Duchess exhorted me to do so. I would not even have run the risk of a doubtful contest. But I came forward at the suggestion of the Duchess, backed by her personal assurance that the seat was certain as being in your Grace's hands. It was no doubt understood that your Grace would not yourself interfere, but it was equally well understood that your Grace's influence was for the time deputed to the Duchess. The Duchess herself will, I am sure, confirm my statement that I had her direct authority for regarding myself as your Grace's candidate.

"I can of course bring an action against Mr. Wise, the gentleman to whom I paid the money, but I feel that as a gentleman I should not do so without reference to your Grace, as circumstances might possibly be brought out in evidence,—I will not say prejudicial to your Grace,—but which would be unbecoming. I cannot, however, think that your Grace will be willing that a poor man like myself, in his search for an entrance into public life, should be mulcted to so heavy an extent in consequence of an error on the part of the Duchess. Should your Grace be able to assist me in my view of getting into Parliament for any other seat I shall be willing to abide the loss I have incurred.

I hardly, however, dare to hope for such assistance. In this case I think your Grace ought to see that I am reimbursed.

"I have the honour to be,
"My Lord Duke,
"Your Grace's very faithful Servant,
"Ferdinand Lopez."

The Duke stood over her in her own room upstairs, with his back to the fireplace and his eyes fixed upon her while she was reading this letter. He gave her ample time, and she did not read it very quickly. Much of it indeed she perused twice, turning very red in the face as she did so. She was thus studious partly because the letter astounded even her, and partly because she wanted time to consider how she would meet his wrath. "Well," said he, "what do you say to that?"

"The man is a blackguard,—of course."

"He is so;—though I do not know that I wish to hear him called such a name by your lips. Let him be what he may he was your friend."

"He was my acquaintance."

"He was the man whom you selected to be your candidate for the borough in opposition to my wishes, and whom you continued to support in direct disobedience to my orders."

"Surely, Plantagenet, we have had all that about disobedience out before."

"You cannot have such things 'out,'—as you call it. Evil-doing will not bury itself out of the way and be done with. Do you feel no shame at having your name mentioned a score of times with reprobation as that man mentions it;—at being written about by such a man as that?"

"Do you want to make me roll in the gutter because I mistook him for a gentleman?"

"That was not all,—nor half. In your eagerness to serve such a miserable creature as this you forgot my entreaties, my commands, my position! I explained to you why I, of all men, and you, of all women, as a part of me, should not do this thing; and yet you did it, mistaking such a cur as that for a man! What am I to do? How am I to free myself from the impediments which you make for me? My enemies I can overcome,—but I cannot escape the pitfalls which are made for me by my own wife. I can only retire into private life and hope to console myself with my children and my books."

There was a reality of tragedy about him which for the moment overcame her. She had no joke ready, no sarcasm, no feminine counter-grumble. Little as she agreed with him when he spoke of the necessity of retiring into private life because a man had written to him such a letter as this, incapable as she was of understanding fully the nature of the irritation which tormented him, still she knew that he was suffering, and acknowledged to herself that she had been the cause of the agony. "I am sorry," she ejaculated at last. "What more can I say?"

"What am I to do? What can be said to the man? Warburton read the letter, and gave it me in silence. He could see the terrible difficulty."

"Tear it in pieces, and then let there be an end of it."

"I do not feel sure but that he has right on his side. He is, as you say, certainly a blackguard, or he would not make such a claim. He is taking advantage of the mistake made by a good-natured woman through her folly and her vanity;"—as he said this the Duchess gave an absurd little pout, but luckily he did not see it,—" and he knows very well that he is doing so. But still he has a show of justice on his side. There was, I suppose, no chance for him at Silverbridge after I had made myself fully understood. The money was absolutely wasted. It was your persuasion and then your continued encouragement that led him on to spend the money."

"Pay it then. The loss will not hurt you."

"Ah;—if we could but get out of our difficulties by paying! Suppose that I do pay it. I begin to think that I must pay it;—that after all I cannot allow such a plea to remain unanswered. But when it is paid;— what then? Do you think such a payment made by the Queen's Minister will not be known to all the newspapers, and that I shall escape the charge of having bribed the man to hold his tongue?"

"It will be no bribe if you pay him because you think you ought."

"But how shall I excuse it? There are things done which are holy as the heavens,—which are clear before God as the light of the sun, which leave no stain on the conscience, and which yet the malignity of man can invest with the very blackness of hell! I shall know why I pay this £500. Because she who of all the world is the nearest and the dearest to me,"—she looked up into his face with amazement, as he stood stretching out both his arms in his energy,—" has in her impetuous folly committed a grievous blunder, from which she would not allow her husband to save her, this sum must be paid to the wretched craven. But I cannot tell the world that. I cannot say abroad that this small sacrifice of money was the justest means of retrieving the injury which you had done."

"Say it abroad. Say it everywhere."

"No, Glencora."

"Do you think that I would have you spare me if it was my fault? And how would it hurt me? Will it be new to any one that I have done a foolish thing? Will the newspapers disturb my peace? I sometimes think, Plantagenet, that I should have been the man, my skin is so thick; and that you should have been the woman, yours is so tender."

"But it is not so."

"Take the advantage, nevertheless, of my toughness. Send him the £500 without a word,—or make Warburton do so, or Mr. Moreton. Make no secret of it. Then if the papers talk about it——"

"A question might be asked about it in the House."

"Or if questioned in any way,—say that I did it. Tell the exact truth. You are always saying that nothing but truth ever serves. Let the truth serve now. I shall not blench. Your saying it all in the House of Lords won't wound me half so much as your looking at me as you did just now."

"Did I wound you? God knows I would not hurt you willingly."

"Never mind. Go on. I know you think that I have brought it all on myself by my own wickedness. Pay this man the money, and then if anything be said about it, explain that it was my fault, and say that you paid the money because I had done wrong."

When he came in she had been seated on a sofa,

which she constantly used herself, and he had stood over her, masterful, imperious, and almost tyrannical. She had felt his tyranny, but had resented it less than usual,—or rather had been less determined in holding her own against him and asserting herself as his equal,—because she confessed to herself that she had injured him. She had, she thought, done but little, but that which she had done had produced this injury. So she had sat and endured the oppression of his standing posture. But now he sat down by her, very close to her, and put his hand upon her shoulder,—almost round her waist.

"Cora," he said, "you do not quite understand it."

"I never understand anything, I think," she answered.

"Not in this case,—perhaps never,—what it is that a husband feels about his wife. Do you think that I could say a word against you, even to a friend?"

"Why not?"

"I never did. I never could. If my anger were at the hottest I would not confess to a human being that you were not perfect,—except to yourself."

"Oh, thank you! If you were to scold me vicariously I should feel it less."

"Do not joke with me now, for I am so much in earnest! And if I could not consent that your conduct should be called in question even by a friend, do you suppose it possible that I could contrive an escape from public censure by laying the blame publicly on you?"

"Stick to the truth;—that's what you always say."

"I certainly shall stick to the truth. A man and his wife are one. For what she does he is responsible."

"They could n't hang you, you know, because I committed a murder."

"I should be willing that they should do so. No;—if I pay this money I shall take the consequences. I shall not do it in any way under the rose. But I wish you would remember—— "

"Remember what? I know I shall never forget all this trouble about that dirty little town, which I never will enter again as long as I live."

"I wish you would think that in all that you do you are dealing with my feelings, with my heartstrings, with my reputation. You cannot divide yourself from me; nor, for the value of it all, would I wish that such division were possible. You say that I am thin-skinned."

"Certainly you are. What people call a delicate organisation,—whereas I am rough and thick and monstrously commonplace."

"Then should you too be thin-skinned for my sake."

"I wish I could make you thick-skinned for your own. It's the only way to be decently comfortable in such a course, rough-and-tumble world as this is."

"Let us both do our best," he said, now putting his arm round her and kissing her. "I think I shall send the man his money at once. It is the least of two evils. And now let there never be a word more about it between us."

Then he left her and went back,—not to the study in which he was wont, when at Matching, to work with his private secretary,—but to a small inner closet of his own, in which many a bitter moment was spent while he thought over that abortive system of decimal coinage by which he had once hoped to make himself one of the great benefactors of his nation, revolving in his mind the troubles which his wife brought upon him, and regretting the golden inanity of the coronet which in the very prime of life had expelled him from the House of Commons. Here he seated himself, and for an hour neither stirred from his seat, nor touched a pen, nor opened a book. He was trying to calculate in his mind what might be the consequences of paying the money to Mr. Lopez. But when the calculation slipped from him,—as it did,—then he demanded of himself whether strict high-minded justice did not call upon him to pay the money let the consequences be what they might. And here his mind was truer to him, and he was able to fix himself to a purpose,—though the resolution to which he came was not, perhaps, wise.

When the hour was over he went to his desk, drew a cheque for £500 in favour of Ferdinand Lopez, and then caused his secretary to send it in the following note:—

"Matching, August 4, 187—.

"Sir,—The Duke of Omnium has read the letter you have addressed to him, dated the 3rd instant. The Duke of Omnium, feeling that you may have been induced to undertake the late contest at Silverbridge by misrepresentations made to you at Gatherum Castle, directs me to enclose a cheque for £500, that being the sum stated by you to have been expended in carrying on the contest at Silverbridge.

"I am, sir,
"Your obedient servant,
"ARTHUR WARBURTON.

"Ferdinand Lopez, Esq."

CHAPTER XVI.

KAURI GUM.

THE reader will no doubt think that Ferdinand Lopez must have been very hardly driven indeed by circumstances before he would have made such an appeal to the Duke as that given in the last chapter. But it was not want of money only that had brought it about. It may be remembered that the £500 had already been once repaid him by his father-in-law,—that special sum having been given to him for that special purpose. And Lopez, when he wrote to the Duke, assured himself that if, by any miracle, his letter should produce pecuniary results in the shape of a payment from the Duke, he would refund the money so obtained to Mr. Wharton. But when he wrote the letter he did not expect to get money,—nor, indeed, did he expect that aid towards another seat, to which he alluded at the close of his letter. He expected probably nothing but to vex the Duke, and to drive the Duke into a correspondence with him.

Though this man had lived nearly all his life in England, he had not quite acquired that knowledge of the way in which things are done which is so general among men of a certain class, and so rare among those beneath them. He had not understood that the Duchess's promise of her assistance at Silverbridge might be taken by him for what it was worth, and that her aid might be used as far as it went,—but that, in the event of its failing him, he was bound in honour to take the result without complaining, whatever that result might be. He felt that a grievous injury had been done him, and that it behoved him to resent that injury,—even though it were against a woman. He just knew that he could not very well write to the Duchess herself,—though there was sometimes present to his mind a plan for attacking her in public, and telling her what evil she had done him. He had half resolved that he would do so in her own garden at The Horns;—but on that occasion the apparition of Arthur Fletcher had disturbed him, and he had vented his anger in another direction. But still his wrath against the Duke and Duchess remained, and he was wont to indulge it with very violent language as he sat upon one of the chairs in Sexty Parker's office, talking somewhat loudly of his own position, of the things that he would do, and of the injury done him. Sexty Parker sympathised with him to the full,—especially as that first £500, which he had received from Mr. Wharton, had gone into Sexty's coffers. At that time Lopez and Sexty were together committed to large speculations in the guano trade, and Sexty's mind was by no means easy in the early periods of the day. As he went into town by his train he would think of his wife and family and of the terrible things that might happen to them. But yet, up to this period, money had always been forthcoming from Lopez when absolutely wanted, and Sexty was quite alive to the fact that he was living with a freedom of expenditure in his own household that he had never known before, and that without apparent damage. Whenever, therefore, at some critical moment, a much-needed sum of money was produced, Sexty would become light-hearted, triumphant, and very sympathetic. "Well;—I never heard such a story," he had said when Lopez was insisting on his wrongs. "That's what the Dukes and Duchesses call honour among thieves! Well, Ferdy, my boy, if you stand that you'll stand anything." In these latter days Sexty had become very intimate indeed with his partner.

"I don't mean to stand it," Lopez had replied, and then on the spot had written the letter which he had dated from Manchester Square. He had certainly contrived to make that letter as oppressive as possible. He had been clever enough to put into it words which were sure to wound the poor Duke and to confound the Duchess. And having written it he was very careful to keep the first draft, so that if occasion came he might use it again and push his vengeance farther. But he certainly had not expected such a result as it produced.

When he received the private secretary's letter with the money he was sitting opposite to his father-in-law at breakfast, while his wife was making the tea. Not many of his letters came to Manchester Square. Sexty Parker's office or his club were more convenient addresses; but in this case he had thought that Manchester Square would have a better sound and appearance. When he opened the letter the cheque of course appeared bearing the Duke's own signature. He had seen that and the amount before he had read the letter, and as he saw it his eye travelled quickly across the table to his father-in-law's face. Mr. Wharton might certainly have seen the cheque and even the amount, probably also the signature, without the slightest suspicion as to the nature of the payment made. As it was, he was eating his toast, and had thought nothing about the letter. Lopez, having concealed the cheque, read the few words which the private secretary had written, and then put the document with its contents into his pocket. "So you think, sir, of going down to Herefordshire on the 15th," he said in a very cheery voice. The cheery voice was still pleasant to the old man, but the young wife had already come to distrust it. She had learned, though she was hardly conscious how the lesson had come to her, that a certain tone of cheeriness indicated, if not deceit, at any rate the concealment of something. It grated against her spirit; and when this tone reached her ears a frown or look of sorrow would cross her brow. And her husband also had perceived that it was so, and knew at such times that he was rebuked. He was hardly aware what doings, and especially what feelings, were imputed to him as faults,—not understanding the lines which separated right from wrong; but he knew that he was often condemned by his wife, and he lived in fear that he should also be condemned by his wife's father. Had it been his wife only he thought that he could soon have quenched her condemnation. He would soon have made her tired of showing her disapproval. But he had put himself into the old man's house, where the old man could see not only him but his treatment of his wife, and the old man's good-will and good opinion were essential to him. Yet he could not restrain one glance of anger at her when he saw that look upon her face.

"I suppose I shall," said the barrister. "I must go somewhere. My going need not disturb you."

"I think we have made up our mind," said Lopez,

"to take a cottage at Dovercourt. It is not a very lively place, nor yet fashionable. But it is very healthy, and I can run up to town easily. Unfortunately my business won't let me be altogether away this autumn."

"I wish my business would keep me," said the barrister.

"I did not understand that you had made up your mind to go to Dovercourt," said Emily. He had spoken to Mr. Wharton of their joint action in the matter, and as the place had only once been named by him to her, she resented what seemed to be a falsehood. She knew that she was to be taken or left as it suited him. If he had said boldly,—"We'll go to Dovercourt. That's what I've settled on. That's what will suit me," she would have been contented. She quite understood that he meant to have his own way in such things. But it seemed to her that he wanted to be a tyrant without having the courage necessary for tyranny.

"I thought you seemed to like it," he said.

"I don't dislike it at all."

"Then, as it suits my business, we might as well consider it settled." So saying, he left the room and went off to the City. The old man was still sipping his tea and lingering over his breakfast in a way that was not usual with him. He was generally anxious to get away to Lincoln's Inn, and on most mornings had left the house before his son-in-law. Emily of course remained with him, sitting silent in her place opposite to the teapot, meditating perhaps on her prospects of happiness at Dovercourt,—a place of which she had never heard even the name two days ago, and in which it was hardly possible that she should find even an acquaintance. In former years these autumn months, passed in Herefordshire, had been the delight of her life.

Mr. Wharton also had seen the cloud on his daughter's face, and had understood the nature of the little dialogue about Dovercourt. And he was aware,—had been aware since they had both come into his house,—that the young wife's manner and tone to her husband was not that of perfect conjugal sympathy. He had already said to himself more than once that she had made her bed for herself, and must lie upon it. She was the man's wife, and must take her husband as he was. If she suffered under this man's mode and manner of life, he, as her father, could not assist her,—could do nothing for her, unless the man should become absolutely cruel. He had settled that within his own mind already;—but yet his heart yearned towards her, and when he thought that she was unhappy he longed to comfort her and tell her that she still had a father. But the time had not come as yet in which he could comfort her by sympathising with her against her husband. There had never fallen from her lips a syllable of complaint. When she had spoken to him a chance word respecting her husband, it had always carried with it some tone of affection. But still he longed to say to her something which might tell her that his heart was soft towards her. "Do you like the idea of going to this place?" he said.

"I don't at all know what it will be like. Ferdinand says it will be cheap."

"Is that of such vital consequence?"

"Ah;—yes; I fear it is."

This was very sad to him. Lopez had already had from him a considerable sum of money, having not yet been married twelve months, and was now living in London almost free of expense. Before his marriage he had always spoken of himself, and had contrived to be spoken of, as a wealthy man, and now he was obliged to choose some small English sea-side place to which to retreat, because thus he might live at a low rate! Had they married as poor people there would have been nothing to regret in this;—there would be nothing that might not be done with entire satisfaction. But, as it was, it told a bad tale for the future! "Do you understand his money matters, Emily?"

"Not at all, papa."

"I do not in the least mean to make inquiry. Perhaps I should have asked before;—but if I did make inquiry now it would be of him. But I think a wife should know."

"I know nothing."

"What is his business?"

"I have no idea. I used to think he was connected with Mr. Mills Happerton and with Messrs. Hunky & Sons."

"Is he not connected with Hunky's house?"

"I think not. He has a partner of the name of Parker, who is,—who is not, I think, quite—quite a gentleman. I never saw him."

"What does he do with Mr. Parker?"

"I believe they buy guano."

"Ah;—that, I fancy, was only one affair."

"I 'm afraid he lost money, papa, by that election at Silverbridge."

"I paid that," said Mr. Wharton sternly. Surely

he should have told his wife that he had received that money from her family!

"Did you? That was very kind. I am afraid, papa, we are a great burden on you."

"I should not mind it, my dear, if there were confidence and happiness. What matter would it be to me whether you had your money now or hereafter, so that you might have it in the manner that would be most beneficial to you? I wish he would be open with me, and tell me everything."

"Shall I let him know that you say so?"

He thought for a minute or two before he answered her. Perhaps the man would be more impressed if the message came to him through his wife. "If you think that he will not be annoyed with you, you may do so."

"I don't know why he should,—but if it be right, that must be borne. I am not afraid to say anything to him."

"Then tell him so. Tell him that it will be better that he should let me know the whole condition of his affairs. God bless you, dear." Then he stooped over her, and kissed her, and went his way to Stone Buildings.

It was not as he sat at the breakfast-table that Ferdinand Lopez made up his mind to pocket the Duke's money and to say nothing about it to Mr. Wharton. He had been careful to conceal the cheque, but he had done so with the feeling that the matter was one to be considered in his own mind before he took any step. As he left the house, already considering it, he was inclined to think that the money must be surrendered. Mr. Wharton had very generously paid his electioneering expenses, but had not done so simply with the view of making him a present of money. He wished the Duke had not taken him at his word. In handing this cheque over to Mr. Wharton he would be forced to tell the story of his letter to the Duke, and he was sure that Mr. Wharton would not approve of his having written such a letter. How could any one approve of his having applied for a sum of money which had already been paid to him? How could such a one as Mr. Wharton,—an old-fashioned English gentleman,—approve of such an application being made under any circumstances? Mr. Wharton would very probably insist on having the cheque sent back to the Duke,—which would be a sorry end to the triumph as at present achieved. And the more he thought of it the more sure he was that it would be imprudent to mention to Mr. Wharton his application to the Duke. The old men of the present day were, he said to himself, such fools that they understood nothing. And then the money was very convenient to him. He was intent on obtaining Sexty Parker's consent to a large speculation, and knew that he could not do so without a show of funds. By the time, therefore, that he had reached the City he had resolved that at any rate for the present he would use the money and say nothing about it to Mr. Wharton. Was it not spoil got from the enemy by his own courage and cleverness? When he was writing his acknowledgment for the money to Warburton he had taught himself to look upon the sum extracted from the Duke as a matter quite distinct from the payment made to him by his father-in-law.

It was evident on that day to Sexty Parker that his partner was a man of great resources. Though things sometimes looked very bad, yet money always " turned up." Some of their buyings and sellings had answered pretty well. Some had been great failures. No great stroke had been made as yet, but then the great stroke was always being expected. Sexty's fears were greatly exaggerated by the feeling that the coffee and guano were not always real coffee and guano. His partner, indeed, was of opinion that in such a trade as this they were following there was no need at all of real coffee and real guano, and explained his theory with considerable eloquence. "If I buy a ton of coffee and keep it six weeks, why do I buy it and keep it, and why does the seller sell it instead of keeping it? The seller sells it because he thinks he can do best by parting with it now at a certain price. I buy it because I think I can make money by keeping it. It is just the same as though we were to back our opinions. He backs the fall. I back the rise. You need n't have coffee and you need n't have guano to do this. Indeed the possession of the coffee or the guano is only a very clumsy addition to the trouble of your profession. I make it my study to watch the markets;—but I need n't buy everything I see in order to make money by my labour and intelligence." Sexty Parker before his lunch always thought that his partner was wrong, but after that ceremony he almost daily became a convert to the great doctrine. Coffee and guano still had to be bought because the world was dull and would not learn the tricks of trade as taught by Ferdinand Lopez,—also possibly because somebody might want such articles,—but our enterprising hero looked for a time in which no such dull burden should be imposed on him.

On this day, when the Duke's £500 was turned into

the business, Sexty yielded in a large matter which his partner had been pressing upon him for the last week. They bought a cargo of kauri gum, coming from New Zealand. Lopez had reasons for thinking that kauri gum must have a great rise. There was an immense demand for amber, and kauri gum might be used as a substitute, and in six months' time would be double its present value. This unfortunately was a real cargo. He could not find an individual so enterprising as to venture to deal in a cargo of kauri gum after his fashion. But the next best thing was done. The real cargo was bought and his name and Sexty's name were on the bills given for the goods. On that day he returned home in high spirits, for he did believe in his own intelligence and good fortune.

CHAPTER XVII.

MR. WHARTON INTENDS TO MAKE A NEW WILL.

On that afternoon, immediately on the husband's return to the house, his wife spoke to him as her father had desired. On that evening Mr. Wharton was dining at his club, and therefore there was the whole evening before them; but the thing to be done was disagreeable, and therefore she did it at once,—rushing into the matter almost before he had seated himself in the arm-chair which he had appropriated to his use in the drawing-room. "Papa was talking about our affairs after you left this morning, and he thinks that it would be so much better if you would tell him all about them."

"What made him talk of that to-day?" he said, turning at her almost angrily and thinking at once of the Duke's cheque.

"I suppose it is natural that he should be anxious about us, Ferdinand;—and the more natural as he has money to give if he chooses to give it."

"I have asked him for nothing lately;—though, by George, I intend to ask him and that very roundly. Three thousand pounds is n't much of a sum of money for your father to have given you."

"And he paid the election bill;—did n't he?"

"He has been complaining of that behind my back,—has he? I did n't ask him for it. He offered it. I was n't such a fool as to refuse, but he need n't bring that up as a grievance to you."

"It was n't brought up as a grievance. I was saying that your standing had been a heavy expenditure——"

"Why did you say so? What made you talk about it at all? Why should you be discussing my affairs behind my back?"

"To my own father! And that too when you are telling me every day that I am to induce him to help you!"

"Not by complaining that I am poor. But how did it all begin?" She had to think for a moment before she could recollect how it did begin. "There has been something," he said, "which you are ashamed to tell me."

"There is nothing that I am ashamed to tell you. There never has been and never will be anything." And she stood up as she spoke, with open eyes and extended nostrils. "Whatever may come, however wretched it may be, I shall not be ashamed of myself."

"But of me!"

"Why do you say so? Why do you try to make unhappiness between us?"

"You have been talking of—my poverty."

"My father asked why you should go to Dovercourt,—and whether it was because it would save expense."

"You want to go somewhere?"

"Not at all. I am contented to stay in London. But I said that I thought the expense had a good deal to do with it. Of course it has."

"Where do you want to be taken? I suppose Dovercourt is not fashionable."

"I want nothing."

"If you are thinking of travelling abroad, I can't spare the time. It is n't an affair of money, and you had no business to say so. I thought of the place because it is quiet and because I can get up and down easily. I am sorry that I ever came to live in this house."

"Why do you say that, Ferdinand?"

"Because you and your father make cabals behind my back. If there is anything I hate it is that kind of thing."

"You are very unjust," she said to him, sobbing. "I have never caballed. I have never done anything against you. Of course papa ought to know."

"Why ought he to know? Why is your father to have the right of inquiry into all my private affairs?"

"Because you want his assistance. It is only natural. You always tell me to get him to assist you. He spoke most kindly, saying that he would like to know how the things are."

"Then he won't know. As for wanting his assistance, of course I want the fortune which he ought to give you. He is man of the world enough to know that as I am in business capital must be useful to me. I should have thought that you would understand as much as that yourself."

"I do understand it, I suppose."

"Then why don't you act as my friend rather than his? Why don't you take my part? It seems to me that you are much more his daughter than my wife."

"That is most unfair."

"If you had any pluck you would make him understand that for your sake he ought to say what he means to do, so that I might have the advantage of the fortune which I suppose he means to give you some day. If you had the slightest anxiety to help me you could influence him. Instead of that you talk to him about my poverty. I don't want him to think that I am a pauper. That's not the way to get round a man like your father, who is rich himself and who thinks it a disgrace in other men not to be rich too."

"I can't tell him in the same breath that you are rich and that you want money."

"Money is the means by which men make money. If he was confident of my business he'd shell out his cash quick enough! It is because he has been taught to think that I am in a small way. He'll find his mistake some day."

"You won't speak to him then?"

"I don't say that at all. If I find that it will answer my own purpose I shall speak to him. But it would be very much easier to me if I could get you to be cordial in helping me."

Emily by this time quite knew what such cordiality meant. He had been so free in his words to her that there could be no mistake. He had instructed her to "get round" her father. And now again he spoke of her influence over her father. Although her illusions were all melting away,—oh, so quickly vanishing,—still she knew that it was her duty to be true to her husband, and to be his wife rather than her father's daughter. But what could she say on his behalf, knowing nothing of his affairs? She had no idea what was his business, what was his income, what amount of money she ought to spend as his wife. As far as she could see,—and her common sense in seeing such things was good,—he had no regular income, and was justified in no expenditure. On her own account she would ask for no information. She was too proud to request that from him which should be given to her without any request. But in her own defence she must tell him that she could use no influence with her father as she knew none of the circumstances by which her father would be guided. "I cannot help you in the manner you mean," she said, "because I know nothing myself."

"You know that you can trust me to do the best with your money if I could get hold of it, I suppose?" She certainly did not know this, and held her tongue. "You could assure him of that?"

"I could only tell him to judge for himself."

"What you mean is that you 'd see me d———d before you would open your mouth for me to the old man!"

He had never sworn at her before, and now she burst out into a flood of tears. It was to her a terrible outrage. I do not know that a woman is very much the worse because her husband may forget himself on an occasion and "rap out an oath at her," as he would call it when making the best of his own sin. Such an offence is compatible with uniform kindness, and most affectionate consideration. I have known ladies who would think little or nothing about it,—who would go no farther than the mildest protest,—"Do remember where you are!" or, "My dear John!"—if no stranger were present. But then a wife should be initiated into it by degrees; and there are different tones of bad language, of which by far the most general is the good-humoured tone. We all of us know men who never damn their servants, or any inferiors, or strangers, or women,—who in fact keep it all for their bosom friends; and if a little does sometimes flow over in the freedom of domestic life, the wife is apt to remember that she is the bosomest of her husband's friends, and so to pardon the transgression. But here the word had been uttered with all its foulest violence, with virulence and vulgarity. It seemed to the victim to be the sign of a terrible crisis in her early married life, —as though the man who had so spoken to her could never again love her, never again be kind to her, never again be sweetly gentle and like a lover. And as he spoke it he looked at her as though he would like to tear her limbs asunder. She was frightened as well as horrified and astounded. She had not a word to say to him. She did not know in what language to make her complaint of such treatment. She burst into tears, and throwing herself on the sofa hid her face in her hands. "You provoke me to be violent," he said. But still she could not speak to him. "I come away from the City tired with work and troubled with a thousand things, and you have not a kind word to say to me." Then there was a pause, during which she still sobbed. "If your father has anything to say to me, let him say it. I shall not run away. But as to going to him of my own accord with a story as long as my arm about my own affairs, I don't mean to do it." Then he paused a moment again. "Come, old girl, cheer up! Don't pretend to be broken-hearted because I used a hard word. There are worse things than that to be borne in the world."

"I—I—I was so startled, Ferdinand."

"A man can't always remember that he is n't with

another man. Don't think anything more about it; but do bear this in mind,—that, situated as we are, your influence with your father may be the making or the marring of me." And so he left the room.

She sat for the next ten minutes thinking of it all. The words which he had spoken were so horrible that she could not get them out of her mind,—could not bring herself to look upon them as a trifle. The darkness of his countenance still dwelt with her,—and that absence of all tenderness, that coarse un-marital and yet marital roughness, which should not at any rate have come to him so soon. The whole man too was so different from what she had thought him to be. Before their marriage no word as to money had ever reached her ears from his lips. He had talked to her of books,—and especially of poetry. Shakespeare and Molière, Dante, and Goethe had been or had seemed to be dear to him. And he had been full of fine ideas about women, and about men in their intercourse with women. For his sake she had separated herself from all her old friends. For his sake she had hurried into a marriage altogether distasteful to her father. For his sake she had closed her heart against that other lover. Trusting altogether in him she had ventured to think that she had known what was good for her better than all those who had been her counsellors, and had given herself to him utterly. Now she was awake; her dream was over; and the natural language of the man was still ringing in her ears!

They met together at dinner and passed the evening without a further allusion to the scene which had been acted. He sat with a magazine in his hand, every now and then making some remark intended to be pleasant but which grated on her ears as being fictitious. She would answer him,—because it was her duty to do so, and because she would not condescend to sulk; but she could not bring herself even to say to herself that all should be with her as though that horrid word had not been spoken. She sat over her work till ten, answering him when he spoke in a voice which was also fictitious, and then took herself off to her bed that she might weep alone. It would, she knew, be late before he would come to her.

On the next morning there came a message to him as he was dressing. Mr. Wharton wished to speak to him. Would he come down before breakfast, or would he call on Mr. Wharton in Stone Buildings? He sent down word that he would do the latter at an hour he fixed, and then did not show himself in the breakfast-room till Mr. Wharton was gone. "I 've got to go to your father to-day," he said to his wife, "and I thought it best not to begin till we come to the regular business. I hope he does not mean to be unreasonable." To this she made no answer. "Of course you think the want of reason will be all on my side."

"I don't know why you should say so."

"Because I can read your mind. You do think so. You 've been in the same boat with your father all your life, and you can't get out of that boat and get into mine. I was wrong to come and live here. Of course it was not the way to withdraw you from his influence." She had nothing to say that would not anger him, and was therefore silent. "Well; I must do the best I can by myself, I suppose. Good-bye," and so he was off.

"I want to know," said Mr. Wharton, on whom was

thrown by premeditation on the part of Lopez the task of beginning the conversation,—"I want to know what is the nature of your operations. I have never been quite able to understand it."

"I do not know that I quite understand it myself," said Lopez, laughing.

"No man alive," continued the old barrister almost solemnly, "has a greater objection to thrust himself into another man's affairs than I have. And as I did n't ask the question before your marriage,—as perhaps I ought to have done,—I should not do so now, were it not that the disposition of some part of the earnings of my life must depend on the condition of your affairs." Lopez immediately perceived that it behoved him to be very much on the alert. It might be that if he showed himself to be very poor, his father-in-law would see the necessity of assisting him at once; or, it might be, that unless he could show himself to be in prosperous circumstances, his father-in-law would not assist him at all. "To tell you the plain truth, I am minded to make a new will. I had of course made arrangements as to my property before Emily's marriage. Those arrangements I think I shall now alter. I am greatly distressed with Everett; and from what I see and from a few words which have dropped from Emily, I am not, to tell you the truth, quite happy as to your position. If I understand rightly you are a general merchant, buying and selling goods in the market?"

"That 's about it, sir."

"What capital have you in the business?"

"What capital?"

"Yes;—how much did you put into it at starting?"

MR. WHARTON INTENDS TO MAKE A NEW WILL. 207

Lopez paused a moment. He had got his wife. The marriage could not be undone. Mr. Wharton had money enough for them all, and would not certainly discard his daughter. Mr. Wharton could place him on a really firm footing, and might not improbably do so if he could be made to feel some confidence in his son-in-law. At this moment there was much doubt with the son-in-law whether he had better not tell the simple truth. "It has gone in by degrees," he said. "Altogether I have had about £8,000 in it." In truth he had never been possessed of a shilling.

"Does that include the £3,000 you had from me?"

"Yes; it does."

"Then you have married my girl and started into the world with a business based on £5,000, and which had so far miscarried that within a month or two after your marriage you were driven to apply to me for funds!"

"I wanted money for a certain purpose."

"Have you any partner, Mr. Lopez?" This address was felt to be very ominous.

"Yes. I have a partner who is possessed of capital. His name is Parker."

"Then his capital is your capital."

"Well;—I can't explain it, but it is not so."

"What is the name of your firm?"

"We have n't a registered name."

"Have you a place of business?"

"Parker has a place of business in Little Tankard Yard."

Mr. Wharton turned to a directory and found out Parker's name. "Mr. Parker is a stockbroker. Are you also a stockbroker?"

"No,—I am not."

"Then, sir, it seems to me that you are a commercial adventurer?"

"I am not at all ashamed of the name, Mr. Wharton. According to your manner of reckoning, half the business in the City of London is done by commercial adventurers. I watch the markets and buy goods,—and sell them at a profit. Mr. Parker is a moneyed man, who happens also to be a stockbroker. We can very easily call ourselves merchants, and put up the names of Lopez and Parker over the door."

"Do you sign bills together?"

"Yes."

"As Lopez and Parker?"

"No. I sign them and he signs them. I trade also by myself, and so, I believe, does he."

"One other question, Mr. Lopez. On what income have you paid income-tax for the last three years?"

"On £2,000 a year," said Lopez. This was a direct lie.

"Can you make out any schedule showing your exact assets and liabilities at the present time?"

"Certainly I can."

"Then do so, and send it to me before I go into Herefordshire. My will as it stands at present would not be to your advantage. But I cannot change it till I know more of your circumstances than I do now." And so the interview was over.

CHAPTER XVIII.

MRS. SEXTY PARKER.

THOUGH Mr. Wharton and Lopez met every day for the next week, nothing more was said about the schedule. The old man was thinking about it every day, and so also was Lopez. But Mr. Wharton had made his demand, and, as he thought, nothing more was to be said on the subject. He could not continue the subject as he would have done with his son. But as day after day passed by he became more and more convinced that his son-in-law's affairs were not in a state which could bear to see the light. He had declared his purpose of altering his will in the man's favour, if the man would satisfy him. And yet nothing was done and nothing was said.

Lopez had come among them and robbed him of his daughter. Since the man had become intimate in his house he had not known an hour's happiness. The man had destroyed all the plans of his life, broken through into his castle, and violated his very hearth. No doubt he himself had vacillated. He was aware of that, and in his present mood was severe enough in judging himself. In his desolation he had tried to take the man to his heart,—had been kind to him, and had even opened his house to him. He had told himself that as the man was the husband of his daughter he had better make the best of it. He had endeavoured to make the best of it, but between him and the man there were such differences that they were poles asunder. And now it became clear to him that the man was, as he had declared to the man's face, no better than an adventurer!

By his will as it at present stood he had left two-thirds of his property to Everett, and one-third to his daughter, with arrangements for settling her share on her children, should she be married and have children at the time of his death. This will had been made many years ago, and he had long since determined to alter it, in order that he might divide his property equally between his children;—but he had postponed the matter, intending to give a large portion of Emily's share to her directly on her marriage with Arthur Fletcher. She had not married Arthur Fletcher;—but still it was necessary that a new will should be made.

When he left town for Herefordshire he had not yet made up his mind how this should be done. He had at one time thought that he would give some considerable sum to Lopez at once, knowing that to a man in business such assistance would be useful. And he had not altogether abandoned that idea, even when he had asked for the schedule. He did not relish the thought of giving his hard-earned money to Lopez, but, still, the man's wife was his daughter, and he must do the best that he could for her. Her taste in marrying the man was inexplicable to him. But that was done;—and now how might he best arrange his affairs so as to serve her interests?

About the middle of August he went to Herefordshire and she to the sea-side in Essex,—to the little place which Lopez had selected. Before the end of the month the father-in-law wrote a line to his son-in-law.

"Dear Lopez," (not without premeditation had he departed from the sternness of that "Mr. Lopez," which in his anger he had used at his chambers,)—

"When we were discussing your affairs I asked you for a schedule of your assets and liabilities. I can make no new arrangement of my property till I receive this. Should I die leaving my present will as the instrument under which my property would be conveyed to my heirs, Emily's share would go into the hands of trustees for the use of herself and her possible children. I tell you this that you may understand that it is for your own interest to comply with my requisition.

"Yours,
"A. WHARTON."

Of course questions were asked him as to how the newly married couple were getting on. At Wharton these questions were mild and easily put off. Sir Alured was contented with a slight shake of his head, and Lady Wharton only remarked for the fifth or sixth time that "it was a pity." But when they all went to Longbarns, the difficulty became greater. Arthur was not there, and old Mrs. Fletcher was in full strength. "So the Lopezes have come to live with you in Manchester Square?" Mr. Wharton acknowledged that it was so with an affirmative grunt. "I hope he's a pleasant inmate." There was a scorn in the old woman's voice as she said this, which ought to have provoked any man.

"More so than most men would be," said Mr. Wharton.

"Oh, indeed!"

"He is courteous and forbearing, and does not

think that everything around him should be suited to his own peculiar fancies."

"I am glad that you are contented with the marriage, Mr. Wharton."

"Who has said that I am contented with it? No one ought to understand or to share my discontent so cordially as yourself, Mrs. Fletcher;—and no one ought to be more chary of speaking of it. You and I had hoped other things, and old people do not like to be disappointed. But I need n't paint the devil blacker than he is."

"I 'm afraid that, as usual, he is rather black."

"Mother," said John Fletcher, "the thing has been done and you might as well let it be. We are all sorry that Emily has not come nearer to us; but she has had a right to choose for herself, and I for one wish,—as does my brother also,—that she may be happy in the lot she has chosen."

"His conduct to Arthur at Silverbridge was so nice!" said the pertinacious old woman.

"Never mind his conduct, mother. What is it to us?"

"That 's all very well, John; but according to that nobody is to talk about anybody."

"I would much prefer at any rate," said Mr. Wharton, "that you would not talk about Mr. Lopez in my hearing."

"Oh; if that is to be so, let it be so. And now I understand where I am." Then the old woman shook herself, and endeavoured to look as though Mr. Wharton's soreness on the subject were an injury to her as robbing her of a useful topic.

"I don't like Lopez, you know," Mr. Wharton said

to John Fletcher afterwards. " How would it be possible that I should like such a man? But there can be no good got by complaints. It is not what your mother suffers, or what even I may suffer,—or, worse again, what Arthur may suffer, that makes the sadness of all this. What will be her life? That is the question. And it is too near me, too important to me, for the endurance either of scorn or pity. I was glad that you asked your mother to be silent."

"I can understand it," said John. "I do not think that she will trouble you again."

In the meantime Lopez received Mr. Wharton's letter at Dovercourt, and had to consider what answer he should give to it. No answer could be satisfactory, —unless he could impose a false answer on his father-in-law so as to make it credible. The more he thought of it, the more he believed that this would be impossible. The cautious old lawyer would not accept unverified statements. A certain sum of money,—by no means illiberal as a present,—he had already extracted from the old man. What he wanted was a further and a much larger grant. Though Mr. Wharton was old he did not want to have to wait for the death even of an old man. The next two or three years,—probably the very next year,—might be the turning point of his life. He had married the girl, and ought to have the girl's fortune,—down on the nail! That was his idea; and the old man was robbing him in not acting up to it. As he thought of this he cursed his ill-luck. The husbands of other girls had their fortunes conveyed to them immediately on their marriage. What would not £20,000 do for him, if he could get it into his hand? And so he taught himself to regard the old man as a robber and himself as a victim. Who among us is there that does not teach himself the same lesson? And then too how cruelly, how damnably he had been used by the Duchess of Omnium! And now Sexty Parker, whose fortune he was making for him, whose fortune he at any rate intended to make, was troubling him in various ways. "We 're in a boat together," Sexty had said. "You 've had the use of my money, and by heavens you have it still. I don't see why you should be so stiff. Do you bring your missis to Dovercourt, and I 'll take mine, and let 'em know each other." There was a little argument on the subject, but Sexty Parker had the best of it, and in this way the trip to Dovercourt was arranged.

Lopez was in a very good humour when he took his wife down, and he walked her round the terraces and esplanades of that not sufficiently well-known marine paradise, now bidding her admire the sea and now laughing at the finery of the people, till she became gradually filled with an idea that as he was making himself pleasant, she also ought to do the same. Of course she was not happy. The gilding had so completely and so rapidly been washed off her idol that she could not be very happy. But she also could be good-humoured. "And now," said he, smiling, "I have got something for you to do for me,—something that you will find very disagreeable."

"What is it? It won't be very bad, I 'm sure."

"It will be very bad, I 'm afraid. My excellent but horribly vulgar partner, Mr. Sextus Parker, when he found that I was coming here, insisted on bringing his wife and children here also. I want you to know them."

"Is that all? She must be very bad indeed if I can't put up with that."

"In one sense she is n't bad at all. I believe her to be an excellent woman, intent on spoiling her children and giving her husband a good dinner every day. But I think you 'll find that she is,—well,—not quite what you call a lady."

"I shan't mind that in the least. I 'll help her to spoil the children."

"You can get a lesson there, you know," he said, looking into her face. The little joke was one which a young wife might take with pleasure from her husband, but her life had already been too much embittered for any such delight. Yes; the time was coming when that trouble also would be added to her. She dreaded she knew not what, and had often told herself that it would be better that she should be childless.

"Do you like him?" she said.

"Like him. No;—I can't say I like him. He is useful, and in one sense honest."

"Is he not honest in all senses?"

"That 's a large order. To tell you the truth, I don't know any man who is."

"Everett is honest."

"He loses money at play which he can't pay without assistance from his father. If his father had refused, where would then have been his honesty? Sexty is as honest as others, I dare say, but I should n't like to trust him much farther than I can see him. I shan't go up to town to-morrow, and we 'll both look in on them after luncheon."

In the afternoon the call was made. The Parkers,

having children, had dined early, and he was sitting out in a little porch smoking his pipe, drinking whiskey and water, and looking at the sea. His eldest girl was standing between his legs, and his wife, with the other three children round her, was sitting on the doorstep. "I 've brought my wife to see you," said Lopez, holding out his hand to Mrs. Parker, as she rose from the ground.

"I told her that you 'd be coming," said Sexty, "and she wanted me to put off my pipe and little drop of drink; but I said that if Mrs. Lopez was the lady I took her to be she would n't begrudge a hard-working fellow his pipe and glass on a holiday."

There was a soundness of sense in this which mollified any feeling of disgust which Emily might have felt at the man's vulgarity. "I think you are quite right, Mr. Parker. I should be very sorry if,—if——"

"If I was to put my pipe out. Well, I won't. You 'll take a glass of sherry, Lopez? Though I 'm drinking spirits myself, I brought down a hamper of sherry wine. Oh, nonsense;—you must take something. That 's right, Jane. Let us have the stuff and the glasses, and then they can do as they like." Lopez lit a cigar, and allowed his host to pour out for him a glass of "sherry wine," while Mrs. Lopez went into the house with Mrs. Parker and the children.

Mrs. Parker opened herself out to her new friend immediately. She hoped that they two might see "a deal of each other;—that is, if you don't think me too pushing." Sextus, she said, was so much away, coming down to Dovercourt only every other day! And then, within the half-hour which was consumed by Lopez with his cigar, the poor woman got upon the general troubles of her life. Did Mrs. Lopez think that "all this speckelation was just the right thing?"

"I don't think that I know anything about it, Mrs. Parker."

"But you ought;—ought n't you, now? Don't you think that a wife ought to know what it is that her husband is after;—specially if there 's children? A good bit of the money was mine, Mrs. Lopez; and though I don't begrudge it, not one bit, if any good is to come out of it to him or them, a woman does n't like what her father has given her should be made ducks and drakes of."

"But are they making ducks and drakes?"

"When he don't tell me I 'm always afeared. And I 'll tell you what I know just as well as two and two. When he comes home a little flustered, and then takes more than his regular allowance, he 's been at something as don't quite satisfy him. He 's never that way when he 's done a good day's work at his regular business. He takes to the children then, and has one glass after his dinner, and tells me all about it,—down to the shillings and pence. But it 's very seldom he 's that way now."

"You may think it very odd, Mrs. Parker, but I don't in the least know what my husband is—in business."

"And you never ask?"

"I have n't been very long married, you know;— only about ten months."

"I 'd had my fust by that time."

"Only nine months, I think, indeed."

"Well; I was n't very long after that. But I took care to know what it was he was a doing of in the City long before that time. And I did use to know everything, till——" She was going to say, till Lopez had come upon the scene. But she did not wish, at any rate as yet, to be harsh to her new friend.

"I hope it is all right," said Emily.

"Sometimes he's as though the Bank of England was all his own. And there's been more money come into the house;—that I must say. And there is n't an open-handeder one than Sexty anywhere. He 'd like to see me in a silk gown every day of my life;—and as for the children, there 's nothing smart enough for them. Only I 'd sooner have a little and safe, than anything ever so fine, and never be sure whether it was n't going to come to an end."

"There I agree with you, quite."

"I don't suppose men feels it as we do; but, oh, Mrs. Lopez, give me a little, safe, so that I may know that I shan't see my children want. When I thinks what it would be to have them darlings' little bellies empty, and nothing in the cupboard, I get that low that I 'm nigh fit for Bedlam."

In the meantime the two men outside the porch were discussing their affairs in somewhat the same spirit. At last Lopez showed his friend Wharton's letter, and told him of the expected schedule. "Schedule be d——d, you know," said Lopez. "How am I to put down a rise of 12*s.* 6*d.* a ton on kauri gum in a schedule? But when you come to 2,000 tons it 's £1,250."

"He 's very old;—is n't he?"

"But as strong as a horse."

"He 's got the money?"

"Yes;—he has got it safe enough. There 's no doubt about the money."

"What he talks about is only a will. Now you want the money at once."

"Of course I do;—and he talks to me as if I were some old fogy with an estate of my own. I must concoct a letter and explain my views; and the more I can make him understand how things really are the better. I don't suppose he wants to see his daughter come to grief."

"Then the sooner you write it the better," said Mr. Parker.

CHAPTER XIX.

"HE WANTS TO GET RICH TOO QUICK."

As they strolled home Lopez told his wife that he had accepted an invitation to dine the next day at the Parkers' cottage. In doing this his manner was not quite so gentle as when he had asked her to call on them. He had been a little ruffled by what had been said, and now exhibited his temper. "I don't suppose it will be very nice," he said, "but we may have to put up with worse things than that."

"I have made no objection."

"But you don't seem to take to it very cordially."

"I had thought that I got on very well with Mrs. Parker. If you can eat your dinner with them, I'm sure that I can. You do not seem to like him altogether, and I wish you had got a partner more to your taste."

"Taste, indeed! When you come to this kind of thing it is n't a matter of taste. The fact is that I am in that fellow's hands to an extent I don't like to think of, and don't see my way out of it unless your father will do as he ought to do. You altogether refuse to help me with your father, and you must, therefore, put up with Sexty Parker and his wife. It is quite on the cards that worse things may come even than Sexty Parker." To this she made no immediate answer, but walked on, increasing her pace, not only unhappy, but also very angry. It was becoming a matter of doubt to her whether she could continue to bear these repeated attacks about her father's money. "I see how it is," he continued. "You think that a husband should bear all the troubles of life, and that a wife should never be made to hear of them."

"Ferdinand," she said, "I declare I did not think that any man could be so unfair to a woman as you are to me."

"Of course! Because I have n't got thousands a year to spend on you I am unfair."

"I am content to live in any way that you may direct. If you are poor, I am satisfied to be poor. If you are even ruined, I am content to be ruined."

"Who is talking about ruin?"

"If you are in want of everything, I also will be in want and will never complain. Whatever our joint lot may bring to us I will endure, and will endeavour to endure with cheerfulness. But I will not ask my father for money, either for you or for myself. He knows what he ought to do. I trust him implicitly."

"And me not at all."

"He is, I know, in communication with you about what should be done. I can only say,—tell him everything."

"My dear, that is a matter in which it may be possible that I understand my own interest best."

"Very likely. I certainly understand nothing, for I do not even know the nature of your business. How can I tell him that he ought to give you money?"

"You might ask him for your own."

"I have got nothing. Did I ever tell you that I had?"

"You ought to have known."

"Do you mean that when you asked me to marry you I should have refused you because I did not know what money papa would give me? Why did you not ask papa?"

"Had I known him then as well as I do now you may be quite sure that I should have done so."

"Ferdinand, it will be better that we should not speak about my father. I will in all things strive to do as you would have me, but I cannot hear him abused. If you have anything to say, go to Everett."

"Yes;—when he is such a gambler that your father won't even speak to him. Your father will be found dead in his bed some day, and all his money will have been left to some cursed hospital." They were at their own door when this was said, and she, without further answer, went up to her bedroom.

All these bitter things had been said, not because Lopez had thought that he could further his own views by saying them;—he knew indeed that he was injuring himself by every display of ill-temper;—but she was in his power, and Sexty Parker was rebelling. He thought a good deal that day on the delight he would have in "kicking that ill-conditioned cur," if only he could afford to kick him. But his wife was his own, and she must be taught to endure his will, and must be made to know that though she was not to be kicked, yet she was to be tormented and ill-used. And it might be possible that he should so cow her spirit as to bring her to act as he should direct. Still, as he walked alone along the sea-shore, he knew that it would be better for him to control his temper.

On that evening he did write to Mr. Wharton,—as follows,—and he dated his letter from Little Tankard

Yard, so that Mr. Wharton might suppose that that was really his own place of business, and that he was there, at his work:—

"My dear Sir,—You have asked for a schedule of my affairs, and I have found it quite impossible to give it. As it was with the merchants whom Shakespeare and the other dramatists described,—so it is with me. My caravels are out at sea, and will not always come home in time. My property at this moment consists of certain shares of cargoes of jute, kauri gum, guano, and sulphur, worth altogether at the present moment something over £26,000, of which Mr. Parker possesses the half;—but then of this property only a portion is paid for,—perhaps something more than a half. For the other half our bills are in the market. But in February next these articles will probably be sold for considerably more than £30,000. If I had £5,000 placed to my credit now, I should be worth about £15,000 by the end of next February. I am engaged in sundry other smaller ventures, all returning profits;—but in such a condition of things it is impossible that I should make a schedule.

"I am undoubtedly in the condition of a man trading beyond his capital. I have been tempted by fair offers, and what I think I may call something beyond an average understanding of such matters, to go into ventures beyond my means. I have stretched my arm out too far. In such a position it is not perhaps unnatural that I should ask a wealthy father-in-law to assist me. It is certainly not unnatural that I should wish him to do so.

"I do not think that I am a mercenary man. When

I married your daughter I raised no question as to her fortune. Being embarked in trade I no doubt thought that her means,—whatever they might be,—would be joined to my own. I know that a sum of £20,000, with my experience in the use of money, would give us a noble income. But I would not condescend to ask a question which might lead to a supposition that I was marrying her for her money and not because I loved her.

"You now know, I think, all that I can tell you. If there be any other questions I would willingly answer them. It is certainly the case that Emily's fortune, whatever you may choose to give her, would be of infinitely greater use to me now,—and consequently to her,—than at a future date which I sincerely pray may be very long deferred.

"Believe me to be, your affectionate son-in-law,
"FERDINAND LOPEZ.
"A. Wharton, Esq."

This letter he himself took up to town on the following day, and there posted, addressing it to Wharton Hall. He did not expect very great results from it. As he read it over, he was painfully aware that all his trash about caravels and cargoes of sulphur would not go far with Mr. Wharton. But it might go farther than nothing. He was bound not to neglect Mr. Wharton's letter to him. When a man is in difficulty about money, even a lie,—even a lie that is sure to be found out to be a lie,—will serve his immediate turn better than silence. There is nothing that the courts hate so much as contempt;—not even perjury. And Lopez felt that Mr. Wharton was the judge before whom he was bound to plead.

He returned to Dovercourt on that day, and he and his wife dined with the Parkers. No woman of her age had known better what were the manners of ladies and gentlemen than Emily Wharton. She had thoroughly understood that when in Herefordshire she was surrounded by people of that class, and that when she was with her aunt, Mrs. Roby, she was not quite so happily placed. No doubt she had been terribly deceived by her husband,—but the deceit had come from the fact that his manners gave no indication of his character. When she found herself in Mrs. Parker's little sitting-room, with Mr. Parker making florid speeches to her, she knew that she had fallen among people for whose society she had not been intended. But this was a part, and only a very trifling part, of the punishment which she felt that she deserved. If that, and things like that, were all, she would bear them without a murmur.

"Now I call Dovercourt a dooced nice little place," said Mr. Parker, as he helped her to the "bit of fish," which he told her he had brought down with him from London.

"It is very healthy, I should think."

"Just the thing for the children, ma'am. You've none of your own, Mrs. Lopez, but there's a good time coming. You were up to-day, were n't you, Lopez? Any news?"

"Things seemed to be very quiet in the City."

"Too quiet, I 'm afraid. I hate having 'em quiet. You must come and see me in Little Tankard Yard some of these days, Mrs. Lopez. We can give you a glass of cham. and the wing of a chicken;—can't we, Lopez?"

"I don't know. It's more than you ever gave me," said Lopez, trying to look good-humoured.

"But you ain't a lady."

"Or me," said Mrs. Parker.

"You're only a wife. If Mrs. Lopez will make a day of it we'll treat her well in the City;—won't we, Ferdinand?" A black cloud came across "Ferdinand's" face, but he said nothing. Emily of a sudden drew herself up, unconsciously,—and then at once relaxed her features and smiled. If her husband chose that it should be so, she would make no objection.

"Upon my honour, Sexty, you are very familiar," said Mrs. Parker.

"It's a way we have in the City," said Sexty. Sexty knew what he was about. His partner called him Sexty, and why should n't he call his partner Ferdinand?

"He'll call you Emily before long," said Lopez.

"When you call my wife Jane I shall,—and I've no objection in life. I don't see why people ain't to call each other by their Christian names. Take a glass of champagne, Mrs. Lopez. I brought down half-a-dozen to-day so that we might be jolly. Care killed a cat. Whatever we call each other, I'm very glad to see you here, Mrs. Lopez, and I hope it's the first of a great many. Here's your health."

It was all his ordering, and if he bade her dine with a crossing-sweeper she would do it. But she could not but remember that not long since he had told her that his partner was not a person with whom she could fitly associate; and she did not fail to perceive that he must be going down in the world to admit such association for her after he had so spoken. And as she sipped the mixture which Sexty called champagne, she thought of Herefordshire and the banks of the Wye, and,—alas, alas,—she thought of Arthur Fletcher. Nevertheless, come what might, she would do her duty, even though it might call upon her to sit at dinner with Mr. Parker three days in the week. Lopez was her husband, and would be the father of her child, and she would make herself one with him. It mattered not what people might call him,—or even her. She had acted on her own judgment in marrying him, and had been a fool; and now she would bear the punishment without complaint.

When dinner was over Mrs. Parker helped the servant to remove the dinner things from the single sitting-room, and the two men went out to smoke their cigars in the covered porch. Mrs. Parker herself took out the whiskey and hot water, and sugar and lemons, and then returned to have a little matronly discourse with her guest. "Does Mr. Lopez ever take a drop too much?" she asked.

"Never," said Mrs. Lopez.

"Perhaps it don't affect him as it do Sexty. He ain't a drinker;—certainly not. And he's one that works hard every day of his life. But he's getting fond of it these last twelve months, and though he don't take very much it hurries him and flurries him. If I speaks at night he gets cross;—and in the morning when he gets up, which he always do regular, though it's ever so bad with him, then I haven't the heart to scold him. It's very hard sometimes for a wife to know what to do, Mrs. Lopez."

"Yes, indeed." Emily could not but think how soon she herself had learned that lesson.

"Of course I'd do anything for Sexty,—the father of my bairns, and has always been a good husband to me. You don't know him, of course, but I do. A right good man at bottom;—but so weak!"

"If he,—if he,—injures his health, shouldn't you talk to him quietly about it?"

"It isn't the drink as is the evil, Mrs. Lopez, but that which makes him drink. He's not one as goes a mucker merely for the pleasure. When things are going right he'll sit out in our arbour at home, and smoke pipe after pipe, playing with the children, and one glass of gin and water cold will see him to bed. Tobacco, dry, do agree with him, I think. But when he comes to three or four goes of hot toddy, I know it's not as it should be."

"You should restrain him, Mrs. Parker."

"Of course I should;—but how? Am I to walk off with the bottle and disgrace him before the servant girl? Or am I to let the children know as their father takes too much? If I was as much as to make one fight of it, it'd be all over Ponders End that he's a drunkard; —which he ain't. Restrain him;—oh yes! If I could restrain that gambling instead of regular business! That's what I'd like to restrain."

"Does he gamble?"

"What is it but gambling that he and Mr. Lopez is a doing together? Of course, ma'am, I don't know you, and you are different from me. I ain't foolish enough not to know all that. My father stood in Smithfield and sold hay, and your father is a gentleman as has been high up in the Courts all his life. But it's your husband is a doing this."

"Oh, Mrs. Parker!"

"He is then. And if he brings Sexty and my little ones to the workhouse, what 'll be the good then of his guano and his gum?"

"Is it not all in the fair way of commerce?"

"I 'm sure I don't know about commerce, Mrs. Lopez, because I 'm only a woman; but it can't be fair. They goes and buys things that they have n't got the money to pay for, and then waits to see if they 'll turn up trumps. Is n't that gambling?"

"I cannot say. I do not know." She felt now that her husband had been accused, and that part of the accusation had been levelled at herself. There was something in her manner of saying these few words which the poor complaining woman perceived, feeling immediately that she had been inhospitable and perhaps unjust. She put out her hand softly, touching the other woman's arm, and looking up into her guest's face. "If this is so, it is terrible," said Emily.

"Perhaps I ought n't to speak so free."

"Oh yes;—for your children, and yourself, and your husband."

"It 's them,—and him. Of course it 's not your doing, and Mr. Lopez, I 'm sure, is a very fine gentleman. And if he gets wrong one way, he 'll get himself right in another." Upon hearing this Emily shook her head. "Your papa is a rich man, and won't see you and yours come to want. There 's nothing more to come to me or Sexty let it be ever so."

"Why does he do it?"

"Why does who do it?"

"Your husband. Why don't you speak to him as you do to me, and tell him to mind only his proper business?"

"Now you are angry with me."

"Angry! No;—indeed I am not angry. Every word that you say is good, and true, and just what you ought to say. I am not angry, but I am terrified. I know nothing of my husband's business. I cannot tell you that you should trust to it. He is very clever, but——"

"But—what, ma'am?"

"Perhaps I should say that he is ambitious."

"You mean he wants to get rich too quick, ma'am."

"I'm afraid so."

"Then it's just the same with Sexty. He's ambitious too. But what's the good of being ambitious, Mrs. Lopez, if you never know whether you're on your head or your heels? And what's the good of being ambitious if you're to get into the workhouse? I know what that means. There's one or two of them sort of men gets into Parliament, and has houses as big as the Queen's palace, while hundreds of them has their wives and children in the gutter. Who ever hears of them? Nobody. It don't become any man to be ambitious who has got a wife and family. If he's a bachelor, why, of course, he can go to the Colonies. There's Mary Jane and the two little ones right down on the sea, with their feet in the salt water. Shall we put on our hats, Mrs. Lopez, and go and look after them?" To this proposition Emily assented, and the two ladies went out after the children.

"Mix yourself another glass," said Sexty to his partner.

"I'd rather not. Don't ask me again. You know I never drink and I don't like being pressed."

"By George!—You are particular."

"What 's the use of teasing a fellow to do a thing he does n't like?"

"You won't mind me having another?"

"Fifty if you please, so that I 'm not forced to join you."

"Forced! It 's liberty 'all here, and you can do as you please. Only when a fellow will take a drop with me he 's better company."

"Then I 'm d——d bad company, and you 'd better get somebody else to be jolly with. To tell you the truth, Sexty, I suit you better at business than at this sort of thing. I 'm like Shylock, you know."

"I don't know about Shylock, but I 'm blessed if I think you suit me very well at anything. I 'm putting up with a deal of ill-usage, and when I try to be happy with you, you won't drink, and you tell me about Shylock. He was a Jew, was n't he?"

"That is the general idea."

"Then you ain't very much like him, for they 're a sort of people that always have money about 'em."

"How do you suppose he made his money to begin with? What an ass you are!"

"That 's true. I am. Ever since I began putting my name on the same bit of paper with yours I 've been an ass."

"You 'll have to be one a bit longer yet;—unless you mean to throw up everything. At this present moment you are six or seven thousand pounds richer than you were before you first met me."

"I wish I could see the money."

"That 's like you. What 's the use of money you

can see? How are you to make money out of money by looking at it? I like to know that my money is fructifying."

"I like to know that it's all there,—and I did know it before I ever saw you. I'm blessed if I know it now. Go down and join the ladies, will you? You ain't much of a companion up here."

Shortly after that Lopez told Mrs. Parker that he had already bade adieu to her husband, and then he took his wife to their own lodgings.

CHAPTER XX.

AS FOR LOVE!

The time spent by Mrs. Lopez at Dovercourt was by no means one of complete happiness. Her husband did not come down very frequently, alleging that his business kept him in town, and that the journey was too long. When he did come he annoyed her either by moroseness and tyranny, or by an affectation of loving good-humour, which was the more disagreeable alternative of the two. She knew that he had no right to be good-humoured, and she was quite able to appreciate the difference between fictitious love and love that was real. He did not while she was at Dovercourt speak to her again directly about her father's money,— but he gave her to understand that he required from her very close economy. Then again she referred to the brougham which she knew was to be in readiness on her return to London; but he told her that he was the best judge of that. The economy which he demanded was that comfortless heart-rending economy which nips the practiser at every turn, but does not betray itself to the world at large. He would have her save out of her washerwoman and linendraper, and yet have a smart gown and go in a brougham. He begrudged her postage stamps, and stopped the subscription at Mudie's, though he insisted on a front seat in the Dovercourt church, paying half a guinea more for it than he would for a place at the side. And then before their sojourn at the place had come to an end he left her for a while absolutely penniless, so that when the butcher and baker called for their money she could not pay them. That was a dreadful calamity to her, and of which she was hardly able to measure the real worth. It had never happened to her before to have to refuse an application for money that was due. In her father's house such a thing, as far as she knew, had never happened. She had sometimes heard that Everett was impecunious, but that had simply indicated an additional call upon her father. When the butcher came the second time she wrote to her husband in an agony. Should she write to her father for a supply? She was sure that her father would not leave them in actual want. Then he sent her a cheque, enclosed in a very angry letter. Apply to her father! Had she not learned as yet that she was not to lean on her father any longer, but simply on him? And was she such a fool as to suppose that a tradesman could not wait a month for his money?

During all this time she had no friend,—no person to whom she could speak,—except Mrs. Parker. Mrs. Parker was very open and very confidential about the business, really knowing very much more about it than did Mrs. Lopez. There was some sympathy and confidence between her and her husband, though they had latterly been much lessened by Sexty's conduct. Mrs. Parker talked daily about the business now that her mouth had been opened, and was very clearly of opinion that it was not a good business. "Sexty don't think it good himself," she said.

"Then why does he go on with it?"

"Business is a thing, Mrs. Lopez, as people can't

drop out of just at a moment. A man gets hisself entangled, and must free hisself as best he can. I know he's terribly afeared;—and sometimes he does say such things of your husband!" Emily shrunk almost into herself as she heard this. "You must n't be angry, for indeed it 's better you should know all."

"I 'm not angry; only very unhappy. Surely Mr. Parker could separate himself from Mr. Lopez if he pleased?"

"That 's what I say to him. Give it up, though it be ever so much as you 've to lose by him. Give it up, and begin again. You 've always got your experience, and if it 's only a crust you can earn, that 's sure and safe. But then he declares that he means to pull through yet. I know what men are at when they talk of pulling through, Mrs. Lopez. There should n't be no need of pulling through. It should all come just of its own accord,—little and little; but safe." Then, when the days of their marine holiday were coming to an end,—in the first week in October,—the day before the return of the Parkers to Ponders End, she made a strong appeal to her new friend. "You ain't afraid of him; are you?"

"Of my husband?" said Mrs. Lopez. "I hope not. Why should you ask?"

"Believe me, a woman should never be afraid of 'em. I never would give in to be bullied and made little of by Sexty. I 'd do a'most anything to make him comfortable, I 'm that soft-hearted. And why not, when he 's the father of my children? But I 'm not going not to say a thing if I thinks it right, because I 'm afeard."

"I think I could say anything if I thought it right."

"Then tell him of me and my babes,—as how I can

never have a quiet night while this is going on. It is n't that they two men are fond of one another. Nothing of the sort! Now you;—I 've got to be downright fond of you, though, of course, you think me common." Mrs. Lopez would not contradict her, but stooped forward and kissed her cheek. " I 'm downright fond of you, I am," continued Mrs. Parker, snuffling and sobbing, " but they two men are only together because Mr. Lopez wants to gamble, and Parker has got a little money to gamble with." This aspect of the thing was so terrible to Mrs. Lopez that she could only weep and hide her face. " Now, if you would tell him just the truth! Tell him what I say, and that I 've been a-saying it! Tell him it 's for my children I 'm a-speaking, who won't have bread in their very mouths if their father 's squeezed dry like a sponge! Sure, if you 'd tell him this, he would n't go on!" Then she paused a moment, looking up into the other woman's face. " He 'd have some bowels of compassion;—would n't he now? "

" I 'll try," said Mrs. Lopez.

" I know you 're good and kind-hearted, my dear. I saw it in your eyes from the very first. But them men, when they get on at money-making,—or money-losing, which makes 'em worse,—are like tigers clawing one another. They don't care how many they kills, so that they has the least bit for themselves. There ain't no fear of God in it, nor yet no mercy, nor e'er a morsel of heart. It ain't what I call manly,—not that longing after other folks' money. When it 's come by hard work, as I tell Sexty,—by the very sweat of his brow,—oh,—it 's sweet as sweet. When he 'd tell me that he 'd made his three pound, or his five pound, or, perhaps, his ten pound in a day, and 'd calculate it up, how much it 'd come to if he did that every day, and where we could go to, and what we could do for the children, I loved to hear him talk about his money. But now———! why, it's altered the looks of the man altogether. It's just as though he was a-thirsting for blood."

Thirsting for blood! Yes, indeed. It was the very idea that had occurred to Mrs. Lopez herself when her husband had bade her to "get round her father." No; —it certainly was not manly. There certainly was neither fear of God in it, nor mercy. Yes;—she would try. But as for bowels of compassion in Ferdinand Lopez———; , she, the young wife, had already seen enough of her husband to think that he was not to be moved by any prayers on that side. Then the two women bade each other farewell. "Parker has been talking of my going to Manchester Square," said Mrs. Parker, "but I shan't. What 'd I be in Manchester Square? And, besides, there 'd better be an end of it. Mr. Lopez 'd turn Sexty and me out of the house at a moment's notice if it was n't for the money."

"It's papa's house," said Mrs. Lopez, not, however, meaning to make an attack on her husband.

"I suppose so, but I shan't come to trouble no one; and we live ever so far away, at Ponders End,—out of your line altogether, Mrs. Lopez. But I've taken to you, and will never think ill of you any way;—only do as you said you would."

"I will try," said Mrs. Lopez.

In the meantime Lopez had received from Mr. Wharton an answer to his letter about the missing caravels, which did not please him. Here is the letter:—

"My dear Lopez,—I cannot say that your statement is satisfactory, nor can I reconcile it to your assurance to me that you have made a trade income for some years past of £2,000 a year. I do not know much of business, but I cannot imagine such a result from such a condition of things as you describe. Have you any books; and, if so, will you allow them to be inspected by any accountant I may name?

"You say that a sum of £20,000 would suit your business better now than when I 'm dead. Very likely. But with such an account of the business as that you have given me, I do not know that I feel disposed to confide the savings of my life to assist so very doubtful an enterprise. Of course whatever I may do to your advantage will be done for the sake of Emily and her children, should she have any. As far as I can see at present, I shall best do my duty to her, by leaving what I may have to leave to her, to trustees, for her benefit and that of her children.

"Yours truly,
"A. Wharton."

This, of course, did not tend to mollify the spirit of the man to whom it was written, or to make him gracious towards his wife. He received the letter three weeks before the lodgings at Dovercourt were given up,—but during these three weeks he was very little at the place, and when there did not mention the letter. On these occasions he said nothing about business, but satisfied himself with giving strict injunctions as to economy. Then he took her back to town on the day after her promise to Mrs. Parker that she would "try." Mrs. Parker had told her that no woman ought to be afraid to speak to her husband, and, if necessary, to speak roundly on such subjects. Mrs. Parker was certainly not a highly educated lady, but she had impressed Emily with an admiration for her practical good sense and proper feeling. The lady who was a lady had begun to feel that in the troubles of her life she might find a much less satisfactory companion than the lady who was not a lady. She would do as Mrs. Parker had told her. She would not be afraid. Of course it was right that she should speak on such a matter. She knew herself to be an obedient wife. She had borne all her unexpected sorrows without a complaint, with a resolve that she would bear all for his sake,—not because she loved him, but because she had made herself his wife. Into whatever calamities he might fall, she would share them. Though he should bring her utterly into the dirt, she would remain in the dirt with him. It seemed probable to her that it might be so,—that they might have to go into the dirt;—and if it were so, she would still be true to him. She had chosen to marry him, and she would be his true wife. But, as such, she would not be afraid of him. Mrs. Parker had told her that "a woman should never be afraid of 'em," and she believed in Mrs. Parker. In this case, too, it was clearly her duty to speak,—for the injury being done was terrible, and might too probably become tragical. How could she endure to think of that woman and her children, should she come to know that the husband of the woman and the father of the children had been ruined by her husband?

Yes,—she would speak to him. But she did fear. It is all very well for a woman to tell herself that she will encounter some anticipated difficulty without fear,

—or for a man either. The fear cannot be overcome by will. The thing, however, may be done, whether it be leading a forlorn hope, or speaking to an angry husband,—in spite of fear. She would do it; but when the moment for doing it came, her very heart trembled within her. He had been so masterful with her, so persistent in repudiating her interference, so exacting in his demands for obedience, so capable of making her miserable by his moroseness when she failed to comply with his wishes, that she could not go to her task without fear. But she did feel that she ought not to be afraid, or that her fears, at any rate, should not be allowed to restrain her. A wife, she knew, should be prepared to yield, but yet was entitled to be her husband's counsellor. And it was now the case that in this matter she was conversant with cirumstances which were unknown to her husband. It was to her that Mrs. Parker's appeal had been made, and with a direct request from the poor woman that it should be repeated to her husband's partner.

She found that she could not do it on the journey home from Dovercourt, nor yet on that evening. Mrs. Dick Roby, who had come back from a sojourn at Boulogne, was with them in the Square, and brought her dear friend Mrs. Leslie with her, and also Lady Eustace. The reader may remember that Mr. Wharton had met these ladies at Mrs. Dick's house some months before his daughter's marriage, but he certainly had never asked them into his own. On this occasion Emily had given them no invitation, but had been told by her husband that her aunt would probably bring them in with her. "Mrs. Leslie and Lady Eustace!" she exclaimed with a little shudder. "I suppose your aunt may bring a couple of friends with her to see you, though it is your father's house?" he had replied. She had said no more, not daring to have a fight on that subject at present, while the other matter was pressing on her mind. The evening had passed away pleasantly enough, she thought, to all except herself. Mrs. Leslie and Lady Eustace had talked a great deal, and her husband had borne himself quite as though he had been a wealthy man and the owner of the house in Manchester Square. In the course of the evening Dick Roby came in and Major Pountney, who since the late affairs at Silverbridge had become intimate with Lopez. So that there was quite a party; and Emily was astonished to hear her husband declare that he was only watching the opportunity of another vacancy in order that he might get into the House, and expose the miserable duplicity of the Duke of Omnium. And yet this man, within the last month, had taken away her subscription at Mudie's, and told her that she should n't wear things that wanted washing! But he was able to say ever so many pretty little things to Lady Eustace, and had given a new fan to Mrs. Dick, and talked of taking a box for Mrs. Leslie at The Gaiety.

But on the next morning before breakfast she began. "Ferdinand," she said, "while I was at Dovercourt I saw a good deal of Mrs. Parker."

"I could not help that. Or rather you might have helped it if you pleased. It was necessary that you should meet, but I did n't tell you that you were to see a great deal of her."

"I liked her very much."

"Then I must say you 've got a very odd taste. Did you like him?"

"No. I did not see so much of him, and I think that the manners of women are less objectionable than those of men. But I want to tell you what passed between her and me."

"If it is about her husband's business she ought to have held her tongue, and you had better hold yours now."

This was not a happy beginning, but still she was determined to go on. "It was, I think, more about your business than his."

"Then it was infernal impudence on her part, and you should not have listened to her for a moment."

"You do not want to ruin her and her children!"

"What have I to do with her and her children? I did not marry her, and I am not their father. He has got to look to that."

"She thinks that you are enticing him into risks which he cannot afford."

"Am I doing anything for him that I ain't doing for myself! If there is money made, will not he share it? If money has to be lost, of course he must do the same." Lopez in stating his case omitted to say that whatever capital was now being used belonged to his partner. "But women when they get together talk all manner of nonsense. Is it likely that I shall alter my course of action because you tell me that she tells you that he tells her that he is losing money? He is a half-hearted fellow who quails at every turn against him. And when he is crying drunk I dare say he makes a poor mouth to her."

"I think, Ferdinand, it is more than that. She says that——"

"To tell you the truth, Emily, I don't care a d——
what she says. Now give me some tea."

The roughness of this absolutely quelled her. It
was not now that she was afraid of him,—not at this
moment, but that she was knocked down as though by
a blow. She had been altogether so unused to such
language that she could not get on with her matter in
hand, letting the bad word pass by her as an unmeaning expletive. She wearily poured out the cup of tea
and sat herself down silent. The man was too strong
for her, and would be so always. She told herself at
this moment that language such as that must always
absolutely silence her. Then, within a few minutes, he
desired her, quite cheerfully, to ask her uncle and aunt
to dinner the day but one following, and also to ask
Lady Eustace and Mrs. Leslie. "I will pick up a
couple of men which will make us all right," he said.

This was in every way horrible to her. Her father
had been back in town, had not been very well, and
had been recommended to return to the country. He
had consequently removed himself,—not to Herefordshire,—but to Brighton, and was now living at an hotel,
almost within an hour of London. Had he been at
home he certainly would not have invited Mrs. Leslie
and Lady Eustace to his house. He had often expressed a feeling of dislike to the former lady in the
hearing of his son-in-law, and had ridiculed his sister-in-law for allowing herself to be made acquainted with
Lady Eustace, whose name had at one time been very
common in the mouths of people. Emily also felt that
she was hardly entitled to give a dinner-party in his
house in his absence. And, after all that she had lately

heard about her husband's poverty, she could not understand how he should wish to incur the expense. "You would not ask Mrs. Leslie here!" she said.

"Why should we not ask Mrs. Leslie?"

"Papa dislikes her."

"But 'papa,' as you call him, is n't going to meet her."

"He has said that he does n't know what day he may be home. And he does more than dislike her. He disapproves of her."

"Nonsense! She is your aunt's friend. Because your father once heard some cock-and-bull story about her, and because he has always taken upon himself to criticise your aunt's friends, I am not to be civil to a person I like."

"But, Ferdinand, I do not like her myself. She never was in this house till the other night."

"Look here, my dear, Lady Eustace can be useful to me, and I cannot ask Lady Eustace without asking her friend. You do as I bid you,—or else I shall do it myself."

She paused for a moment, and then she positively refused. "I cannot bring myself to ask Mrs. Leslie to dine in this house. If she comes to dine with you of course I shall sit at the table, but she will be sure to see that she is not welcome."

"It seems to me that you are determined to go against me in everything I propose."

"I don't think you would say that if you knew how miserable you made me."

"I tell you that that other woman can be very useful to me."

"In what way useful?"

"Are you jealous, my dear?"

"Certainly not of Lady Eustace,—nor of any woman. But it seems so odd that such a person's services should be required."

"Will you do as I tell you, and ask them? You can go round and tell your aunt about it. She knows that I mean to ask them. Lady Eustace is a very rich woman, and is disposed to do a little in commerce. Now do you understand?"

"Not in the least," said Emily.

"Why shouldn't a woman who has money buy coffee as well as buy shares?"

"Does she buy shares?"

"By George, Emily, I think that you're a fool."

"I dare say I am, Ferdinand. I do not in the least know what it all means. But I do know this, that you ought not, in papa's absence, to ask people to dine here whom he particularly dislikes, and whom he would not wish to have in his house."

"You think that I am to be governed by you in such a matter as that?"

"I do not want to govern you."

"You think that a wife should dictate to a husband as to the way in which he is to do his work, and the partners he may be allowed to have in his business, and the persons whom he may ask to dinner! Because you have been dictating to me on all these matters. Now, look here, my dear. As to my business, you had better never speak to me about it any more. I have endeavoured to take you into my confidence and to get you to act with me, but you have declined that, and have preferred to stick to your father. As to my partners, whether I may choose to have Sexty

Parker or Lady Eustace, I am a better judge than you. And as to asking Mrs. Leslie and Lady Eustace or any other persons to dinner, as I am obliged to make even the recreations of life subservient to its work, I must claim permission to have my own way." She had listened, but when he paused she made no reply. "Do you mean to do as I bid you and ask these ladies?"

"I cannot do that. I know that it ought not to be done. This is papa's house, and we are living here as his guests."

"D—— your papa!" he said, as he burst out of the room. After a quarter of an hour he put his head again into the room and saw her sitting, like a statue, exactly where he had left her. "I have written the notes both to Lady Eustace and to Mrs. Leslie," he said. "You can't think it any sin at any rate to ask your aunt."

"I will see my aunt," she said.

"And remember I am not going to be your father's guest, as you call it. I mean to pay for the dinner myself, and to send in my own wines. Your father shall have nothing to complain of on that head."

"Could you not ask them to Richmond, or to some hotel?" she said.

"What; in October! If you think that I am going to live in a house in which I can't invite a friend to dinner, you are mistaken." And with that he took his departure.

The whole thing had now become so horrible to her that she felt unable any longer to hold up her head. It seemed to her to be sacrilege that these women should come and sit in her father's room; but when she spoke of her father her husband had cursed him with scorn! Lopez was going to send food and wine into the house, which would be gall and wormwood to her father. At one time she thought she would at once write to her father and tell him of it all,—or perhaps telegraph to him; but she could not do so without letting her husband know what she had done, and then he would have justice on his side in calling her disobedient. Were she to do that, then it would indeed be necessary that she should take part against her husband.

She had brought all this misery on herself and on her father because she had been obstinate in thinking that she could with certainty read a lover's character. As for love,—that of course had died away in her heart,—imperceptibly, though, alas, so quickly! It was impossible that she could continue to love a man who from day to day was teaching her mean lessons, and who was ever doing mean things, the meanness of which was so little apparent to himself that he did not scruple to divulge them to her. How could she love a man who would make no sacrifice either to her comfort, her pride, or her conscience? But still she might obey him,—if she could feel sure that obedience to him was a duty. Could it be a duty to sin against her father's wishes, and to assist in profaning his house and abusing his hospitality after this fashion? Then her mind again went back to the troubles of Mrs. Parker, and her absolute inefficiency in that matter. It seemed to her that she had given herself over, body and soul and mind, to some evil genius, and that there was no escape.

"Of course we'll come," Mrs. Roby had said to

her when she went round the corner into Berkeley Street early in the day. "Lopez spoke to me about it before."

"What will papa say about it, Aunt Harriet?"

"I suppose he and Lopez understand each other."

"I do not think papa will understand this."

"I am sure Mr. Wharton would not lend his house to his son-in-law, and then object to the man he had lent it to asking a friend to dine with him. And I am sure that Mr. Lopez would not consent to occupy a house on those terms. If you don't like it, of course we won't come."

"Pray don't say that. As these other women are to come, pray do not desert me. But I cannot say I think it is right." Mrs. Dick, however, only laughed at her scruples.

In the course of the evening Emily got letters addressed to herself, from Lady Eustace and Mrs. Leslie, informing her that they would have very much pleasure in dining with her on the day named. And Lady Eustace went on to say, with much pleasantry, that she always regarded little parties, got up without any ceremony, as being the pleasantest, and that she should come on this occasion without any ceremonial observance. Then Emily was aware that her husband had not only written the notes in her name, but had put into her mouth some studied apology as to the shortness of the invitation. Well! She was the man's wife, and she supposed that he was entitled to put any words that he pleased into her mouth.

CHAPTER XXI.

"HAS HE ILL-TREATED YOU?"

LOPEZ relieved his wife from all care as to provision for his guests. "I've been to a shop in Wigmore Street," he said, "and everything will be done. They'll send in a cook to make the things hot, and your father won't have to pay even for a crust of bread."

"Papa does n't mind paying for anything," she said in her indignation.

"It is all very pretty for you to say so, but my experience of him goes just the other way. At any rate there will be nothing to be paid for. Stewam and Sugarscraps will send in everything, if you'll only tell the old fogies downstairs not to interfere." Then she made a little request. Might she ask Everett, who was now in town? "I've already got Major Pountney and Captain Gunner," he said. She pleaded that one more would make no difference. "But that's just what one more always does. It destroys everything, and turns a pretty little dinner into an awkward feed. We won't have him this time. Pountney'll take you, and I'll take her ladyship. Dick will take Mrs. Leslie, and Gunner will have Aunt Harriet. Dick will sit opposite to me, and the four ladies will sit at the four corners. We shall be very pleasant, but one more would spoil us."

She did speak to the "old fogies" downstairs,—the housekeeper, who had lived with her father since she was a child, and the butler, who had been there still longer, and the cook, who, having been in her place only three years, resigned impetuously within half an hour after the advent of Mr. Sugarscraps' head man. The "fogies" were indignant. The butler expressed his intention of locking himself up in his own peculiar pantry, and the housekeeper took upon herself to tell her young mistress that "Master would n't like it." Since she had known Mr. Wharton such a thing as cooked food being sent into the house from a shop had never been so much as heard of. Emily, who had hitherto been regarded in the house as a rather strong-minded young woman, could only break down and weep. Why, oh why, had she consented to bring herself and her misery into her father's house? She could at any rate have prevented that by explaining to her father the unfitness of such an arrangement.

The "party" came. There was Major Pountney, very fine, rather loud, very intimate with the host, whom on one occasion he called "Ferdy, my boy," and very full of abuse of the Duke and Duchess of Omnium. "And yet she was a good creature when I knew her," said Lady Eustace. Pountney suggested that the Duchess had not then taken up politics. "I 've got out of her way," said Lady Eustace, "since she did that." And there was Captain Gunner, who defended the Duchess, but who acknowledged that the Duke was the "most consumedly stuck-up coxcomb" then existing. "And the most dishonest," said Lopez, who had told his new friends nothing about the repayment of the election expenses. And Dick was there.

He liked these little parties, in which a good deal of wine could be drunk, and at which ladies were not supposed to be very stiff. The major and the captain, and Mrs. Leslie and Lady Eustace, were such people as he liked,—all within the pale, but having a piquant relish of fastness and impropriety. Dick was wont to declare that he hated the world in buckram. Aunt Harriet was triumphant in a manner which disgusted Emily, and which she thought to be most disrespectful to her father;—but in truth Aunt Harriet did not now care very much for Mr. Wharton, preferring the friendship of Mr. Wharton's son-in-law. Mrs. Leslie came in gorgeous clothes, which, as she was known to be very poor, and to have attached herself lately with almost more than feminine affection to Lady Eustace, were at any rate open to suspicious cavil. In former days Mrs. Leslie had taken upon herself to say bitter things about Mr. Lopez, which Emily could now have repeated, to that lady's discomfiture, had such a mode of revenge suited her disposition. With Mrs. Leslie there was Lady Eustace, pretty as ever, and sharp and witty, with the old passion for some excitement, the old proneness to pretend to trust everybody, and the old incapacity for trusting anybody. Ferdinand Lopez had lately been at her feet, and had fired her imagination with stories of the grand things to be done in trade. Ladies do it? Yes; why not women as well as men? Any one might do it who had money in his pocket and experience to tell him, or to tell her, what to buy and what to sell. And the experience, luckily, might be vicarious. At the present moment half the jewels worn in London were,—if Ferdinand Lopez knew anything about it,—bought from the proceeds of such commerce. Of course there were misfortunes. But these came from a want of that experience which Ferdinand Lopez possessed, and which he was quite willing to place at the service of one whom he admired so thoroughly as he did Lady Eustace. Lady Eustace had been charmed, had seen her way into a new and most delightful life,—but had not yet put any of her money into the hands of Ferdinand Lopez.

I cannot say that the dinner was good. It may be a doubt whether such tradesmen as Messrs. Stewam and Sugarscraps do ever produce good food;—or whether, with all the will in the world to do so, such a result is within their power. It is certain, I think, that the humblest mutton chop is better eating than any "Supreme of chicken after martial manner,"—as I have seen the dish named in a French bill of fare, translated by a French pastry cook for the benefit of his English customers,—when sent in from Messrs. Stewam and Sugarscraps even with their best exertions. Nor can it be said that the wine was good, though Mr. Sugarscraps, when he contracted for the whole entertainment, was eager in his assurance that he procured the very best that London could produce. But the outside look of the things was handsome, and there were many dishes, and enough of servants to hand them, and the wines, if not good, were various. Probably Pountney and Gunner did not know good wines. Roby did, but was contented on this occasion to drink them bad. And everything went pleasantly, with perhaps a little too much noise;—everything except the hostess, who was allowed by general consent to be sad and silent;—till there came a loud double rap at the door.

"There's papa," said Emily, jumping up from her seat.

Mrs. Dick looked at Lopez, and saw at a glance that for a moment his courage had failed him. But he recovered himself quickly. "Hadn't you better keep your seat, my dear?" he said to his wife. "The servants will attend to Mr. Wharton, and I will go to him presently."

"Oh no," said Emily, who by this time was almost at the door.

"You didn't expect him,—did you?" asked Dick Roby.

"Nobody knew when he was coming. I think he told Emily that he might be here any day."

"He's the most uncertain man alive," said Mrs. Dick, who was a good deal scared by the arrival, though determined to hold up her head and exhibit no fear.

"I suppose the old gentleman will come in and have some dinner," whispered Captain Gunner to his neighbour Mrs. Leslie.

"Not if he knows I'm here," replied Mrs. Leslie, tittering. "He thinks that I am,—oh, something a great deal worse than I can tell you."

"Is he given to be cross?" asked Lady Eustace, also affecting to whisper.

"Never saw him in my life," answered the major, "but I shouldn't wonder if he was. Old gentlemen generally are cross. Gout, and that kind of thing, you know."

For a minute or two the servants stopped their ministrations, and things were very uncomfortable; but Lopez, as soon as he had recovered himself, directed Mr. Sugarscraps' men to proceed with the banquet.

"We can eat our dinner, I suppose, though my father-in-law has come back," he said. "I wish my wife was not so fussy, though that is a kind of thing, Lady Eustace, that one has to expect from young wives." The banquet did go on, but the feeling was general that a misfortune had come upon them, and that something dreadful might possibly happen.

Emily, when she rushed out, met her father in the hall, and ran into his arms. "Oh, papa!" she exclaimed.

"What's all this about?" he asked, and as he spoke he passed on through the hall to his own room at the back of the house. There were of course many evidences on all sides of the party,—the strange servants, the dishes going in and out, the clatter of glasses, and the smell of viands. "You've got a dinner-party," he said. "Had you not better go back to your friends?"

"No, papa."

"What is the matter, Emily? You are unhappy."

"Oh, so unhappy!"

"What is it all about? Who are they? Whose doing is it,—yours or his? What makes you unhappy?"

He was now seated in his arm-chair, and she threw herself on her knees at his feet. "He would have them. You must n't be angry with me. You won't be angry with me;—will you?"

He put his hand upon her head, and stroked her hair. "Why should I be angry with you because your husband has asked friends to dinner?" She was so unlike her usual self that he knew not what to make of it. It had not been her nature to kneel and to ask for pardon, or to be timid and submissive. "What is it, Emily, that makes you like this?"

"He should n't have had the people."

"Well;—granted. But it does not signify much. Is your Aunt Harriet there?"

"Yes."

"It can't be very bad, then."

"Mrs. Leslie is there, and Lady Eustace,—and two men I don't like."

"Is Everett here?"

"No;—he would n't have Everett."

"Ought n't you to go to them?"

"Don't make me go. I should only cry. I have been crying all day, and the whole of yesterday." Then she buried her face upon his knees, and sobbed as though she would break her heart.

He could n't at all understand it. Though he distrusted his son-in-law, and certainly did not love him, he had not as yet learned to hold him in aversion. When the connection was once made he had determined to make the best of it, and had declared to himself that as far as manners went the man was well enough. He had not as yet seen the inside of the man, as it had been the sad fate of the poor wife to see him. It had never occurred to him that his daughter's love had failed her, or that she could already be repenting what she had done. And now, when she was weeping at his feet and deploring the sin of the dinner-party,—which, after all, was a trifling sin,—he could not comprehend the feelings which were actuating her. "I suppose your Aunt Harriet made up the party," he said.

"He did it."

"Your husband?"

"Yes;—he did it. He wrote to the women in my

name when I refused." Then Mr. Wharton began to perceive that there had been a quarrel. "I told him Mrs. Leslie ought n't to come here."

"I don't love Mrs. Leslie,—nor, for the matter of that, Lady Eustace. But they won't hurt the house, my dear."

"And he has had the dinner sent in from a shop."

"Why could n't he let Mrs. Williams do it?" As he said this, the tone of his voice became for the first time angry.

"Cook has gone away. She would n't stand it. And Mrs. Williams is very angry. And Barker would n't wait at table."

"What 's the meaning of it all?"

"He would have it so. Oh, papa, you don't know what I 've undergone. I wish,—I wish we had not come here. It would have been better anywhere else."

"What would have been better, dear?"

"Everything. Whether we lived or died, it would have been better. Why should I bring my misery to you? Oh, papa, you do not know,—you can never know."

"But I must know. Is there more than this dinner to disturb you?"

"Oh yes;—more than that. Only I could n't bear that it should be done in your house."

"Has he——ill-treated you?"

Then she got up, and stood before him. "I do not mean to complain. I should have said nothing only that you have found us in this way. For myself, I will bear it all, whatever it may be. But, papa, I want you to tell him that we must leave this house."

"He has got no other home for you."

"He must find one. I will go anywhere. I don't care where it is. But I won't stay here. I have done it myself, but I won't bring it upon you. I could bear it all if I thought that you would never see me again."

"Emily!"

"Yes;—if you would never see me again. I know it all, and that would be best." She was now walking about the room. "Why should you see it all?"

"See what, my love?"

"See his ruin, and my unhappiness, and my baby. Oh,—oh,—oh!"

"I think so very differently, Emily, that under no circumstances will I have you taken to another home. I cannot understand much of all this as yet, but I suppose I shall come to see it. If Lopez be, as you say, ruined, it is well that I have still enough for us to live on. This is a bad time just now to talk about your husband's affairs."

"I did not mean to talk about them, papa."

"What would you like best to do now,—now at once. Can you go down again to your husband's friends?"

"No;—no;—no."

"As for the dinner, never mind about that. I can't blame him for making use of my house in my absence as far as that goes,—though I wish he could have contented himself with such a dinner as my servants could have prepared for him. I will have some tea here."

"Let me stay with you, papa, and make it for you."

"Very well, dear. I do not mean to be ashamed to enter my own dining-room. I shall, therefore, go in and make your apologies." Thereupon Mr. Wharton walked slowly forth and marched into the dining-room.

"Oh, Mr. Wharton," said Mrs. Dick, "we did n't expect you."

"Have you dined yet, sir?" asked Lopez.

"I dined early," said Mr. Wharton. "I should not now have come in to disturb you, but that I have found Mrs. Lopez unwell, and she has begged me to ask you to excuse her."

"I will go to her," said Lopez, rising.

"It is not necessary," said Wharton. "She is not ill, but hardly able to take her place at table." Then Mrs. Dick proposed to go to her dear niece; but Mr. Wharton would not allow it, and left the room, having succeeded in persuading them to go on with their dinner. Lopez certainly was not happy during the evening, but he was strong enough to hide his misgivings, and to do his duty as host with seeming cheerfulness.

CHAPTER XXII.

"WHERE IS GUATEMALA?"

THOUGH his daughter's words to him had been very wild they did almost more to convince Mr. Wharton that he should not give money to his son-in-law than even the letters which had passed between them. To Emily herself he spoke very little as to what had occurred that evening. "Papa," she said, "do not ask me anything more about it. I was very miserable,— because of the dinner." Nor did he at that time ask her any questions, contenting himself with assuring her that, at any rate at present, and till after her baby should have been born, she must remain in Manchester Square. "He won't hurt me," said Mr. Wharton, and then added with a smile, "he won't want to have any more dinner-parties while I am here."

Nor did he make any complaint to Lopez as to what had been done, or even allude to the dinner. But when he had been back about a week he announced to his son-in-law his final determination as to money. "I had better tell you, Lopez, what I mean to do, so that you may not be left in doubt. I shall not intrust any further sum of money into your hands on behalf of Emily."

"You can do as you please, sir,—of course."

"Just so. You have had what to me is a very considerable sum,—though I fear that it did not go for much in your large concerns."

"It was not very much, Mr. Wharton."

"I dare say not. Opinions on such a matter differ, you know. At any rate, there will be no more. At present I wish Emily to live here, and you, of course, are welcome here also. If things are not going well with you, this will, at any rate, relieve you from immediate expense."

"My calculations, sir, have never descended to that."

"Mine are more minute. The necessities of my life have caused me to think of these little things. When I am dead there will be provision for Emily made by my will,—the income going to trustees for her benefit, and the capital to her children after her death. I thought it only fair to you that this should be explained."

"And you will do nothing for me?"

"Nothing;—if that is nothing. I should have thought that your present maintenance and the future support of your wife and children would have been regarded as something."

"It is nothing;—nothing!"

"Then let it be nothing. Good morning."

Two days after that Lopez recurred to the subject. "You were very explicit with me the other day, sir."

"I meant to be so."

"And I will be equally so to you now. Both I and your daughter are absolutely ruined unless you reconsider your purpose."

"If you mean money by reconsideration,—present money to be given to you,—I certainly shall not reconsider it. You may take my solemn assurance that I will give you nothing that can be of any service to you in trade."

"Then, sir,—I must tell you my purpose, and give you my assurance, which is equally solemn. Under those circumstances I must leave England, and try my fortune in Central America. There is an opening for me at Guatemala, though not a very hopeful one."

"Guatemala!"

"Yes;—friends of mine have a connection there. I have not broken it to Emily yet, but under these circumstances she will have to go."

"You will not take her to Guatemala!"

"Not take my wife, sir? Indeed I shall. Do you suppose that I would go away and leave my wife a pensioner on your bounty? Do you think that she would wish to desert her husband? I don't think you know your daughter."

"I wish you had never known her."

"That is neither here nor there, sir. If I cannot succeed in this country I must go elsewhere. As I have told you before, £20,000 at the present moment would enable me to surmount all my difficulties, and make me a very wealthy man. But unless I can command some such sum by Christmas everything here must be sacrificed."

"Never in my life did I hear so base a proposition," said Mr. Wharton.

"Why is it base? I can only tell you the truth."

"So be it. You will find that I mean what I have said."

"So do I, Mr. Wharton."

"As to my daughter, she must, of course, do as she thinks fit."

"She must do as I think fit, Mr. Wharton."

"I will not argue with you. Alas, alas; poor girl!"

"Poor girl, indeed! She is likely to be a poor girl if she is treated in this way by her father. As I understand that you intend to use, or to try to use, authority over her, I shall take steps for removing her at once from your house." And so the interview was ended.

Lopez had thought the matter over, and had determined to "brazen it out," as he himself called it. Nothing further was, he thought, to be got by civility and obedience. Now he must use his power. His idea of going to Guatemala was not an invention of the moment, nor was it devoid of a certain basis of truth. Such a suggestion had been made to him some time since by Mr. Mills Happerton. There were mines in Guatemala which wanted, or at some future day might want, a resident director. The proposition had been made to Lopez before his marriage, and Mr. Happerton probably had now forgotten all about it;—but the thing was of service now. He broke the matter very suddenly to his wife. "Has your father been speaking to you of my plans?"

"Not lately;—not that I remember."

"He could not speak of them without your remembering, I should think. Has he told you that I am going to Guatemala?"

"Guatemala! Where is Guatemala, Ferdinand?"

"You can answer my question though your geography is deficient."

"He has said nothing about your going anywhere."

"You will have to go,—as soon after Christmas as you may be fit."

"But where is Guatemala;—and for how long, Ferdinand?"

"Guatemala is in Central America, and we shall

probably settle there for the rest of our lives. I have got nothing to live on here."

During the next two months this plan of seeking a distant home and a strange country was constantly spoken of in Manchester Square, and did receive corroboration from Mr. Happerton himself. Lopez renewed his application, and received a letter from that gentleman saying that the thing might probably be arranged if he were in earnest. "I am quite in earnest," Lopez said as he showed this letter to Mr. Wharton. "I suppose Emily will be able to start two months after her confinement. They tell me that babies do very well at sea."

During this time, in spite of his threat, he continued to live with Mr. Wharton in Manchester Square, and went every day into the City,—whether to make arrangements and receive instructions as to Guatemala, or to carry on his old business, neither Emily nor her father knew. He never at this time spoke about his affairs to either of them, but daily referred to her future expatriation as a thing that was certain. At last there came up the actual question,—whether she were to go or not. Her father told her that though she was doubtless bound by law to obey her husband, in such a matter as this she might defy the law. "I do not think that he can actually force you on board the ship," her father said.

"But if he tells me that I must go?"

"Stay here with me," said the father. "Stay here with your baby. I'll fight it out for you. I'll so manage that you shall have all the world on your side."

Emily at that moment came to no decision, but on the following day she discussed the matter with Lopez himself. "Of course you will go with me," he said, when she asked the question.

"You mean that I must, whether I wish to go or not."

"Certainly you must. Good G——! where is a wife's place? Am I to go out without my child, and without you, while you are enjoying all the comforts of your father's wealth at home? That is not my idea of life."

"Ferdinand, I have been thinking about it very much. I must beg you to allow me to remain. I ask it of you as if I were asking my life."

"Your father has put you up to this."

"No;—not to this."

"To what then?"

"My father thinks that I should refuse to go."

"He does; does he?"

"But I shall not refuse. I shall go if you insist upon it. There shall be no contest between us about that."

"Well; I should hope not."

"But I do implore you to spare me."

"That is very selfish, Emily."

"Yes," she said,—"yes. I cannot contradict that. But so is the man selfish who prays the judge to spare his life."

"But you do not think of me. I must go."

"I shall not make you happier, Ferdinand."

"Do you think that it is a fine thing for a man to live in such a country as that all alone?"

"I think he would be better so than with a wife he does not—love."

"Who says I do not love you?"

"Or with one who does—not—love him." This she

said very slowly, very softly, but looking up into his eyes as she said it.

"Do you tell me that to my face?"

"Yes;—what good can I do now by lying? You have not been to me as I thought you would be."

"And so, because you have built up some castle in the air that has fallen to pieces, you tell your husband to his face that you do not love him, and that you prefer not to live with him. Is that your idea of duty?"

"Why have you been so cruel?"

"Cruel! What have I done? Tell me what cruelty. Have I beat you? Have you been starved? Have I not asked and implored your assistance,—only to be refused? The fact is that your father and you have found out that I am not a rich man, and you want to be rid of me. Is that true or false?"

"It is not true that I want to be rid of you because you are poor."

"I do not mean to be rid of you. You will have to settle down and do your work as my wife in whatever place it may suit me to live. Your father is a rich man, but you shall not have the advantage of his wealth unless it comes to you, as it ought to come, through my hands. If your father would give me the fortune which ought to be yours there need be no going abroad. He cannot bear to part with his money, and therefore we must go. Now you know all about it." She was then turning to leave him, when he asked her a direct question. "Am I to understand that you intend to resist my right to take you with me?"

"If you bid me go,—I shall go."

"It will be better, as you will save both trouble and exposure."

Of course she told her father what had taken place, but he could only shake his head, and sit groaning over his misery in his chambers. He had explained to her what he was willing to do on her behalf, but she declined his aid. He could not tell her that she was wrong. She was the man's wife, and out of that terrible destiny she could not now escape. The only question with him was whether it would not be best to buy the man,—give him a sum of money to go, and to go alone. Could he have been quit of the man even for £20,000, he would willingly have paid the money. But the man would either not go, or would come back as soon as he had got the money. His own life, as he passed it now, with this man in the house with him, was horrible to him. For Lopez, though he had more than once threatened that he would carry his wife to another home, had taken no steps towards getting that other home ready for her.

During all this time Mr. Wharton had not seen his son. Everett had gone abroad just as his father returned to London from Brighton, and was still on the Continent. He received his allowance punctually, and that was the only intercourse which took place between them. But Emily had written to him, not telling him much of her troubles,—only saying that she believed that her husband would take her to Central America early in the spring, and begging him to come home before she went.

Just before Christmas her baby was born, but the poor child did not live a couple of days. She herself at the time was so worn with care, so thin and wan and wretched, that looking in the glass she hardly knew her own face. "Ferdinand," she said to him, "I know he will not live. The doctor says so."

"Nothing thrives that I have to do with," he answered gloomily.

"Will you not look at him?"

"Well; yes. I have looked at him, have I not? I wish to God that where he is going I could go with him."

"I wish I was;—I wish I was going," said the poor mother. Then the father went out, and before he had returned to the house the child was dead. "Oh, Ferdinand, speak one kind word to me now," she said.

"What kind word can I speak when you have told me that you do not love me? Do you think that I can forget that because,—because he has gone?"

"A woman's love may always be won back again by kindness."

"Psha! How am I to kiss and make pretty speeches with my mind harassed as it is now?" But he did touch her brow with his lips before he went away.

The infant was buried, and then there was not much show of mourning in the house. The poor mother would sit gloomily alone day after day, telling herself that it was perhaps better that she should have been robbed of her treasure than have gone forth with him into the wide, unknown, harsh world with such a father as she had given him. Then she would look at all the preparations she had made,—the happy work of her fingers when her thoughts of their future use were her sweetest consolation,—and weep till she would herself feel that there never could be an end to her tears.

The second week in January had come, and yet nothing further had been settled as to this Guatemala project. Lopez talked about it as though it was certain, and even told his wife that as they would move so soon it would not be now worth while for him to take other lodgings for her. But when she asked as to her own preparations,—the wardrobe necessary for the long voyage and her general outfit,—he told her that three weeks or a fortnight would be enough for all, and that he would give her sufficient notice. "Upon my word, he is very kind to honour my poor house as he does," said Mr. Wharton.

"Papa, we will go at once if you wish it," said his daughter.

"Nay, Emily; do not turn upon me. I cannot but be sensible to the insult of his daily presence; but even that is better than losing you."

Then there occurred a ludicrous incident,—or combination of incidents,—which, in spite of their absurdity, drove Mr. Wharton almost frantic. First there came to him the bill from Messrs. Stewam and Sugarscraps for the dinner. At this time he kept nothing back from his daughter. "Look at that!" he said. The bill was absolutely made out in his name.

"It is a mistake, papa."

"Not at all. The dinner was given in my house, and I must pay for it. I would sooner do so than that he should pay it,—even if he had the means." So he paid Messrs. Stewam and Sugarscraps £25 9s. 6d., begging them as he did so never to send another dinner into his house, and observing that he was in the habit of entertaining his friends at less than three guineas a head. "But Château Yquem and Côte d'Or!" said

Mr. Sugarscraps. "Château fiddlesticks!" said Mr. Wharton, walking out of the house with his receipt.

Then came the bill for the brougham,—for the brougham from the very day of their return to town after their wedding trip. This he showed to Lopez. Indeed, the bill had been made out to Lopez, and sent to Mr. Wharton with an apologetic note. "I did n't tell him to send it," said Lopez.

"But will you pay it?"

"I certainly shall not ask you to pay it." But Mr. Wharton at last did pay it, and he also paid the rent of the rooms in the Belgrave Mansion, and between £30 and £40 for dresses which Emily had got at Lewes and Allenby's under her husband's orders in the first days of their married life in London.

"Oh, papa, I wish I had not gone there," she said.

"My dear, anything that you may have had I do not grudge in the least. And even for him, if he would let you remain here, I would pay willingly. I would supply all his wants if he would only—go away."

CHAPTER XXIII.

MR. SLIDE'S REVENGE.

"Do you mean to say, my lady, that the Duke paid 'is electioneering bill down at Silverbridge?"

"I do mean to say so, Mr. Slide." Lady Eustace nodded her head, and Mr. Quintus Slide opened his mouth.

"Goodness gracious!" said Mrs. Leslie, who was sitting with them. They were in Lady Eustace's drawing-room, and the patriotic editor of the People's Banner was obtaining from a new ally information which might be useful to the country.

"But 'ow do you know, Lady Eustace? You'll pardon the persistency of my inquiries, but when you come to public information accuracy is everything. I never trust myself to mere report. I always travel up to the very fountain 'ead of truth."

"I know it," said Lizzy Eustace oracularly.

"Um—m!" The editor as he ejaculated the sound looked at her ladyship with admiring eyes,—with eyes that were intended to flatter. But Lizzie had been looked at so often in so many ways, and was so well accustomed to admiration, that this had no effect on her at all. "'E did n't tell you himself; did 'e, now?"

"Can you tell me the truth as to trusting him with my money?"

"Yes, I can."

"Shall I be safe if I take the papers which he calls bills of sale?"

"One good turn deserves another, my lady."

"I don't want to make a secret of it, Mr. Slide. Pountney found it out. You know the major?"

"Yes, I know Major Pountney. He was at Gatherum 'imself, and got a little bit of cold shoulder;—did n't he?"

"I dare say he did. What has that to do with it? You may be sure that Lopez applied to the Duke for his expenses at Silverbridge, and that the Duke sent him the money."

"There 's no doubt about it, Mr. Slide," said Mrs. Leslie. "We got it all from Major Pountney. There was some bet between him and Pountney, and he had to show Pountney the cheque."

"Pountney saw the money," said Lady Eustace.

Mr. Slide stroked his hand over his mouth and chin as he sat thinking of the tremendous national importance of this communication. The man who had paid the money was the Prime Minister of England,—and was, moreover, Mr. Slide's enemy! "When the right 'and of fellowship has been rejected, I never forgive," Mr. Slide has been heard to say. Even Lady Eustace, who was not particular as to the appearance of people, remarked afterwards to her friend that Mr. Slide had looked like the devil as he was stroking his face. "It 's very remarkable," said Mr. Slide; "very remarkable!"

"You won't tell the major that we told you," said her ladyship.

"Oh dear, no. I only just wanted to 'ear how it was. And as to embarking your money, my lady, with Ferdinand Lopez,—I would n't do it."

"Not if I get the bills of sale? It's for rum, and they say rum will go up to any price."

"Don't, Lady Eustace. I can't say any more,—but don't. I never mention names. But don't."

Then Mr. Slide went at once in search of Major Pountney, and having found the major at his club extracted from him all that he knew about the Silverbridge payment. Pountney had really seen the Duke's cheque for £500. "There was some bet,—eh, major?" asked Mr. Slide.

"No, there was n't. I know who has been telling you. That's Lizzie Eustace, and just like her mischief. The way of it was this;—Lopez, who was very angry, had boasted that he would bring the Duke down on his marrow-bones. I was laughing at him as we sat at dinner one day afterwards, and he took out the cheque and showed it me. There was the Duke's own signature for £500,—'Omnium,' as plain as letters could make it." Armed with this full information, Mr. Slide felt that he had done all that the most punctilious devotion to accuracy could demand of him, and immediately shut himself up in his cage at the People's Banner office and went to work.

This occurred about the first week in January. The Duke was then at Matching with his wife and a very small party. The singular arrangement which had been effected by the Duchess in the early autumn had passed off without any wonderful effects. It had been done by her in pique, and the result had been apparently so absurd that it had at first frightened her. But in the end it answered very well. The Duke took great pleasure in Lady Rosina's company, and enjoyed the comparative solitude which enabled him to work all day without interruption. His wife protested that it was just what she liked, though it must be feared that she soon became weary of it. To Lady Rosina it was of course a Paradise on earth. In September, Phineas Finn and his wife came to them, and in October there were other relaxations and other business. The Prime Minister and his wife visited their Sovereign, and he made some very useful speeches through the country on his old favourite subject of decimal coinage. At Christmas, for a fortnight, they went to Gatherum Castle and entertained the neighbourhood,—the nobility and squirearchy dining there on one day, and the tenants and other farmers on another. All this went very smoothly, and the Duke did not become outrageously unhappy because the People's Banner made sundry severe remarks on the absence of Cabinet Councils through the autumn.

After Christmas they returned to Matching, and had some of their old friends with them. There was the Duke of St. Bungay and the Duchess, and Phineas Finn and his wife, and Lord and Lady Cantrip, Barrington Erle, and one or two others. But at this period there came a great trouble. One morning as the Duke sat in his own room after breakfast he read an article in the People's Banner, of which the following sentences were a part: "We wish to know by whom were paid the expenses incurred by Mr. Ferdinand Lopez during the late contest at Silverbridge. It may be that they were paid by that gentleman himself,—in which case we shall have nothing further to say, not caring at the present moment to inquire whether those expenses were or were not excessive. It may be that they were paid by subscription among his political friends,—and if so, again we shall be satisfied. Or it is possible that funds were supplied by a new political club of which we have lately heard much, and with the action of such a body we of course have nothing to do. If an assurance can be given to us by Mr. Lopez or his friends that such was the case we shall be satisfied.

"But a report has reached us, and we may say more than a report, which makes it our duty to ask this question. Were those expenses paid out of the private pocket of the present Prime Minister? If so, we maintain that we have discovered a blot in that nobleman's character which it is our duty to the public to expose. We will go further and say that if it be so,—if these expenses were paid out of the private pocket of the Duke of Omnium, it is not fit that that nobleman should any longer hold the high office which he now fills.

"We know that a peer should not interfere in elections for the House of Commons. We certainly know that a Minister of the Crown should not attempt to purchase parliamentary support. We happen to know also the almost more than public manner,—are we not justified in saying the ostentation?—with which at the last election the Duke repudiated all that influence with the borough which his predecessors, and we believe he himself, had so long exercised. He came forward telling us that he, at least, meant to have clean hands;—that he would not do as his forefathers had done;—that he would not even do as he himself had done in former years. What are we to think of the Duke of Omnium as a Minister of this country, if, after such assurances, he has out of his own pocket paid the electioneering expenses of a candidate at Silverbridge?"

There was much more in the article, but the passages

quoted will suffice to give the reader a sufficient idea of the accusation made, and which the Duke read in the retirement of his own chamber.

He read it twice before he allowed himself to think of the matter. The statement made was at any rate true to the letter. He had paid the man's electioneering expenses. That he had done so from the purest motives he knew and the reader knows;—but he could not even explain those motives without exposing his wife. Since the cheque was sent he had never spoken of the occurrence to any human being,—but he had thought of it very often. At the time his private secretary, with much hesitation, almost with trepidation, had counselled him not to send the money. The Duke was a man with whom it was very easy to work, whose courtesy to all dependent on him was almost exaggerated, who never found fault, and was anxious as far as possible to do everything for himself. The comfort of those around him was always matter of interest to him. Everything he held, he held as it were in trust for the enjoyment of others. But he was a man whom it was very difficult to advise. He did not like advice. He was so thin-skinned that any counsel offered to him took the form of criticism. When cautioned what shoes he should wear,—as had been done by Lady Rosina; or what wine or what horses he should buy, as was done by his butler and coachman, he was thankful, taking no pride to himself for knowledge as to shoes, wine, or horses. But as to his own conduct, private or public, as to any question of politics, as to his opinions and resolutions, he was jealous of interference. Mr. Warburton therefore had almost trembled when asking the Duke whether he was quite sure about sending the money to Lopez. "Quite sure," the Duke had answered, having at that time made up his mind. Mr. Warburton had not dared to express a further doubt, and the money had been sent. But from the moment of sending it doubts had repeated themselves in the Prime Minister's mind.

Now he sat with the newspaper in his hand thinking of it. Of course it was open to him to take no notice of the matter,—to go on as though he had not seen the article, and to let the thing die if it would die. But he knew Mr. Quintus Slide and his paper well enough to be sure that it would not die. The charge would be repeated in the People's Banner till it was copied into other papers; and then the further question would be asked,—Why had the Prime Minister allowed such an accusation to remain unanswered? But if he did notice it, what notice should he take of it? It was true. And surely he had a right to do what he liked with his own money so long as he disobeyed no law. He had bribed no one. He had spent his money with no corrupt purpose. His sense of honour had taught him to think that the man had received injury through his wife's imprudence, and that he therefore was responsible as far as the pecuniary loss was concerned. He was not ashamed of the thing he had done;—but yet he was ashamed that it should be discussed in public.

Why had he allowed himself to be put into a position in which he was subject to such grievous annoyance? Since he had held his office he had not had a happy day, nor,—so he told himself,—had he received from it any slightest gratification, nor could he buoy himself up with the idea that he was doing good service for his country. After a while he walked into the next room and showed the paper to Mr. Warburton. "Perhaps you were right," he said, "when you told me not to send that money."

"It will matter nothing," said the private secretary when he had read it,—thinking, however, that it might matter much, but wishing to spare the Duke.

"I was obliged to repay the man as the Duchess had,—had encouraged him. The Duchess had not quite,—quite understood my wishes." Mr. Warburton knew the whole history now, having discussed it all with the Duchess more than once.

"I think your Grace should take no notice of the article."

No notice was taken of it, but three days afterwards there appeared a short paragraph in large type,—beginning with a question. "Does the Duke of Omnium intend to answer the question asked by us last Friday? Is it true that he paid the expenses of Mr. Lopez when that gentleman stood for Silverbridge? The Duke may be assured that the question shall be repeated till it is answered." This the Duke also saw and took to his private secretary.

"I would do nothing at any rate till it be noticed in some other paper," said the private secretary. "The People's Banner is known to be scandalous."

"Of course it is scandalous. And, moreover, I know the motives and the malice of the wretched man who is the editor. But the paper is read, and the foul charge if repeated will become known, and the allegation made is true. I did pay the man's election expenses;—and, moreover, to tell the truth openly as I do not scruple to do to you, I am not prepared to state publicly the reason why I did so. And nothing but that reason could justify me."

"Then I think your Grace should state it."

"I cannot do so."

"The Duke of St. Bungay is here. Would it not be well to tell the whole affair to him?"

"I will think of it. I do not know why I should have troubled you."

"Oh, my lord!"

"Except that there is always some comfort in speaking even of one's trouble. I will think about it. In the meantime you need perhaps not mention it again."

"Who? I? Oh, certainly not."

"I did not mean to others,—but to myself. I will turn it in my mind and speak of it when I have decided anything." And he did think about it,—thinking of it so much that he could hardly get the matter out of his mind day or night. To his wife he did not allude to it at all. Why trouble her with it? She had caused the evil, and he had cautioned her as to the future. She could not help him out of the difficulty she had created. He continued to turn the matter over in his thoughts till he so magnified it, and built it up into such proportions, that he again began to think that he must resign. It was, he thought, true that a man should not remain in office as Prime Minister who in such a matter could not clear his own conduct.

Then there was a third attack in the People's Banner, and after that the matter was noticed in the Evening Pulpit. This notice the Duke of St. Bungay saw and mentioned to Mr. Warburton. "Has the Duke spoken to you of some allegations made in the press as to the expenses of the late election at Silverbridge?" The old Duke was at this time, and had been for some months, in a state of nervous anxiety about his friend. He had almost admitted to himself that he had been wrong in recommending a politician so weakly organised to take the office of Prime Minister. He had expected the man to be more manly,— had perhaps expected him to be less conscientiously scrupulous. But now, as the thing had been done, it must be maintained. Who else was there to take the office? Mr. Gresham would not. To keep Mr. Daubeny out was the very essence of the Duke of St. Bungay's life,—the turning-point of his political creed, the one grand duty the idea of which was always present to him. And he had, moreover, a most true and most affectionate regard for the man whom he now supported, appreciating the sweetness of his character,—believing still in the Minister's patriotism, intelligence, devotion, and honesty; though he was forced to own to himself that the strength of a man's heart was wanting.

"Yes," said Warburton; "he did mention it."

"Does it trouble him?"

"Perhaps you had better speak to him about it." Both the old Duke and the private secretary were as fearful and nervous about the Prime Minister as a mother is for a weakly child. They could hardly tell their opinions to each other, but they understood one another, and between them they coddled their Prime Minister. They were specially nervous as to what might be done by the Prime Minister's wife, nervous as to what was done by every one who came in contact with him. It had been once suggested by the private secretary that Lady Rosina should be sent for, as she had a soothing effect upon the Prime Minister's spirit.

"Has it irritated him?" asked the Duke.

"Well;—yes, it has;—a little, you know. I think your Grace had better speak to him;—and not perhaps mention my name." The Duke of St. Bungay nodded his head, and said that he would speak to the great man and would not mention any one's name.

And he did speak. "Has any one said anything to you about it?" asked the Prime Minister.

"I saw it in the Evening Pulpit myself. I have not heard it mentioned anywhere."

"I did pay the man's expenses."

"You did!"

"Yes,—when the election was over, and, as far as I can remember, some time after it was over. He wrote to me saying that he had incurred such and such expenses, and asking me to repay him. I sent him a cheque for the amount."

"But why?"

"I was bound in honour to do it."

"But why?"

There was a short pause before this second question was answered. "The man had been induced to stand by representations made to him from my house. He had been, I fear, promised certain support which certainly was not given him when the time came."

"You had not promised it?"

"No;—not I."

"Was it the Duchess?"

"Upon the whole, my friend, I think I would rather not discuss it further, even with you. It is right that you should know that I did pay the money,—and also why I paid it. It may also be necessary that we should consider whether there may be any further probable result from my doing so. But the money has been paid, by me myself,—and was paid for the reason I have stated."

"A question might be asked in the House."

"If so, it must be answered as I have answered you. I certainly shall not shirk any responsibility that may be attached to me."

"You would not like Warburton to write a line to the newspaper?"

"What;—to the People's Banner!"

"It began there, did it? No, not to the People's Banner, but to the Evening Pulpit. He could say, you know, that the money was paid by you, and that the payment had been made because your agents had misapprehended your instructions."

"It would not be true," said the Prime Minister slowly.

"As far as I can understand that was what occurred," said the other Duke.

"My instructions were not misapprehended. They were disobeyed. I think that perhaps we had better say no more about it."

"Do not think that I wish to press you," said the old man tenderly; "but I fear that something ought to be done;—I mean for your own comfort."

"My comfort!" said the Prime Minister. "That has vanished long ago;—and my peace of mind, and my happiness."

"There has been nothing done which cannot be explained with perfect truth. There has been no impropriety."

"I do not know."

"The money was paid simply from an over-nice sense of honour."

"It cannot be explained. I cannot explain it even to you; and how then can I do it to all the gaping fools of the country who are ready to trample upon a man simply because he is in some way conspicuous among them?"

After that the old Duke again spoke to Mr. Warburton, but Mr. Warburton was very loyal to his chief. "Could one do anything by speaking to the Duchess?" said the old Duke.

"I think not."

"I suppose it was her Grace who did it all."

"I cannot say. My own impression is that he had better wait till the Houses meet, and then, if any question is asked, let it be answered. He himself would do it in the House of Lords, or Mr. Finn or Barrington Erle, in our House. It would surely be enough to explain that his Grace had been made to believe that the man had received encouragement at Silverbridge from his own agents, which he himself had not intended should be given, and that therefore he had thought it right to pay the money. After such an explanation what more could any one say?"

"You might do it yourself."

"I never speak."

"But in such a case as that you might do so; and then there would be no necessity for him to talk to another person on the matter."

So the affair was left for the present, though the allusions to it in the People's Banner were still continued. Nor did any other of the Prime Minister's colleagues dare to speak to him on the subject. Barrington Erle and Phineas Finn talked of it among themselves, but they did not mention it even to the Duchess. She would have gone to her husband at once; and they were too careful of him to risk such a proceeding.

It certainly was the case that among them they coddled the Prime Minister.

CHAPTER XXIV.

CODDLING THE PRIME MINISTER.

PARLIAMENT was to meet on the 12th of February, and it was of course necessary that there should be a Cabinet Council before that time. The Prime Minister, about the end of the third week in January, was prepared to name a day for this, and did so, most unwillingly. But he was then ill, and talked both to his friend the old Duke and his private secretary of having the meeting held without him. "Impossible!" said the old Duke.

"If I could not go it would have to be possible."

"We could all come here if it were necessary."

"Bring fourteen or fifteen ministers out of town because a poor creature such as I am is ill!" But in truth the Duke of St. Bungay hardly believed in his illness. The Prime Minister was unhappy rather than ill.

By this time everybody in the House,—and almost everybody in the country who read the newspapers,—had heard of Mr. Lopez and his election expenses,—except the Duchess. No one had yet dared to tell her. She saw the newspapers daily, but probably did not read them very attentively. Nevertheless she knew that something was wrong. Mr. Warburton hovered about the Prime Minister more tenderly than usual; the Duke of St. Bungay was more concerned; the world around her was more mysterious, and her husband more wretched. "What is it that's going on?" she said one day to Phineas Finn.

"Everything,—in the same dull way as usual."

"If you don't tell me I'll never speak to you again. I know there is something wrong."

"The Duke, I'm afraid, is not quite well."

"What makes him ill? I know well when he's ill and when he's well. He's troubled by something."

"I think he is, Duchess. But as he has not spoken to me I am loath to make guesses. If there be anything, I can only guess at it."

Then she questioned Mrs. Finn, and got an answer which, if not satisfactory, was at any rate explanatory. "I think he is uneasy about that Silverbridge affair."

"What Silverbridge affair?"

"You know that he paid the expenses which that man Lopez says that he incurred."

"Yes;—I know that."

"And you know that that other man Slide has found it out, and published it all in the People's Banner?"

"No!"

"Yes, indeed. And a whole army of accusations has been brought against him. I have never liked to tell you, and yet I do not think that you should be left in the dark."

"Everybody deceives me," said the Duchess angrily.

"Nay;—there has been no deceit."

"Everybody keeps things from me. I think you will kill me among you. It was my doing. Why do they attack him? I will write to the papers. I encouraged the man after Plantagenet had determined that he should not be assisted,—and, because I had done so, he paid the man his beggarly money. What is there to hurt him in that? Let me bear it. My back is broad enough."

"The Duke is very sensitive."

"I hate people to be sensitive. It makes them cowards. A man when he is afraid of being blamed, dares not at last even show himself, and has to be wrapped up in lamb's-wool."

"Of course men are differently organised."

"Yes;—but the worst of it is, that when they suffer from this weakness, which you call sensitiveness, they think that they are made of finer material than other people. Men should n't be made of Sevres china, but of good stone earthenware. However, I don't want to abuse him, poor fellow."

"I don't think you ought."

"I know what that means. You do want to abuse me. So they 've been bullying him about the money he paid to that man Lopez. How did anybody know anything about it?"

"Lopez must have told of it," said Mrs. Finn.

"The worst, my dear, of trying to know a great many people is that you are sure to get hold of some that are very bad. Now that man is very bad. Yet they say he has married a nice wife."

"That's often the case, Duchess."

"And the contrary;—is n't it, my dear? But I shall have it out with Plantagenet. If I have to write letters to all the newspapers myself, I 'll put it right." She certainly coddled her husband less than the others; and, indeed, in her heart of hearts disapproved altogether of the coddling system. But she was wont at this particular time to be somewhat tender to him because she was aware that she herself had been imprudent. Since he had discovered her interference at Silverbridge, and had made her understand its pernicious results, she had been,—not, perhaps, shamefaced, for that word describes a condition to which hardly any series of misfortunes could have reduced the Duchess of Omnium,—but inclined to quiescence by feelings of penitence. She was less disposed than heretofore to attack him with what the world of yesterday calls "chaff," or with what the world of to-day calls "cheek." She would not admit to herself that she was cowed;—but the greatness of the game and the high interest attached to her husband's position did in some degree dismay her. Nevertheless she executed her purpose of "having it out with Plantagenet."—"I have just heard," she said, having knocked at the door of his own room, and having found him alone,—"I have just heard, for the first time, that there is a row about the money you paid to Mr. Lopez."

"Who told you?"

"Nobody told me,—in the usual sense of the word. I presumed that something was the matter, and then I got it out from Marie. Why had you not told me?"

"Why should I tell you?"

"But why not? If anything troubled me I should tell you. That is, if it troubled me much."

"You take it for granted that this does trouble me much." He was smiling as he said this, but the smile passed very quickly from his face. "I will not, however, deceive you. It does trouble me."

"I knew very well that something was wrong."

"I have not complained."

"One can see as much as that without words. What

is it that you fear? What can the man do to you? What matter is it to you if such a one as that pours out his malice on you? Let it run off like the rain from the housetops. You are too big even to be stung by such a reptile as that." He looked into her face, admiring the energy with which she spoke to him. "As for answering him," she continued to say, "that may or may not be proper. If it should be done, there are people to do it. But I am speaking of your own inner self. You have a shield against your equals, and a sword to attack them with if necessary. Have you no armour of proof against such a creature as that? Have you nothing inside you to make you feel that he is too contemptible to be regarded?"

"Nothing," he said.

"Oh, Plantagenet!"

"Cora, there are different natures which have each their own excellencies and their own defects. I will not admit that I am a coward, believing as I do that I could dare to face necessary danger. But I cannot endure to have my character impugned,—even by Mr. Slide and Mr. Lopez."

"What matter,—if you are in the right? Why blench if your conscience accuses you of no fault? I would not blench even if it did. What;—is a man to be put in the front of everything, and then to be judged as though he could give all his time to the picking of his steps?"

"Just so! And he must pick them more warily than another."

"I do not believe it. You see all this with jaundiced eyes. I read somewhere the other day that the great ships have always little worms attached to them, but that the great ships swim on and know nothing of the worms."

"The worms conquer at last."

"They should n't conquer me! After all, what is it that they say about the money? That you ought not to have paid it?"

"I begin to think that I was wrong to pay it."

"You certainly were not wrong. I had led the man on. I had been mistaken. I had thought that he was a gentleman. Having led him on at first, before you had spoken to me, I did not like to go back from my word. I did go to the man at Silverbridge who sells the pots, and no doubt the man, when thus encouraged, told it all to Lopez. When Lopez went to the town he did suppose that he would have what the people call the Castle interest."

"And I had done so much to prevent it!"

"What 's the use of going back to that now, unless you want me to put my neck down to be trodden on? I am confessing my own sins as fast as I can."

"God knows I would not have you trodden on."

"I am willing,—if it be necessary. Then came the question;—as I had done this evil, how was it to be rectified? Any man with a particle of spirit would have taken his rubs and said nothing about it. But as this man asked for the money, it was right that he should have it. If it is all made public he won't get very well out of it."

"What does that matter to me?"

"Nor shall I;—only luckily I do not mind it."

"But I mind it for you."

"You must throw me to the whale. Let somebody say in so many words that the Duchess did so and so.

It was very wicked, no doubt; but they can't kill me,—nor yet dismiss me. And I won't resign. In point of fact, I shan't be a penny the worse for it."

"But I should resign."

"If all the Ministers in England were to give up as soon as their wives do foolish things, that question about the Queen's Government would become very difficult."

"They may do foolish things, dear; and yet——"

"And yet what?"

"And yet not interfere in politics."

"That's all you know about it, Plantagenet. Does n't everybody know that Mrs. Daubeny got Dr. Mac-Fuzlem made a bishop, and that Mrs. Gresham got her husband to make that hazy speech about women's rights, so that nobody should know which way he meant to go? There are others just as bad as me, only I don't think they get blown up so much. You do now as I ask you."

"I could n't do it, Cora. Though the stain were but a little spot, and the thing to be avoided political destruction, I could not ride out of the punishment by fixing that stain on my wife. I will not have your name mentioned. A man's wife should be talked about by no one."

"That's highfaluting, Plantagenet."

"Glencora, in these matters you must allow me to judge for myself, and I will judge. I will never say that I did n't do it;—but that it was my wife who did."

"Adam said so,—because he chose to tell the truth."

"And Adam has been despised ever since,—not because he ate the apple, but because he imputed the eating of it to a woman. I will not do it. We have had enough of this now." Then she turned to go away;—

but he called her back. "Kiss me, dear," he said. Then she stooped over him and kissed him. "Do not think I am angry with you because the thing vexes me. I am dreaming always of some day when we may go away together with the children, and rest in some pretty spot, and live as other people live."

"It would be very stupid," she muttered to herself as she left the room.

He did go up to town for the Cabinet meeting. Whatever may have been done at that august assembly there was certainly no resignation, or the world would have heard it. It is probable, too, that nothing was said about these newspaper articles. Things if left to themselves will generally die at last. The old Duke and Phineas Finn and Barrington Erle were all of opinion that the best plan for the present was to do nothing. "Has anything been settled?" the Duchess asked Phineas when he came back.

"Oh yes;—the Queen's Speech. But there is n't very much in it."

"But about the payment of this money?"

"I have n't heard a word about it," said Phineas.

"You 're just as bad as all the rest, Mr. Finn, with your pretended secrecy. A girl with her first sweetheart is n't half so fussy as a young Cabinet Minister."

"The Cabinet Ministers get used to it sooner, I think," said Phineas Finn.

Parliament had already met before Mr. Slide had quite determined in what way he would carry on the war. He could indeed go on writing pernicious articles about the Prime Minister ad infinitum,—from year's end to year's end. It was an occupation in which he took delight, and for which he imagined himself to be peculiarly well suited. But readers will become tired even of abuse if it be not varied. And the very continuation of such attacks would seem to imply that they were not much heeded. Other papers had indeed taken the matter up,—but they had taken it up only to drop it. The subject had not been their own. The little discovery had been due not to their acumen, and did not therefore bear with them the highest interest. It had almost seemed as though nothing would come of it;—for Mr. Slide in his wildest ambition could have hardly imagined the vexation and hesitation, the nervousness and serious discussions which his words had occasioned among the great people at Matching. But certainly the thing must not be allowed to pass away as a matter of no moment. Mr. Slide had almost worked his mind up to real horror as he thought of it. What! A prime minister, a peer, a great duke,—put a man forward as a candidate for a borough, and, when the man was beaten, pay his expenses! Was this to be done,—to be done and found out, and then nothing come of it in these days of purity, when a private member of Parliament, some mere nobody, loses his seat because he has given away a few bushels of coals or a score or two of rabbits! Mr. Slide's energetic love of public virtue was scandalised as he thought of the probability of such a catastrophe. To his thinking public virtue consisted in carping at men high placed, in abusing ministers and judges and bishops,—and especially in finding out something for which they might be abused. His own public virtue was in this matter very great, for it was he who had ferreted out the secret. For his intelligence and energy in that matter the country owed him much. But the country would pay him nothing, would give him none of the credit he desired, would rob him of this special opportunity of declaring a dozen times that the People's Banner was the surest guardian of the people's liberty,—unless he could succeed in forcing the matter further into public notice. "How terrible is the apathy of the people at large," said Mr. Slide to himself, "when they cannot be wakened by such a revelation as this!"

Mr. Slide knew very well what ought to be the next step. Proper notice should be given and a question should be asked in Parliament. Some gentleman should declare that he had noticed such and such statements in the public press, and that he thought it right to ask whether such and such payments had been made by the Prime Minister. In his meditations Mr. Slide went so far as to arrange the very words which the indignant gentleman should utter, among which words was a graceful allusion to a certain public-spirited newspaper. He did even go so far as to arrange a compliment to the editor,—but in doing so he knew that he was thinking only of that which ought to be, and not of that which would be. The time had not come as yet in which the editor of a newspaper in this country received a tithe of the honour due to him. But the question in any form, with or without a compliment to the People's Banner, would be the thing that was now desirable.

Who was to ask the question? If public spirit were really strong in the country there would be no difficulty on that point. The crime committed had been so horrible that all the great politicians of the country ought to compete for the honour of asking it. What greater service can be trusted to the hands of a great man than that of exposing the sins of the rulers of the nation? So thought Mr. Slide. But he knew that he was in advance of the people, and that the matter would not be seen in the proper light by those who ought so to see it. There might be a difficulty in getting any peer to ask the question in the House in which the Prime Minister himself sat, and even in the other House there was now but little of that acrid, indignant opposition upon which, in Mr. Slide's opinion, the safety of the nation altogether depends.

When the statement was first made in the People's Banner, Lopez had come to Mr. Slide at once and had demanded his authority for making it. Lopez had found the statement to be most injurious to himself. He had been paid his election expenses twice over, making a clear profit of £500 by the transaction; and, though the matter had at one time troubled his conscience, he had already taught himself to regard it as one of those bygones to which a wise man seldom refers. But now Mr. Wharton would know that he had been cheated, should this statement reach him. "Who gave you authority to publish all this?" asked Lopez, who at this time had become intimate with Mr. Slide.

"Is it true, Lopez?" asked the editor.

"Whatever was done was done in private,—between me and the Duke."

"Dukes, my dear fellow, can't be private, and certainly not when they are Prime Ministers."

"But you 've no right to publish these things about me."

"Is it true? If it 's true I have got every right to publish it. If it 's not true, I 've got the right to ask the question. If you will 'ave to do with Prime Ministers you can't 'ide yourself under a bushel. Tell me this;—is it true? You might as well go 'and in 'and with me in the matter. You can't 'urt yourself. And if you oppose me,—why I shall oppose you."

"You can't say anything of me."

"Well;—I don't know about that. I can generally 'it pretty 'ard if I feel inclined. But I don't want to 'it you. As regards you I can tell the story one way, —or the other, just as you please." Lopez, seeing it in the same light, at last agreed that the story should be told in a manner not inimical to himself. The present project of his life was to leave his troubles in England,—Sexty Parker being the worst of them,—and get away to Guatemala. In arranging this the good word of Mr. Slide might not benefit him, but his ill word might injure him. And then, let him do what he would, the matter must be made public. Should Mr. Wharton hear of it,—as of course he would,—it must be brazened out. He could not keep it from Mr. Wharton's ears by quarrelling with Quintus Slide.

"It was true," said Lopez.

"I knew it before just as well as though I had seen it. I ain't often very wrong in these things. You asked him for the money,—and threatened him."

"I don't know about threatening him."

"'E would n't have sent it else."

"I told him that I had been deceived by his people in the borough, and that I had been put to expense through the misrepresentations of the Duchess. I don't think I did ask for the money. But he sent a cheque, and of course I took it."

"Of course;—of course. You could n't give me a copy of your letter."

"Never kept a copy." He had a copy in his breast

coat-pocket at that moment, and Slide did not for a moment believe the statement made. But in such discussions one man hardly expects truth from another. Mr. Slide certainly never expected truth from any man. "He sent the cheque almost without a word," said Lopez.

"He did write a note, I suppose?"

"Just a few words."

"Could you let me 'ave that note?"

"I destroyed it at once." This was also in his breast pocket at the time.

"Did 'e write it 'imself?"

"I think it was his private secretary, Mr. Warburton."

"You must be sure, you know. Which was it?"

"It was Mr. Warburton."

"Was it civil?"

"Yes, it was. If it had been uncivil I should have sent it back. I'm not the man to take impudence even from a duke."

"If you'll give me those two letters, Lopez, I'll stick to you through thick and thin. By heavens, I will! Think what the People's Banner is. You may come to want that kind of thing some of these days." Lopez remained silent, looking into the other man's eager face. "I shouldn't publish them, you know; but it would be so much to me to have the evidence in my hands. You might do worse, you know, than make a friend of me."

"You won't publish them?"

"Certainly not. I shall only refer to them."

Then Lopez pulled a bundle of papers out of his pocket. "There they are," he said.

"Well," said Slide, when he had read them; "it is one of the rummest transactions I ever 'eard of. Why did 'e send the money? That's what I want to know. As far as the claim goes, you 'ad n't a leg to stand on."

"Not legally."

"You 'ad n't a leg to stand on any way. But that does n't much matter. He sent the money, and the sending of the money was corrupt. Who shall I get to ask the question? I suppose young Fletcher would n't do it?"

"They 're birds of a feather," said Lopez.

"Birds of a feather do fall out sometimes. Or Sir Orlando Drought? I wonder whether Sir Orlando would do it. If any man ever 'ated another Sir Orlando Drought must 'ate the Duke of Omnium."

"I don't think he 'd let himself down to that kind of thing."

"Let 'imself down! I don't see any letting down in it. But those men who have been in Cabinets do stick to one another even when they are enemies. They think themselves so mighty that they ought n't to be 'andled like other man. But I'll let 'em know that I'll 'andle 'em. A Cabinet Minister or a cowboy is the same to Quintus Slide when he has got his pen in 'is 'and."

On the next morning there came out another article in the People's Banner, in which the writer declared that he had in his own possession the damnatory correspondence between the Prime Minister and the late candidate at Silverbridge. "The Prime Minister may deny the fact," said the article. "We do not think it probable, but it is possible. We wish to be fair and above-board in everything. And therefore we at once inform the noble Duke that the entire correspondence is in our hands." In saying this Mr. Quintus Slide thought that he had quite kept the promise which he made when he said that he would only refer to the letters.

CHAPTER XXV.

"I CAN SLEEP HERE TO-NIGHT, I SUPPOSE?"

THAT scheme of going to Guatemala had been in the first instance propounded by Lopez with the object of frightening Mr. Wharton into terms. There had, indeed, been some previous thoughts on the subject,—some plan projected before his marriage; but it had been resuscitated mainly with the hope that it might be efficacious to extract money. When by degrees the son-in-law began to feel that even this would not be operative on his father-in-law's purse,—when under this threat neither Wharton nor Emily gave way,—and when, with the view of strengthening his threat, he renewed his inquiries as to Guatemala and found that there might still be an opening for him in that direction,—the threat took the shape of a true purpose, and he began to think that he would in real earnest try his fortunes in a new world. From day to day things did not go well with him, and from day to day Sexty Parker became more unendurable. It was impossible for him to keep from his partner this plan of emigration,—but he endeavoured to make Parker believe that the thing, if done at all, was not to be done till all his affairs were settled,—or in other words all his embarrassments cleared by downright money payments, and that Mr. Wharton was to make these payments on the condition that he thus expatriated himself. But Mr. Wharton had made no such promise. Though the threatened day came nearer and nearer he could not bring himself to purchase a short respite for his daughter by paying money to a scoundrel,—which payment he felt sure would be of no permanent service. During all this time Mr. Wharton was very wretched. If he could have freed his daughter from her marriage by half his fortune he would have done it without a second thought. If he could have assuredly purchased the permanent absence of her husband, he would have done it at a large price. But let him pay what he would, he could see his way to no security. From day to day he became more strongly convinced of the rascality of this man who was his son-in-law, and who was still an inmate in his own house. Of course he had accusations enough to make within his own breast against his daughter, who, when the choice was open to her, would not take the altogether fitting husband provided for her, but had declared herself to be broken-hearted forever unless she were allowed to throw herself away upon this wretched creature. But he blamed himself almost as much as he did her. Why had he allowed himself to be so enervated by her prayers at last as to surrender everything,—as he had done? How could he presume to think that he should be allowed to escape, when he had done so little to prevent this misery?

He spoke to Emily about it,—not often indeed, but with great earnestness. "I have done it myself," she said, "and I will bear it."

"Tell him you cannot go till you know to what home you are going."

"That is for him to consider. I have begged him to let me remain, and I can say no more. If he chooses to take me, I shall go."

Then he spoke to her about money. "Of course I have money," he said. "Of course I have enough both for you and Everett. If I could do any good by giving it to him, he should have it."

"Papa," she answered, "I will never again ask you to give him a single penny. That must be altogether between you and him. He is what they call a speculator. Money is not safe with him."

"I shall have to send it you when you are in want."

"When I am—dead there will be no more to be sent. Do not look like that, papa. I know what I have done, and I must bear it. I have thrown away my life. It is just that. If baby had lived it would have been different." This was about the end of January, and then Mr. Wharton heard of the great attack made by Mr. Quintus Slide against the Prime Minister, and heard, of course, of the payment alleged to have been made to Ferdinand Lopez by the Duke on the score of the election at Silverbridge. Some persons spoke to him on the subject. One or two friends at the club asked him what he supposed to be the truth in the matter, and Mrs. Roby inquired of him on the subject. "I have asked Lopez," she said, "and I am sure from his manner that he did get the money."

"I don't know anything about it," said Mr. Wharton.

"If he did get it I think he was very clever." It was well known at this time to Mrs. Roby that the Lopez marriage had been a failure, that Lopez was not a rich man, and that Emily, as well as her father, was discontented and unhappy. She had latterly heard of the Guatemala scheme, and had of course expressed her horror. But she sympathised with Lopez rather than with his wife, thinking that if Mr. Wharton would only open his pockets wide enough things might still be right. " It was all the Duchess's fault, you know," she said to the old man.

"I know nothing about it, and when I want to know I certainly shall not come to you. The misery he has brought upon me is so great that it makes me wish that I had never seen any one who knew him."

"It was Everett who introduced him to your house."

"It was you who introduced him to Everett."

"There you are wrong,—as you so often are, Mr. Wharton. Everett met him first at the club."

"What's the use of arguing about it? It was at your house that Emily met him. It was you that did it. I wonder you can have the face to mention his name to me."

"And the man living all the time in your own house!"

Up to this time Mr. Wharton had not mentioned to a single person the fact that he had paid his son-in-law's election expenses at Silverbridge. He had given him the cheque without much consideration, with the feeling that by doing so he would in some degree benefit his daughter; and had since regretted the act, finding that no such payment from him could be of any service to Emily. But the thing had been done,—and there had been, so far, an end of it. In no subsequent discussion would Mr. Wharton have alluded to it, had not circumstances now as it were driven it back upon his mind. And since the day on which he had paid that money he had been, as he declared to himself, swindled over and over again by his son-in-law. There was the dinner in Manchester Square, and after that the brougham, and the rent, and a score of bills, some of which he had paid and some declined to pay! And yet he had said but little to the man himself of all these injuries. Of what use was it to say anything? Lopez would simply reply that he had asked him to pay nothing. "What is it all," Lopez had once said, "to the fortune I had a right to expect with your daughter?" "You had no right to expect a shilling," Wharton had said. Then Lopez had shrugged his shoulders, and there had been an end of it.

But now, if this rumour were true, there had been positive dishonesty. From whichever source the man might have got the money first, if the money had been twice got, the second payment had been fraudulently obtained. Surely if the accusation had been untrue Lopez would have come to him and declared it to be false, knowing what must otherwise be his thoughts. Lately, in the daily worry of his life, he had avoided all conversation with the man. He would not allow his mind to contemplate clearly what was coming. He entertained some irrational, undefined hope that something would at last save his daughter from the threatened banishment. It might be, if he held his own hand tight enough, that there would not be money enough even to pay for her passage out. As for her outfit Lopez would of course order what he wanted and have the bills sent to Manchester Square. Whether or not this was being done neither he nor Emily knew. And thus matters went on without much speech between the two men. But now the old barrister thought that he was bound to speak. He therefore waited on a certain morning till Lopez had come down, having previously desired his daughter to leave the room. "Lopez," he asked, "what is this that the newspapers are saying about your expenses at Silverbridge?"

Lopez had expected the attack and had endeavoured to prepare himself for it. "I should have thought, sir, that you would not have paid much attention to such statements in a newspaper."

"When they concern myself, I do. I paid your electioneering expenses."

"You certainly subscribed £500 towards them, Mr. Wharton."

"I subscribed nothing, sir. There was no question of a subscription,—by which you intend to imply contribution from various sources. You told me that the contest cost you £500 and that sum I handed to you, with the full understanding on your part, as well as on mine, that I was paying for the whole. Was that so?"

"Have it your own way, sir."

"If you are not more precise, I shall think that you have defrauded me."

"Defrauded you!"

"Yes, sir;—defrauded me, or the Duke of Omnium. The money is gone, and it matters little which. But if that be so I shall know that either from him or from me you have raised money under false pretences."

"Of course, Mr. Wharton, from you I must bear whatever you may choose to say."

"Is it true that you have applied to the Duke of Omnium for money on account of your expenses at Silverbridge, and is it true that he has paid you money on that score?"

"Mr. Wharton, as I said just now, I am bound to hear and to bear from you anything that you may choose to say. Your connection with my wife and your age alike restrain my resentment. But I am not bound to answer your questions when they are accompanied by such language as you have chosen to use, and I refuse to answer any further questions on this subject."

"Of course I know that you have taken the money from the Duke."

"Then why do you ask me?"

"And of course I know that you are as well aware as I am of the nature of the transaction. That you can brazen it out without a blush only proves to me that you have got beyond the reach of shame!"

"Very well, sir."

"And you have no further explanation to make?"

"What do you expect me to say? Without knowing any of the facts of the case,—except the one, that you contributed £500 to my election expenses,—you take upon yourself to tell me that I am a shameless, fraudulent swindler. And then you ask for a further explanation! In such a position is it likely that I shall explain anything;—that I can be in a humour to be explanatory? Just turn it all over in your own mind, and ask yourself the question."

"I have turned it over in my own mind, and I have asked myself the question, and I do not think it probable that you should wish to explain anything. I shall take steps to let the Duke know that I as your father-in-law had paid the full sum which you had stated that you had spent at Silverbridge."

"Much the Duke will care about that."

"And after what has passed I am obliged to say that the sooner you leave this house the better I shall be pleased."

"Very well, sir. Of course I shall take my wife with me."

"That must be as she pleases."

"No, Mr. Wharton. That must be as I please. She belongs to me,—not to you or to herself. Under your influence she has forgotten much of what belongs to the duty of a wife, but I do not think that she will so far have forgotten herself as to give me more trouble than to bid her come with me when I desire it."

"Let that be as it may, I must request that you, sir, will absent yourself. I will not entertain as my guest a man who has acted as you have done in this matter, —even though he be my son-in-law."

"I can sleep here to-night, I suppose?"

"Or to-morrow if it suits you. As for Emily she can remain here, if you will allow her to do so."

"That will not suit me," said Lopez.

"In that case, as far as I am concerned, I shall do whatever she may ask me to do. Good morning."

Mr. Wharton left the room, but did not leave the house. Before he did so he would see his daughter; and, thinking it probable that Lopez would also choose to see his wife, he prepared to wait in his own room. But, in about ten minutes, Lopez started from the hall door in a cab, and did so without going upstairs. Mr. Wharton had reason to believe that his son-in-law was almost destitute of money for immediate purposes. Whatever he might have would at any rate be serviceable to him before he started. Any home for Emily must be expensive; and no home in their present circumstances could be so reputable for her as one under her father's roof. He therefore almost hoped that she might still be left with him till that horrid day should come,—if it ever did come,—in which she would be taken away from him forever. "Of course, papa, I shall go if he bids me," she said, when he told her all that he thought right to tell her of that morning's interview.

"I hardly know how to advise you," said the father, meaning in truth to bring himself round to the giving of some advice adverse to her husband's will.

"I want no advice, papa."

"Want no advice! I never knew a woman who wanted it more."

"No, papa. I am bound to do as he tells me. I know what I have done. When some poor wretch has got himself into perpetual prison by his misdeeds, no advice can serve him then. So it is with me."

"You can at any rate escape from your prison."

"No;—no. I have a feeling of pride which tells me that as I chose to become the wife of my husband, —as I insisted on it in opposition to all my friends,— as I would judge for myself,—I am bound to put up with my choice. If this had come upon me through the authority of others, if I had been constrained to marry him, I think I could have reconciled myself to deserting him. But I did it myself, and I will abide by it. When he bids me go, I shall go." Poor Mr. Wharton went to his chambers, and sat there the whole day without taking a book or a paper into his hands. Could there be no rescue, no protection, no relief! He turned over in his head various plans, but in a vague and useless manner. What if the Duke were to prosecute Lopez for the fraud! What if he could induce Lopez to abandon his wife,—pledging himself by some deed not to return to her,—for, say, twenty or even thirty thousand pounds! What if he himself were to carry his daughter away to the Continent, half forcing and half persuading her to make the journey! Surely there might be some means found by which the man might be frightened into compliance. But there he sat,—and did nothing. And in the evening he ate a solitary mutton chop at the Jolly Blackbird, because he could not bear to face even his club, and then returned to his chambers,—to the great disgust of the old woman who had them in charge at nights. And at about midnight he crept away to his own house, a wretched old man.

Lopez when he left Manchester Square did not go in search of a new home for himself and his wife, nor during the whole of the day did he trouble himself on that subject. He spent most of the day at the rooms in Coleman Street of the San Juan Mining Association, of which Mr. Mills Happerton had once been Chairman. There was now another Chairman and other Directors; but Mr. Mills Happerton's influence had so far remained with the Company as to enable Lopez to become well known in the Company's offices, and acknowledged as a claimant for the office of resident manager at San Juan in Guatemala. Now the present project was this,—that Lopez was to start on behalf of the Company early in May, that the Company was to pay his own personal expenses out to Guatemala, and that they should allow him while there a salary of £1,000 a year for managing the affairs of the mine. As far as this offer went, the thing was true enough. It was true that Lopez had absolutely secured the place. But he had done so subject to the burden of one very serious stipulation. He was to become proprietor of fifty shares in the mine, and to pay up £100 each on those shares.

It was considered that the man who was to get £1,000 a year in Guatemala for managing the affair should at any rate assist the affair, and show his confidence in the affair to an extent as great as that. Of course the holder of these fifty shares would be as fully entitled as any other shareholder to that twenty per cent. which those who promoted the mine promised as the immediate result of the speculation.

At first Lopez had hoped that he might be enabled to defer the actual payment of the £5,000 till after he had sailed. When once out in Guatemala as manager, as manager he would doubtless remain. But by degrees he found that the payment must actually be made in advance. Now there was nobody to whom he could apply but Mr. Wharton. He was, indeed, forced to declare at the office that the money was to come from Mr. Wharton, and had given some excellent but fictitious reason why Mr. Wharton would not pay the money till February.

And in spite of all that had come and gone he still did hope that if the need to go were actually there he might even yet get the money from Mr. Wharton. Surely Mr. Wharton would sooner pay such a sum than be troubled at home with such a son-in-law. Should the worst come to the worst, of course he could raise the money by consenting to leave his wife at home. But this was not part of his plan, if he could avoid it. Five thousand pounds would be a very low price at which to sell his wife, and all that he might get from his connection with her. As long as he kept her with him he was in possession at any rate of all that Mr. Wharton would do for her. He had not therefore as yet made his final application to his father-in-law for the money, having found it possible to postpone the payment till the middle of February. His quarrel with Mr. Wharton this morning he regarded as having little or no effect upon his circumstances. Mr. Wharton would not give him the money because he loved him, nor yet from personal respect, nor from any sense of duty as to what he might owe to a son-in-law. It would be simply given as the price by which his absence might be purchased, and his absence would not be the less desirable because of this morning's quarrel.

But, even yet, he was not quite resolved as to going to Guatemala. Sexty Parker had been sucked nearly dry, and was in truth at this moment so violent with indignation and fear and remorse that Lopez did not dare to show himself in Little Tankard Yard; but still there were, even yet, certain hopes in that direction from which great results might come. If a certain new spirit which had just been concocted from the bark of trees in Central Africa, and which was called Bios, could only be made to go up in the market, everything might be satisfactorily arranged. The hoardings of London were already telling the public that if it wished to get drunk without any of the usual troubles of intoxication it must drink Bios. The public no doubt does read the literature of the hoardings, but then it reads so slowly! This Bios had hardly been twelve months on the boards as yet! But they were now increasing the size of the letters in the advertisements and the jocundity of the pictures,—and the thing might be done. There was, too, another hope,—another hope of instant moneys by which Guatemala might be staved off, as to which further explanation shall be given in a further chapter.

"I suppose I shall find Dixon a decent sort of a fellow?" said Lopez to the secretary of the Association in Coleman Street.

"Rough, you know."

"But honest?"

"Oh yes;—he's all that."

"If he's honest, and what I call loyal, I don't care a straw for anything else. One does n't expect West-End manners in Guatemala. But I shall have a deal to do with him,—and I hate a fellow that you can't depend on."

"Mr. Happerton used to think a great deal of Dixon."

"That's all right," said Lopez. Mr. Dixon was the underground manager out at the San Juan mine, and was perhaps as anxious for a loyal and honest colleague as was Mr. Lopez. If so, Mr. Dixon was very much in the way to be disappointed.

Lopez stayed at the office all the day studying the affairs of the San Juan mine, and then went to the Progress for his dinner. Hitherto he had taken no steps whatever as to getting lodgings for himself or for his wife.

CHAPTER XXVI.

MR. HARTLEPOD.

WHEN the time came at which Lopez should have left Manchester Square he was still there. Mr. Wharton, in discussing the matter with his daughter,—when wishing to persuade her that she might remain in his house even in opposition to her husband,—had not told her that he had actually desired Lopez to leave it. He had then felt sure that the man would go and would take his wife with him, but he did not even yet know the obduracy and the cleverness and the impregnability of his son-in-law. When the time came, when he saw his daughter in the morning after the notice had been given, he could not bring himself even yet to say to her that he had issued an order for his banishment. Days went by and Lopez was still there, and the old barrister said no further word on the subject. The two men never met;—or met simply in the hall or passages. Wharton himself studiously avoided such meetings, thus denying himself the commonest uses of his own house. At last Emily told him that her husband had fixed the day for her departure. The next Indian mail-packet by which they would leave England would start from Southampton on the 2nd of April, and she was to be ready to go on that day. "How is it to be till then?" the father asked in a low, uncertain voice.

"I suppose I may remain with you."

"And your husband?"

"He will be here too,—I suppose."

"Such a misery,—such a destruction of everything no man ever heard of before!" said Mr. Wharton. To this she made no reply, but continued working at some necessary preparation for her final departure. "Emily," he said, "I will make any sacrifice to prevent it. What can be done? Short of injuring Everett's interests I will do anything."

"I do not know," she said.

"You must understand something of his affairs."

"Nothing whatever. He has told me nothing of them. In earlier days,—soon after our marriage,—he bade me get money from you."

"When you wrote to me for money from Italy?"

"And after that. I have refused to do anything;—to say a word. I told him that it must be between you and him. What else could I say? And now he tells me nothing."

"I cannot think that he should want you to go with him." Then there was again a pause. "Is it because he loves you?"

"Not that, papa."

"Why then should he burden himself with a companion? His money, whatever he has, would go further without such impediment."

"Perhaps he thinks, papa, that while I am with him he has a hold upon you."

"He shall have a stronger hold by leaving you. What is he to gain? If I could only know his price."

"Ask him, papa."

"I do not even know how I am to speak to him again."

Then again there was a pause. "Papa," she said

after a while, "I have done it myself. Let me go. You will still have Everett. And it may be that after a time I shall come back to you. He will not kill me, and it may be that I shall not die."

"By God!" said Mr. Wharton, rising from his chair suddenly, "if there were money to be made by it I believe that he would murder you without a scruple." Thus it was that within eighteen months of her marriage the father spoke to his daughter of her husband.

"What am I to take with me?" she said to her husband a few days later.

"You had better ask your father."

"Why should I ask him, Ferdinand? How should he know?"

"And how should I?"

"I should have thought that you would interest yourself about it."

"Upon my word I have enough to interest me just at present, without thinking of your finery. I suppose you mean what clothes you should have?"

"I was not thinking of myself only."

"You need think of nothing else. Ask him what he pleases to allow you to spend, and then I will tell you what to get."

"I will never ask him for anything, Ferdinand."

"Then you may go without anything. You might as well do it at once, for you will have to do it sooner or later. Or, if you please, go to his tradesmen and say nothing to him about it. They will give you credit. You see how it is, my dear. He has cheated me in a most rascally manner. He has allowed me to marry his daughter, and because I did not make a bargain with him as another man would have done, he denies me the fortune I had a right to expect with you. You know that the Israelites despoiled the Egyptians, and it was taken as a merit on their part. Your father is an Egyptian to me, and I will despoil him. You can tell him that I say so if you please."

And so the days went on till the first week of February had passed, and Parliament had met. Both Lopez and his wife were still living in Manchester Square. Not another word had been said as to that notice to quit, nor an allusion made to it. It was supposed to be a settled thing that Lopez was to start with his wife for Guatemala in the first week in April. Mr. Wharton had himself felt that difficulty as to his daughter's outfit, and had told her that she might get whatever it pleased her on his credit. "For yourself, my dear."

"Papa, I will get nothing till he bids me."

"But you can't go across the world without anything. What are you to do in such a place as that unless you have the things you want?"

"What do poor people do who have to go? What should I do if you had cast me off because of my disobedience?"

"But I have not cast you off."

"Tell him that you will give him so much, and then, if he bids me, I will spend it."

"Let it be so. I will tell him."

Upon that Mr. Wharton did speak to his son-in-law; —coming upon him suddenly one morning in the dining-room. "Emily will want an outfit if she is to go to this place."

"Like other people she wants many things that she cannot get."

"I will tell my tradesmen to furnish her with what she wants, up to,—well,—suppose I say £200. I have spoken to her and she wants your sanction."

"My sanction for spending your money? She can have that very quickly."

"You can tell her so;—or I will do so."

Upon that Mr. Wharton was going, but Lopez stopped him. It was now essential that the money for the shares in the San Juan mine should be paid up, and his father-in-law's pocket was still the source from which the enterprising son-in-law hoped to procure it. Lopez had fully made up his mind to demand it, and thought that the time had now come. And he was resolved that he would not ask it as a favour on bended knee. He was beginning to feel his own power, and trusted that he might prevail by other means than begging. "Mr. Wharton," he said, "you and I have not been very good friends lately."

"No, indeed."

"There was a time,—a very short time,—during which I thought that we might hit it off together, and I did my best. You do not, I fancy, like men of my class."

"Well;—well! You had better go on if there be anything to say."

"I have much to say, and I will go on. You are a rich man, and I am your son-in-law." Mr. Wharton put his left hand up to his forehead, brushing the few hairs back from his head, but he said nothing. "Had I received from you during the last most vital year that assistance which I think I had a right to expect, I also might have been a rich man now. It is no good going back to that." Then he paused, but still Mr. Wharton said nothing. "Now you know what has come to me and to your daughter. We are to be expatriated."

"Is that my fault?"

"I think it is, but I mean to say nothing further of that. This Company which is sending me out, and which will probably be the most thriving thing of the kind which has come up within these twenty years, is to pay me a salary of £1,000 a year as resident manager at San Juan."

"So I understand."

"The salary alone would be a beggarly thing. Guatemala, I take it, is not the cheapest country in the world in which a man can live. But I am to go out as the owner of fifty shares on which £100 each must be paid up, and I am entitled to draw another £1,000 a year as dividend on the profit of those shares."

"That will be twenty per cent."

"Exactly."

"And will double your salary."

"Just so. But there is one little ceremony to be perfected before I can be allowed to enter upon so halcyon a state of existence. The £100 a share must be paid up." Mr. Wharton simply stared at him. "I must have the £5,000 to invest in the undertaking before I can start."

"Well!"

"Now I have not got £5,000 myself, nor any part of it. You do not wish, I suppose, to see either me or your daughter starve. And as for me I hardly flatter myself when I say that you are very anxious to be rid of me. Five thousand pounds is not very much for me to ask of you, as I regard it."

"Such consummate impudence I never met in my life before!"

"Nor perhaps so much unprevaricating downright truth. At any rate such is the condition of my affairs. If I am to go the money must be paid this week. I have, perhaps foolishly, put off mentioning the matter till I was sure that I could not raise the sum elsewhere. Though I feel my claim on you to be good, Mr. Wharton, it is not pleasant to me to make it."

"You are asking me for £5,000 down!"

"Certainly I am."

"What security am I to have?"

"Security?"

"Yes;—that if I pay it I shall not be troubled again by the meanest scoundrel that it has ever been my misfortune to meet. How am I to know that you will not come back to-morrow? How am I to know that you will go at all? Do you think it probable that I will give you £5,000 on your own simple word?"

"Then the scoundrel will stay in England,—and will generally find it convenient to live in Manchester Square."

"I'll be d———d if he does. Look here, sir. Between you and me there can be a bargain, and nothing but a bargain. I will pay the £5,000,—on certain conditions."

"I did n't doubt at all that you would pay it."

"I will go with you to the office of this Company, and will pay for the shares if I can receive assurance there that the matter is as you say, and that the shares will not be placed in your power before you have reached Guatemala."

"You can come to-day, sir, and receive all that assurance."

"And I must have a written undertaking from you,—a document which my daughter can show if it be necessary,—that you will never claim her society again or trouble her with any application."

"You mistake me, Mr. Wharton. My wife goes with me to Guatemala."

"Then I will not pay one penny. Why should I? What is your presence or absence to me except as it concerns her? Do you think that I care for your threats of remaining here? The police will set that right."

"Wherever I go, my wife goes."

"We'll see to that too. If you want the money, you must leave her. Good morning."

Mr. Wharton as he went to his chambers thought the matter over. He was certainly willing to risk the £5,000 demanded if he could rid himself and his daughter of this terrible incubus, even if it were only for a time. If Lopez would but once go to Guatemala, leaving his wife behind him, it would be comparatively easy to keep them apart should he ever return. The difficulty now was not in him but in her. The man's conduct had been so outrageous, so barefaced, so cruel, that the lawyer did not doubt but that he could turn the husband out of his house, and keep the wife, even now, were it not that she was determined to obey the man whom she, in opposition to all her friends, had taken as her master. "I have done it myself and I will bear it," was all the answer she would make when her father strove to persuade her to separate herself from her husband. "You have got Everett," she would say. "When a girl is married she is divided from her family;—and I am divided." But she would willingly stay if Lopez would bid her stay. It now seemed that he could not go without the £5,000; and, when the pressure came upon him, surely he would go and leave his wife.

In the course of that day Mr. Wharton went to the offices of the San Juan mine and asked to see the Director. He was shown up into a half-furnished room, two stories high, in Coleman Street, where he found two clerks sitting upon stools;—and when he asked for the Director was shown into the back room in which sat the secretary. The secretary was a dark, plump little man with a greasy face, who had the gift of assuming an air of great importance as he twisted his chair round to face visitors who came to inquire about the San Juan Mining Company. His name was Hartlepod; and if the San Juan mine "turned out trumps," as he intended that it should, Mr. Hartlepod meant to be a great man in the City. To Mr. Hartlepod Mr. Wharton, with considerable embarrassment, explained as much of the joint history of himself and Lopez as he found to be absolutely necessary. "He has only left the office about half an hour," said Mr. Hartlepod.

"Of course you understand that he is my son-in-law."

"He has mentioned your name to us, Mr. Wharton, before now."

"And he is going out to Guatemala?"

"Oh yes;—he's going out. Has he not told you as much himself?"

"Certainly, sir. And he has told me that he is desirous of buying certain shares in the company before he starts."

"Probably, Mr. Wharton."

"Indeed I believe he cannot go, unless he buys them."

"That may be so, Mr. Wharton. No doubt he has told you all that himself."

"The fact is, Mr. Hartlepod, I am willing, under certain stipulations, to advance him the money." Mr. Hartlepod bowed. "I need not trouble you with private affairs between myself and my son-in-law." Again the secretary bowed. "But it seems to be for his interest that he should go."

"A very great opening indeed, Mr. Wharton. I don't see how a man is to have a better opening. A fine salary! His expenses out paid! One of the very best things that has come up for many years! And as for the capital he is to embark in the affair, he is as safe to get twenty per cent. on it,—as safe,—as safe as the Bank of England."

"He 'll have the shares?"

"Oh yes;—the scrip will be handed to him at once."

"And,—and——"

"If you mean about the mine, Mr. Wharton, you may take my word that it 's all real. It 's not one of those sham things that melt away like snow and leave the shareholders nowhere. There 's the prospectus, Mr. Wharton. Perhaps you have not seen that before. Take it away and cast your eye over it at your leisure." Mr. Wharton put the somewhat lengthy pamphlet into his pocket. "Look at the list of Directors. We 've three members of Parliament, a baronet, and one or two City names that are as good,—as good as the Bank of England. If that prospectus won't make a man confident I don't know what will. Why, Mr. Wharton, you don't think that your son-in-law would get those fifty shares at par unless he was going out as our general local manager. The shares ain't to be had. It's a large concern as far as capital goes. You'll see if you look. About a quarter of a million paid up. But it's all in a box, as one may say. It's among ourselves. The shares ain't in the market. Of course it's not for me to say what should be done between you and your son-in-law. Lopez is a friend of mine, and a man I esteem, and all that. Nevertheless I should n't think of advising you to do this or that,—or not to do it. But when you talk of safety, Mr. Wharton,—why, Mr. Wharton, I don't scruple to tell you, as a man who knows what these things are, that this is an opportunity that does n't come in a man's way perhaps twice in his life."

Mr. Wharton found that he had nothing more to say, and went back to Lincoln's Inn. He knew very well that Mr. Hartlepod's assurances were not worth much. Mr. Hartlepod himself and his belongings, the clerks in his office, the look of the rooms, and the very nature of the praises which he had sung, all of them inspired anything but confidence. Mr. Wharton was a man of the world; and, though he knew nothing of City ways, was quite aware that no man in his senses would lay out £5,000 on the mere word of Mr. Hartlepod. But still he was inclined to make the payment. If only he could secure the absence of Lopez,—if he could be sure that Lopez would in truth go to Guatemala, and if also he could induce the man to go without his wife, he would risk the money. The money would, of course, be thrown away,—but he would throw it away. Lopez no doubt had declared that he would not go without his wife, even though the money were paid for him. But the money was an alluring sum! As the pressure upon the man became greater, Mr. Wharton thought he would probably consent to leave his wife behind him.

In his emergency the barrister went to his attorney and told him everything. The two lawyers were closeted together for an hour, and Mr. Wharton's last words to his old friend were as follows:—" I will risk the money, Walker, or rather I will consent absolutely to throw it away,—as it will be thrown away,—if it can be managed that he shall in truth go to this place without his wife."

END OF VOL. II.

Date Due

RET'D DEC 13 1955

FACULTY

FEB 17 1957

Demco 293-5